THE BOOK OF THE CITY OF LADIES

THE BOOK OF THE CITY OF LADIES

Christine de Pizan

Translated by Earl Jeffrey Richards

Foreword by Marina Warner

PERSEA BOOKS
New York

Library of Congress Cataloging in Publication Data

Pizan, Christine de, ca. 1363-ca. 1431.
  The book of the city of ladies.

  Translation of: Le livre de la cité des dames.
  Includes bibliographical references and index.
  I. Title.
PQ1575.L56E5   1982   843'.2   82-331
ISBN 0-89255-061-9   AACR2

Designed by George Bacso
Design executed by Peter McKenzie

Printed in the United States of America by The Book Press,
Brattleboro, Vermont.
First Edition

CONTENTS

vii   *Contents*

ILLUSTRATIONS

All illustrations are from Christine de Pizan's *Collected Works*, Harley manuscript 4431, and are copyrighted by and courtesy of The British Library, London.

FOREWORD

In one of the most appealing and interesting anecdotes
in this collection of women's lives, Christine de Pizan
describes how Novella, the daughter of a law professor
at the famed university of Bologna, taught in her father's
place when he was busy, and in order to prevent her
beauty from distracting her pupils, drew a curtain in front
of her face. Beauty used to be one of the defining attributes of the female sex, virtually synonymous with feminine form; it was also presumed dangerous, and from Eve
onwards, the naked female face (and form) were thought
so potent they could unman the strongest of men. Novella's curtain did not just disguise her beauty, but her
femaleness. Christine might well have written that Novella drew a curtain over her sex, just as the editor of
Christine's work of military ethics, *The Book of Feats of
Arms and Chivalry*, in 1448, decided to draw a veil over
Christine's sex, and changed the text so that it appeared
to have been written by a man. He was taking an elemen-
tary precaution against losing his readers. A work on the
proper conduct of war, by a woman, would invite slurs of
unreliability.

It was exactly this climate of prejudice that inspired
Christine de Pizan's partisan works in defense of woman-
kind. *The Book of the City of Ladies*, here translated into
accessible contemporary English and at last made available for general readership, is part of Christine's ardent
campaign to rehabilitate her sex in her contemporaries'
eyes.

Although *The Book of the City of Ladies* was written
more than half a millenium ago, it is filled with potent
observations for our times. The *querelle des femmes*— the
woman question in late fourteenth- and fifteenth-century
France— articulated its arguments in much the same way

as today's debate about the equality of women. Here, in *The Book of the City of Ladies*, Christine intersperses her tales of formidable and exemplary heroines of the past with down-to-earth remarks about the wrongs done to women by society's attitudes and opinions. Her tone is not shrill, but forbearing; her comments trenchant; she never whines. She indicts men, Portia-like, from a position of superior benevolence, enacting the drama of women's greater moral qualities by refusing the line of violence or suppliant weakness. Christine de Pizan was born in a court and she was an adept of courtly ways; her strategy in her attack is courteous, and her courtesy, with its appearance of frankness, even artlessness, conceals a fair bit of cunning, and a deal of rage.

Recurring themes with resonance for today provoke in her a controlled indignation. She returns again and again, for instance, to the lack of access women have to education. She praises her own father generously for giving her an education against the conventional objections of her mother, and interjects defiantly that women's minds are "freer and sharper" than men's. She laments the disappointment women of her day felt at the birth of daughters: she gives as its cause the need to provide young women with dowries. Yet today, when the economic reason has failed, the arrival of a girl baby is often greeted with less enthusiasm by grandparents, in-laws. Yet another barbarism that has not been modified in the long interval separating us from Christine appears in her pages: the accusation that women invite rape. Christine exonerates women from this suspicion with a fierce, felt regret, and ends by approving the supreme penalty for rapists. Elsewhere, touching what appears to be a personal note, she also pleads that women can be pretty and enjoy fine clothes without forfeiting their title to chastity. Her anger at the double standard, by which men, raping women, then blame women for allowing them to do so, still rings loud and clear today. She also paints a devastating and unchanged picture of violence in marriage, of drunken beatings and spendthrift husbands.

The Book of the City of Ladies uses a popular medieval convention, of an author's conversation with allegorical figures. In this book, Christine talks to the figures of Reason and Justice, familiar then from iconography as well as theology, but she also creates her own allegorical maiden, *Droiture*, Rectitude, "Right-thinking," "Right-doing." Christine's introduction of this figure into the pageant of the regular female Virtues, Liberal Arts, Heavenly Beatitudes, and other personifications found in the sculpture programs of cathedrals, reveals her mental and emotional bent. In a book like *The City of Ladies*, Christine de Pizan is casting herself as a moral tutor rather than a poet; she is writing to instruct us, to shape our thinking and so incline us to right-thinking and right-doing. When she pleads for education for women, she gives as her reason education's close correlation with good conduct.

The contemporary reader might be unfamiliar with the medieval convention of allegory. Yet the appearance of Reason, Rectitude, and Justice as women reflects the entire purpose of Christine's *Book of the City of Ladies*: to bring back to memory the lives and deeds of virtuous women embodying those qualities, who have been neglected and forgotten by history. She is restoring speech to the silent portion of the past—one of the principal tasks of all historians. *The Book of the City of Ladies* resembles a visit to the shades of the dead, claiming their right to be remembered. Christine, drawing from her reading of classical and Renaissance sources, adds them to our store of knowledge and breaks the narrow molds of female stereotypes. To achieve her vindication of women, Christine alters her source material in the most surprising ways, sometimes refreshing, sometimes bizarre.

Christine praises Medea for her herbal arts and her command of the elements—an interesting and justifiable example of reassessing witchcraft from a positive viewpoint. She thus frees a historical personality from the fears of ignorance and prejudice. But later, when Medea appears again among Christine's stories of women's constancy in love, it is a trifle peculiar to find her story told without a mention of the demented dimension of her despair, with the murder of her children overlooked. Christine actually describes the great prototype of the wronged first wife turning merely "despondent" after Jason leaves her. Similarly, Xanthippe, Socrates's proverbial shrew of a wife, emerges from Christine's pages as loyal and devoted and wise. Modesty also inspires Christine to change the famous story of "Roman charity." The dying old man who is suckled by a young woman is transformed into a female, the girl's mother moreover. Christine's redress of history's judgment can be enterprising and refreshing (it had never occurred to me that Xanthippe might indeed have been maligned), but often the new, virtuous portrait strays toward a stereotype. Christine here is at her best as a storyteller when she writes from personal truth and emotion, and her rebukes rise from within the sting of lived experience.

Christine herself does not seem to distinguish between the levels of reality she seizes with her pen: her own life's lessons merge without interruption into the examples of heroines, legendary and historical. Reading *The Book of the City of Ladies* involves an odd trick of perception, for the circle enclosing Christine, Medusa, the goddess Ops, and Queen Blanche is one and the same without difference of degree, authenticity, or even time scale. Human experience is universal, Christine is telling us, and distance in time constitutes no effective barrier. But it is arresting— and charming— to find that Uranus was "an extremely powerful man in Greece" married to a wife called Vesta, that Minerva figured in Christine's mind as the historical inventor of shorthand, arithmetic, weaving and spinning, the cultivation of the olive, and the forging of armor, and was not just the protagonist in a pagan myth of origin or a symbolic tutelary goddess of specific skills and arts. Christine was a devout Christian woman who saw Minerva as one of her predecessors in wisdom and industry; in the invocation with which she closes *The Book of Feats of*

Arms and Chivalry, Christine asks Minerva to preside over her undertaking, as she is a *"femme Italienne"* like herself. For Christine de Pizan, the centuries that had elapsed since Italy was part of Magna Graecia were but the winking of an eye; Minerva was her inspiration, her ally, and her compatriot.

The Book of the City of Ladies represents a determined and clear-headed woman's attempt to take apart the structure of her contemporaries' prejudices; a reasoned but fierce counter-assault against baiting by the male. Christine was not a moderate; she believed deeply in sexual difference and she diagnosed, in this book and in other works, the nature and causes of sexual antagonism. She was always alive to injustice. Yet Christine, who herself resolved to remain a widow and sang of her decision in a famous *ballade "Seulete suy et seulete vueil estre,"* showed an admirable open mind when she counselled other women not to seek too much independence (even though her words sound like equivocation to our ears), for usually moralists command people to greatness they themselves cannot achieve. But she believed in the possibility of reconciliation: it was largely a matter of the right education leading to moral enlightenment. In this way, *The Book of the City of Ladies* is a work of optimism that is still by no means entirely justified by events. The task Christine de Pizan set herself has still to be done.

MARINA WARNER
London, 1982

INTRODUCTION

Christine de Pizan is at once one of the outstanding writers of world literature and one of the most neglected. Her works reflect pivotal concerns of medieval writers in general and of the woman of letters in particular. Largely devoted to the social, political, and cultural plight of women, they transcend their own time by addressing all sorts and conditions of women. Their claim to our attention goes beyond the narrower concerns of the medievalist, and yet, the immediate human appeal of Christine's works has all too often been forgotten. *The Book of the City of Ladies* occupies a central position within the enormous body of Christine's works. In 1521 Brian Anslay published his *Boke of the Cyte of Ladyes*, the first (and last) English translation of this work. Since then it has hardly been accessible to the public. This new translation makes a neglected classic of world literature available in modern English. Along with the following brief discussion of Christine's life and works and a scholarly evaluation of her importance, it may serve to bring to light a writer whose works belong among literary masterpieces.

Christine was born in 1365 in Venice, where her father, Tommaso di Benvenuto da Pizzano, was engaged as a municipal counselor.[1] Shortly after her birth the French monarch Charles V invited Tommaso to assume the position of court astrologer. Three years later Tommaso's family followed him to Paris. Christine was able to profit from her family's close ties to the court to obtain a good education, encouraged by her father and in spite of her mother's opposition, as she recounts in *The Book of the City of Ladies*, II.36. This situation was extraordinarily unusual for her time.[2]

xix

Charles V died in 1380, leaving his twelve-year-old son Charles VI as his heir. During the young king's minority, the burden of governing was assumed by his uncles, Philip the Bold, duke of Burgundy, and Louis II, duke of Bourbon. The ongoing rivalry between the two regents led to later factional strife which plagued France throughout Charles VI's reign. During this regency Christine's father, Tommaso, lost favor at court, and his fortunes declined rather abruptly. He died sometime around 1385.

In the meantime, Christine, at the age of fifteen, had married Estienne de Castel, a court notary ten years her elder. To judge from Christine's allusions in her work, her marriage was exceptionally happy—indeed, her husband encouraged Christine's learning and literary activity. Then, in 1389, Estienne de Castel died in Beauvais, the victim of an epidemic which broke out while Charles VI and his court were visiting. Widowed at the age of twenty-five, with three small children to support, and no inheritance, Christine turned to writing to earn her living, a vocation which she pursued with remarkable courage and energy as well as ambition.

The highlights of Christine's career alone are the measure of her literary importance. She was recognized as an accomplished lyric poet and served as the official biographer of Charles V. She was also the chief correspondent in the so-called Quarrel of *The Romance of the Rose*, attacking this central work of medieval French literature for being immoral in general and for slandering women in particular. She supported her charges against some of the most formidable Parisian humanists of her day.

Perhaps what is more important is that Christine was a highly respected and widely disseminated voice on the status of women. A large number of Christine's works spring from her deep sense of commitment. In her letters on *The Romance of the Rose*, as well as in *The Book of the City of Ladies*, *The Book of the Three Virtues* (*Le Livre des Trois Vertus*), and her poem on Joan of Arc (*Le Ditié sur Jehanne d'Arc*), Christine sought to demonstrate that women possessed natural affinities for all areas of cultural and social activity.

That Christine wrote several works on commission, leading to the conclusion by some critics that she should be viewed as the "first professional writer," in no way diminishes the literary commitment which informs all her works. In fact, her concern and involvement are manifest even in the physical presentation of her works, for Christine was one of the first vernacular authors who supervised the copying and illuminating of her own books. A sensitivity to the important relationship between text and illumination had hitherto been a feature primarily of medieval Latin works.[3] (As a point of comparison, *The Romance of the Rose*, whose illuminations have attracted considerable attention from scholars, survives in manuscripts copied and illuminated long after the deaths of its authors, Guillaume de Lorris and Jean de Meung.[4]) Characterizing Christine as the "first professional writer" is one pointed example of how Christine's works have been judged according to extrinsic categories, rather than on their own merits. Her works are not easy. Her style reflects the experimental and innovative nature of her prose. Christine chose Latin prose as her model, and the complicated periodic syntax she preferred was a hallmark of stylistic refinement. Christine was, therefore, both a writer and a scholar, welding together an enormous creative drive and a deep love of learning. To say anything less of Christine is to do her a profound disservice.

Christine might best be considered a *polyscribator*, since she wrote on so many diverse subjects. Between 1390 and 1429 she produced a vast corpus of works in verse and prose, whose range shows a technical mastery of the various well-established literary genres of her day and demonstrates an astonishing poetic versatility. In an important sense, Christine's work *is* her life: one can reconstruct her biography on the basis of her works alone.

But because we have so few sources on Christine's life besides Christine's own remarks, a biographical approach to her works affords no new purchase on them. Even the briefest survey of Christine's works reveals her intimate involvement with political events. Christine's repeated appeals for peace, not surprising in an age so wracked by civil strife as the late thirteenth and early fourteenth centuries in France, take their place beside her incessant plea for the recognition of women's contributions to culture and social life as the most remarkable features of her works. These two recurring themes show how Christine was deeply rooted in her own time and also strove for an historical synthesis of universal application. Christine's works address the issues of her day while bearing the deep imprint of her yearning for a universal historical perspective, a yearning which finds its best expression, perhaps, in *The Book of the City of Ladies*.

The following summary of Christine's works documents the most important stages of her career and underscores her enormous range[5]:

Works in Verse
1. *Cent Ballades, Virelays, Rondeaux.* The majority of Christine's shorter lyrical compositions appear to have been written in the first decade following her husband's death. The first twenty *ballades* are profoundly marked by her grief, whereas the remaining works show an increased tendency to experiment with other themes and lyrical forms. These works are found in the first volume of *Œuvres poétiques de Christine de Pisan*, ed. Maurice Roy (Paris, 1886-1891).

2. *L'Epistre au Dieu d'Amours*, written in May 1399, (in Roy's edition, v. II, pp. 1-27), seems to have initiated the Quarrel of *The Romance of The Rose*. In this work, ladies from all social estates complain to Cupid about their detractors, particularly Ovid and Jean de Meung. Sometime after 1402 this work was translated into English by Thomas Hoccleve (found in: *Hoccleve's Minor Poems*, [London, 1932], pp. 72-91).

3. *Le Dit de la Rose*, written February 14, 1402 (in Roy, v. II,

pp. 29-48) marks the culmination of Christine's polemic against *The Romance of the Rose*. Here Christine founds poetically "the Order of the Rose" to reward knights who defend the honor of women.

4. *Le Debat de deux amans*, dating from ca. 1400 (Roy, v. II, 99-109), presents a polemic between two lovers, the one disappointed, the other satisfied in love.

5. *Le Livre des trois jugemens*, (Roy, v. II, pp. 111-157) is a discussion of three different love situations which are submitted to the arbitration of the Seneschal de Hainault to whom the work is dedicated.

6. *Le Livre du dit de Poissy*, from April 1400 (Roy, v. II, pp. 159-222) tells of a visit Christine paid to her daughter at the Dominican convent of Saint-Louis in Poissy (where Christine perhaps retired after the 1418 Burgundian massacres in Paris).

7. *Enseignemens* and *Proverbes moraux*, dated ca. 1400 (Roy, v. III, pp. 27-57), were written for her son Jean Castel. The latter work was particularly popular in England, where Anthony Wydeville, Earl Rivers, executed a translation which Caxton published in 1477 (*The Morale Proverbes of Cristyne*, facsimile edition reprinted New York, 1970).

8. *Le Livre du chemin de long estude*, written between October 5, 1402 and March 20, 1403, is a dream vision in which Christine is led by the sybil of Cumae into another, more perfect world. They arrive in the Court of Reason where the question is discussed who should rule a proposed world empire whose founding would correct the world's faults. Christine receives the mission of returning to Earth with the message from the Court of Reason. The work shows many borrowings from Boethius, Dante, and Mandeville and is available in an edition done by Robert Püschel (Berlin/Paris, 1881, 1887) and in the dissertation of Patricia Bonin Eargle, *An Edition of Christine de Pisan's "Livre du chemin de long estude"* (Ph.D. Diss., University of Georgia, 1973).

9. *Le Livre de la Mutacion de Fortune*, composed between August 1400 and November 1403 (edited by Suzanne Solente in four volumes, [Paris, 1959-1966]), contains 23,636 verses

divided into seven parts. This essay on universal history, the most important and longest of Christine's works in verse, traces the adversities of Fortune in history ("l'influence müable/De Fortune decevable").[6]

10. *Le Ditié de Jehanne d'Arc* is the last known composition of Christine, dated July 31, 1429, when she broke an eleven-year silence to write the only work written in French during Joan of Arc's lifetime in her honor. This work is available in several editions; the best edition, accompanied by an English translation, was prepared by Angus J. Kennedy and Kenneth Varty, "Christine de Pisan's *Ditié de Jehanne d'Arc*," *Nottingham Medieval Studies 18* (1974), pp. 29-55; *19* (1975), pp. 53-76; and issued as a separate monograph in 1978.

Works in Prose

1. *Epistres du débat sur le Roman de la Rose*, written between 1401 and 1403, form Christine's contribution to the exchange of letters on *The Romance of the Rose*. In perhaps the first literary quarrel of its kind, Christine attacked the immorality of the *Rose*. Eric Hicks prepared the best available edition of the relevant documents: *Le Débat sur le "Roman de la Rose,"* (Paris, 1977). These letters appear to be Christine's first works in prose, for she remarks to Guillaume de Tignonville, "ne vous soit a merveille, pour ce que mes autres dictiéz ay acoustuméz a rimoyer, cestui estre en prose" (Hicks, p. 8).[7] Christine's subsequent works favor this new literary medium. The implications of this quarrel for Christine's view of women will be discussed below.

2. *L'Epistre d'Othea*, dated around 1400, consists of one hundred short narratives, each accompanied by an illumination and composed of three parts: a *texte* (usually an octosyllabic quatrain), a *glose* (an explication), and an *allegorie* (a Christian allegorical interpretation, generally speaking, incorporating citations from the Bible and the Church fathers). This work is extraordinarily important for understanding the relation of text and illumination, for Christine appears to have supervised the illumination. Halina Loukopoulos prepared an edition of *L'Epistre d'Othea* as part of her 1977 dissertation *Classical Mythology in the Works of Christine de*

Pisan (University of Michigan). Gianni Mombello has long promised a critical edition.[8] Stephen Scrope translated the work in the middle of the fifteenth century.[9]

3. *Le Livre des fais et bonnes meurs du sage Roy Charles V*, written between January and the end of November 1404, was composed at the request of Philip the Bold and designed as a manual of good government for the French dauphin (edited by Susanne Solente, [Paris, 1936–40], 2 vol.).

4. *Le Livre de la Cité des Dames*, from 1405, is available in an edition prepared by Maureen Curnow as her 1975 Vanderbilt University doctoral dissertation which is scheduled for publication shortly. Another edition has been announced by Monika Lange of the University of Hamburg. Apart from the present translation, this work was translated in 1521 by Bryan Anslay (*The Boke of the Cyte of Ladyes*). An anonymous Flemish translation, done in Bruges in 1475, is available only in manuscript. For further particulars see below.

5. *Le Livre des Trois Vertus* or *Le Trésor de la Cité des Dames*, completed between the spring of 1405 and November 7, 1405, is a follow-up to *The Book of the City of Ladies* and presents a detailed classification of women's roles in contemporary society. In this work Reason, Rectitude, and Justice reappear to Christine. The first part consists of advice and exhortation to queens, princesses, and noblewomen; the second addresses itself to the women of the court and lesser nobility; and the third speaks to bourgeois women and common women. Excerpts of the work are found in Mathilde Laigle, *Le Livre des Trois Vertus de Christine de Pisan et son milieu historique et littéraire*, (Paris, 1912). Speaking of Christine's position in this work, Charity Cannon Willard noted, "There is no indication that Christine expected her contemporaries to do more than accept their place in society; she merely wanted them to make better use of their opportunities."[10]

6. *L'Avision*, dated from 1405, is one of the principal sources of biographical information on Christine, and relates a dream-vision in which Christine meets a variety of allegorical figures: Libera (personification of France who

mourns the civil strife of her children and urges Christine to continue her writing); Dame Opinion, and Dame Philosophie, to whom Christine relates her life.

7. *Le Livre du corps de policie*, composed 1406-1407, is a three-part treatise, inspired by John of Salisbury's *Policraticus*, which is directed to princes, knights, and the people with recommendations for the proper conduct of the various estates, each corresponding to a different part of the body politic.[11]

8. *Sept psaumes allegorisés*, written between June 26, 1409 and January 1, 1410 at the request of Charles le Noble, king of Navarre, present a verset from one of seven penitential psalms (6, 31, 37, 50, 101, 129, 142) followed by a prose meditation which is more "personal" than exegetical in tone.[12]

9. *Le Livre des fais d'armes et de chevalerie*, from 1410, is a manual of instruction for knights and incorporates extensive passages from the translation made by Jean de Vignai of Vegetius' *De re militari*.[13]

10. *Le Livre de la paix*, composed between September 1, 1412 and January 1, 1414 is an exemplary manual directed to the dauphin, Louis, the Duke of Guyenne, exhorting him in particular to the exercise of prudence.[14]

11. *L'Epistre de la prison de vie humaine* is a consolation dedicated to Mary of Berry, daughter of John, duke of Berry, for the many deaths in her family circle, most related to the civil unrest of the time. Christine appears to have been inspired by the pseudo-Seneca's *De remediis fortuitorum* and Boethius' *Consolatio philosophiae* and perhaps Vincent de Beauvais' letter *Consolatio pro morte amici*.[15]

This rapid survey of Christine's works furnishes us with insights into her participation in the intellectual currents of her age. From the list of her patrons alone—John, Duke of Berry, Philip the Bold, John the Fearless, Louis of Orleans and his wife, Valentina Visconti, Charles VI and his wife, Isabella of Bavaria, among others—one can appreciate how intimately Christine was also involved in political events. Christine mentions her free access to royal circles in *Le Livre des fais et bonnes meurs du sage Roy Charles V*: "me suis informee, tant par croniques, comme par pluseurs gens notables encore vivans, jadis de sa vie, condicions, meurs et ordre de vivre et de ses fais particuliers" (v.I, p.9, "I gathered my information concerning his life, surroundings, behavior, life-style, and his specific acts either from chronicles or from talking to famous people who are still alive").

The large number of French translations of Latin and Italian works circulating in French courtly circles at this time indicate how highly receptive French culture was to Italian humanism. Christine appears to have been familiar with the works of Ovid, Boethius, Valerius Maximus, John of Salisbury, Vincent de Beauvais, and Boccaccio, which were all available in French translation. Christine could not have been so well acquainted with these writers without having been concerned with the historical continuity of literary culture. Her striving to write a universal history of women in *The Book of the City of Ladies* is further proof of her sensitivity to historical problems and might indicate that Christine was aware of the well-known topos of *translatio studii*—the theme of the historical transfer of literary culture from Athens to Rome to France which was popularized in many earlier Old French works.[16] Christine's actual familiarity with particular Latin texts is a problem for specialists. We know from her own statement that Christine used translations in *Le Livre du corps de policie* ("ces hystoires cy sont contenues en la translation de Valere, lesqueles choses j'ay cueillis ung pou." Lucas [ed.], p. 66, "these stories are found in the translation of Valerius which I have gathered together a little").[17] However, Christine must have been able to read some Latin in order to follow the Quarrel of *The Romance of the Rose* mentioned above. The important point remains that Christine's *The Book of the City of Ladies* shows us how she used her own erudition to exemplify the affinity of women for learning. Christine's task in *The Book of the City of Ladies* is to transform her own erudition into an emblem of women's potential for erudition, a task at which, it hardly needs to be said, she brilliantly succeeds.

Christine's learnedness served as a springboard for her to address the question of a woman's role in society in more extensive terms. Initially Christine had to establish her credibility by demonstrating her total mastery of literary tradition. Certain basic points need to be reiterated: prior to Christine, no woman had spoken out in the vernacular on issues pertaining to women. Christine insisted that women must be educated. These two facts alone make Christine revolutionary. Her attitude was profoundly feminist in that it involved a complete dedication to the betterment of women's lives and to the alleviation of their suffering. Yet precisely the feminist implications of Christine's work have received very little attention. For example, Ellen Moer's classic *Literary Women* (New York, 1977) makes no mention of Christine. However, Christine cannot be wholly equated with contemporary feminists because of the latter's predominantly secular orientation. Yet there can be no getting around Christine's feminism. It is central to her works and thought. The scholar Millard Meiss argued that Christine set out to disprove "masculine myths." One can begin to appreciate the wide-scale ramifications of Christine's thinking under the aegis of this mission.

Christine's arguments on behalf of women repeatedly invoke historical tradition and Christianity. She cites tradition in order to remold the same tradition to meet her own needs in writing a history from the point of view of women, a radical break with all previous historiography. Christine persistently defends Christian marriage in order to use the ideals of personal conduct implicit in the Church's concept of marriage as a standard. Christine lived in an age when the Church was seen as the Bride of Christ, and therefore, Christian marriage based on the model of Christ's caring for His Church represented the supreme form of ethical responsibility. Her defense of Christian marriage was a call for the highest form of moral commitment between a man and a woman and not an endorsement of institutionalized domination. This strong religious element may not appeal to some modern critics, but it is an historical fact that Christine saw in Christianity a means of overcoming oppression. Her commitment to Christian values recalls that of Martin Luther King—the diction and the very structure of both their dreams of freedom are profoundly suffused with Christian elements. Christine's title for *The Book of the City of Ladies* alludes directly to Augustine's *City of God*. By juxtaposing the two cities Christine did not intend that her City of Ladies rival the City of God, but that her political vision be understood as participating in a Christian tradition of political philosophy.

Within the context of her time, Christine's thought must be viewed as revolutionary. Writing in an important critical anthology on the history of women writers in France, the German critic Dietmar Rieger characterized Christine's views as "ideologically ambivalent, almost conservative."[18] Rieger's opinion represents an old strain in the reception of Christine. Because critics have often taken Christine for conservative, feminists have sometimes hesitated to cite her. Christine's orientation toward the past which has made her so suspect has been misunderstood. In *The Book of the City of Ladies* Christine expands her defense of women to the past and future so that she can expose the utter falseness of "masculine myths" once and for all. Christine sought a more perfect *realization* of the ideals transmitted by the tradition which she had inherited, which she had cultivated, and which she hoped to transform. Christine's unmistakable clarity on the continuity of women's suffering throughout history is an appeal for change, not for the return to some nostalgically idealized past.

Christine explores the universal suffering and oppression of women. While her coming to terms with this suffering and oppression is in part time-bound, it possesses a clear universal appeal. Christine, of course, recognized medieval class structure and did not call for the overthrow of this hierarchy but urged women to accept their place in it. Nevertheless, every woman possessed for Christine the potential for true nobility. Christine took pains to name her new "kingdom of femininity" the City of Ladies rather the City of Women in order to make sure her readers understood her point: all women could find a place in the City of Ladies by realizing their feminine potential. Christine has taken over the traditional term "lady" and invested it with an innovative significance; "lady" for Christine refers to the nobility of the soul rather than the nobility of blood. She transposes the dignity afforded to noble women in the late medieval French class structure to women who have proven their worthiness through their achievements, whether military, political, cultural, or religious. Christine took received intellectual and social categories and used them for her own ends. In this respect her meditations transcend her own time. As such, one must stress the literary genre of *The Book of the City of Ladies*: it is a *universal history of women*, which encompasses the experience of pagan and Christian women up to Christine's present. Precisely this universality sets it apart from its major literary model and antecedent, Boccaccio's *De mulieribus claris* (*Concerning Famous Women*), which confines itself almost exclusively, for reasons to be discussed below, to pagan women.

The Book of the City of Ladies is central to understanding Christine's view of women, but her reflections on this subject began before its composition and continued after its completion. They can be divided chronologically into four periods: (1) the Quarrel of *The Romance of the Rose* (1398-1402), (2) *The Book of the City of Ladies* (1404-1405), (3) the *Livre des Trois Vertus* (1405), (4) the *Ditié de Jehanne d'Arc* (1429). Unfortunately, the traditional approach to Christine's thought has been to say that Christine was a compiler of received notions, a view argued for most strongly by the Christine specialist Gianni Mombello.[19] Mombello has set the tone for the entire subsequent discussion.[20] What the following survey will show is that Christine's originality, particularly on the subject of women, stems from her reorganization of her sources. Christine was able to forge the received notions of her time into a new and original body of thought.

The Quarrel of *The Romance of the Rose* has been a prickly question for scholars for decades. *The Romance of the Rose* was the most popular work in French of the late Middle Ages. In the first part, written around 1225 by Guillaume de Lorris, the dream-vision of the protagonist Amant ("lover") is recounted. Amant dreams that he enters a beautiful garden where he sees the Rose and falls in love. He seeks help from a number of allegorical characters, and his meeting with each is the occasion for an excursus on some aspect of love. Guillaume's part ends without Amant having won the Rose, and some fifty years later Jean de Meung wrote a continuation of 17,000 lines in which the speeches of the allegorical interlocutors are vastly expanded. In the end—to make a very long story short—Amant wins his Rose. Christine objected in part to the treatment of women in *The Romance of the Rose* and, more specifically, to misogynist remarks made in the various speeches. Christine was supported in her attacks against the *Rose* by the influential chancellor of the University of Paris, Jean Gerson. What prompted Christine and Gerson to attack the *Rose* was a moral concern. The French court was left to its own devices during the frequent spells of insanity which plagued Charles VI. Charles' queen, Isabella of Bavaria, led a licentious and frivolous existence. Not surprisingly, Christine and Gerson connected the immorality of their day to the popularity of the *Rose*.[21] Since Christine's opponents in the Quarrel included some of the most distinguished humanists of her age, she tends to be portrayed as anti-humanist and anti-poetry. This characterization is unfortunate and unfair: for Christine, the erudition of women as well as their participation in literary and cultural life are recurrent and important aspects—indeed the essence—of her aesthetic value. Any discussion of Christine's view in the Quarrel of *The Romance of the Rose* must therefore take into consideration her arguments in *The Book of the City of Ladies*. One point which Christine made in the Quarrel must be repeated here: if women had written the books we read, they would have handled things differently, for women know they have been falsely accused ("Mais se femmes eussent les livres fait/Je scay de vray qu'autrement fust de fair/ Car bien scevent qu'a tort sont encoulpees," *Epistre au Dieu d'Amours*, vv. 417-19). This Quarrel was far from being Christine's last word on the subject; indeed she had barely started! *The Book of the City of Ladies* is Christine's commentary on the Quarrel, and its underlying and unstated poetological aim is to refute any suspicion that Christine was either anti-humanist or anti-poetry.

Christine's claim that if women had written the classics, things would have been different is the challenge which preoccupies her in *The Book of the City of Ladies*. It is a strikingly successful attempt to rewrite the history of women. It succeeds at recasting our perception of women because Christine takes an independent approach. Her major point was to urge "men to live up to their own standards," as Douglas Kelly pointed out in his important re-evaluation of Christine as a feminist writer.[22] Christine's recourse to this tactic shows that her argumentation is innovative on its own terms rather than comprising simply a "reaction" to the intellectual categories of the detractors of women. Her view of women is not antithetically constructed; that is, her idealization of women does not represent an automatic antithesis to the demonization of women found in misogynist writers. She is not a prisoner of the literary clichés of her sources and of her opponents. Her refutation of such clichés is accomplished in a masterfully understated way. For example, Christine recalls in *The Book of the City of Ladies* the charge that women are greedy (II.66). Rather than simply arguing, "no, women are not greedy," Christine prefers to explain that what appears as greed is in fact (female) prudence in the face of (male) profligacy. Without being too blunt about it, Christine means that the same men who accuse women of greed are using this charge to camouflage their own squandering. Once the motives for this slander have been examined and its sting removed, Christine then proceeds to demonstrate women's innate generosity. Her argument is straightforward, matter-of-fact, and generous. She offers no counter-clichés in her refutation but succeeds in showing through her mastery of the available examples that her opponents' arguments are specious. Perhaps, thanks to this clear-sightedness, this "psychological" insight (before the "invention" of psychology), Christine's arguments still sound fresh even 575 years after they were first advanced. Subjects such as the fitness of women to govern, the affinity of women for learning, the criminality of rape are but a few of the themes which Christine treats and which could have been taken from current feminist discussions.

Written as a follow-up to *The Book of the City of Ladies*, the *Livre des Trois Vertus* makes use of its predecessor's didactic framework: Reason, Rectitude, and Justice reappear to Christine. The work is a pedagogical treatise rather than a universal history and seeks to advise women on their role in society. Perhaps because of its contemporary appeal, the *Livre des Trois Vertus* enjoyed a far wider distribution than *The Book of the City of Ladies*. The focus of the *Livre des Trois Vertus* was enhanced by the fact that "no such comprehensive description of women in these sections of society had been attempted previously."[23] As such, the *Livre de Trois Vertus* complements the universal historical outlook of *The Book of the City of Ladies*.

This same concern for current issues is reflected in Christine's *Ditié de Jehanne d'Arc* from 1429. Christine went "out of her way to stress that Joan is to be seen as an outstanding, representative member of the female sex,"[24] thanks to whom France owes its salvation. Christine was of course continuing the argument which had started with the Quarrel of *The Romance of the Rose*. Surely Christine would have included Joan of Arc in *The Book of the City of Ladies* had she had the chance.

This brief survey shows how *The Book of the City of Ladies* is the pivotal expression of Christine's views on women. It occupies a unique position within Christine's works, constituting the longest exposition of her opinions on women sparked by the Quarrel of *The Romance of the Rose* and putting forth arguments which later works complement but do not change.

The Book of the City of Ladies consists of a didactic exchange between Christine and three allegorical interlocutors, the virtues Reason, Rectitude, and Justice. Their remarks to Christine aim at imbuing her with an encompassing feminine ideal which uncompromisingly refuses to apologize for women against their detractors but rather seeks to demonstrate the indispensability of feminine contributions to the continuation of human civilization in the political, cultural, spiritual, and practical spheres. The German Romanist Philip August Becker considered that the work was "something between a translation and free invention," referring to Christine's debt to Boccaccio's *De mulieribus claris*. In order to correct such a misleading characterization, one must review Christine's use of sources (whereby one can at the same time establish the literary historical context for the composition of *The Book of the City of Ladies*), her diction and style, and her major lines of argument.

Prior to Christine's work, composed between December 1404 and April 1405, there was only one major literary work in circulation treating "famous women," Boccaccio's *De mulieribus claris*, available to Christine both in the original and in French translation.[25] Boccaccio's purpose in this work was quite simply to write about famous, even notorious, women, regardless of their moral stature. Boccaccio noted in the Proemium that he wished to understand the term "famous" in "a wider sense" (*in ampliorem sensum*) so that he could treat such "upright matrons" as Penelope, Lucretia, and Sulpitia alongside such "pernicious" women as Medea, Flora, and Sempronia. Boccaccio offers his praise of feminine virtue in a negative, back-handed way: since women are so weak in body and slow in mind, they deserve all the more praise when they manage to muster the sufficient "manly courage" (*virilem animum*) for undertaking tasks difficult (even!) for men. Boccaccio avoids mixing famous pagan women and illustrious women from sacred history (except for Eve) because the two classes of women differ fundamentally from one another: by acting according to their religious precepts, the women from sacred history behave almost contrary to human nature (*in adversam persepe humanitati tolerantiam coegere*) and therefore, presumably, disqualify themselves as examples of womanhood. Boccaccio's concluding remarks supply the final criterion according to which he selected his material for the *De mulieribus claris*: illustrious contemporary women are too few to be mentioned. Of course Boccaccio admits that he may have omitted some illustrious women, but not from the present. One might interpret this omission rather crassly in terms of Boccaccio's overall use of sources: if a woman were not discussed in the Latin *auctores* at Boccaccios's disposal, then she did not merit inclusion. Clearly Cicero, Vergil, Ovid, Servius, Flavius Josephus, Valerius Maximus, Augustine, and Orosius were not in any position to discuss Boccaccio's contemporaries! Lacking their authority, Boccaccio seems to have simply concluded that the only illustrious women were those sanctioned and authorized by the received literary canon. Under these circumstances Christine's reception of Boccaccio assumes an added moral dimension apart from the immediate question of sources.

Alfred Jeanroy, the first to examine Christine's debt to Boccaccio, restricted himself primarily to ascertaining parallel content between the *De mulieribus claris* and *The Book of the City of Ladies*[26].Some three-quarters of Christine's accounts are to be found in Boccaccio. Jeanroy found that Christine did not bother herself with "absolute fidelity" to her source; the reproach implicit here is that Christine's suppressions stem from her over-simplified approach to the mass of details which Boccaccio delighted in presenting. Carla Bozzolo examined the relation between *The Book of the City of Ladies* and the *Decameron* on the basis of Christine's adaption of three tales from Boccaccio (the wife of Bernabo, II.9; Ghismonda, IV.1; Lisabetta, IV.5) and arrived at a more positive evaluation: thematic convergence and divergence between the two reveal that Christine's adaption was intelligent and coherent and guided by a desire to mold the Boccaccian narrative to a more concise moral purpose.[27] One might add that this shift of emphasis implies and constitutes a correction of Boccaccio, and precisely this aspect of Christine's reception of Boccaccio has hitherto been somewhat neglected in the scholarly discussion. Needless to say, in *The Book of the City of the Ladies* Christine rejects implicitly all of Boccaccio's principles of selecting illustrious women worthy of literary celebration. Christine writes only about *good* women, whence in part her entirely nongratuitous insistence on the distinction lady/woman (*dame/femme*). While the term *dame* is of course connected to social standing, Christine does not forget the women of the lower classes in her City: they become, thanks to their good deeds or virtue, ladies *honoris causa*. Christine moreover includes such "notorious" women mentioned by Boccaccio in his Proemium as Medea and Sempronia without blinking, and she presents them in a wholly favorable light. For Christine, the ladies whom she praises did not prove their "manly courage" in order to merit inclusion, rather they presented a purer distillation of their own woman-hood. In other words, for Christine there was no intrinsic "problem of the studious woman."[28] That a woman was learned might present some men with a problem (Gerson was moved to bestow the epithet *femina ista virilis* on Christine, but this was probably well intentioned); the problem for a woman was overcoming narrowmindedness. Christine mentions her own mother's opposition to her receiving an education. In an anecdote at once charming and bewildering Christine tells of the Bolognese jurist Giovanni Andrea, who did not hesitate to send his daughter Novella in his place to hold his university lectures, though the university officials had a curtain drawn before her chair so that the students would not be distracted by her beauty. While Boccaccio largely succeeded in not treating women from sacred history in his *De mulieribus claris*, as he explicitly stated, Christine reserves special attention to them: *The Book of the City of Ladies* culminates in an exposition of one martyred virgin saint after another, following the installation of the Virgin Mary as the City's sovereign. Though she never explicitly rejects Boccaccio's pagan/sacred distinction, by incorporating Christian martyrs so prominently in her work, Christine refutes any attempt to restrict the illustriousness of women to pagan Antiquity. Christine's explosion of Boccaccio's categories is even more evident in her inclusion of contemporary examples and in her open-ended invitation to ladies of the past, present, and future to seek refuge in her City.

Christine's reorganization of Boccaccio's *De mulieribus*

claris is clear when one compares an outline of her *The Book of the City of Ladies* with its borrowings from Boccaccio. The following scheme presents the major lines of Christine's arguments and, in pertinent cases, the chapter number from *De mulieribus claris* is given in parentheses, based on the notes in Curnow's edition.[29] This should serve the double purpose of offering a summary of *The Book of the City of Ladies* and of showing how her thematic systematization—which presupposes an extraordinary effort on Christine's part to digest and recast Boccaccio's work—constitutes simultaneously an implicit refutation of her major source. What this survey omits is a close, case-by-case examination of the modifications Christine introduced. In some cases Christine uses Ovid's version in place of Boccaccio's; in others, particularly in part three, she borrows from the standard medieval reference work for history, Vincent de Beauvais' *Speculum historiale*. The overall effect is nevertheless quite consistent: what Boccaccio presents as notorious is reformulated so that fame replaces notoriety.

Part One
1. *Opening*
   2-7   *Appearance of the three Virtues, Reason, Rectitude, and Justice*
   8-26 *Ladies of political and military accomplishment:* Nicaula (43), Fredegund, Blanche, Semiramis (2), Thamiris (49, but Christine uses the version of the *Histoire ancienne jusqu'à César*, an historical compilation in Old French rather than Boccaccio's version), Penthesilea (32, but Christine again uses the *Histoire ancienne*), Zenobia (100), Artemisia (57), Camilla (39), Berenice of Cappadocia (72), and Cloelia (52).
   27-42 *Ladies of learning and skill:* Cornificia (86), Proba (97), Sappho (47), Leontium (40), Manto (30, but Christine seems aware of Dante's treatment of Manto in *Inferno* 20), Medea (17), Circe (38), Nicostrata or Carmenta (27), Minerva (6), Ceres (5), Isis (8), Arachne (18), Panphyles (44), Thamaris (56), Anas-

tasia, Sempronia (76), Irene (59), and Marcia (66).

43-48 *Ladies of prudence*: Gaia Cirilla (46), Dido (42), Ops (3), and Lavinia (41).

Part Two

1-6 *Ladies of vision and prophecy*: the sybils (in spite of some borrowing from Boccaccio, Christine relies on the *Speculum historiale* of Vincent de Beauvais), the sybil Erythrea (21), the sybil Almathea (26), Deborah, Elizabeth, Anna, the Queen of Sheba, Nicostrata or Carmenta (27), Cassandra (35, with details from the *Historie ancienne jusqu'à César*), Basine, Antonia.

7-11 *Examples of filial piety (daughters who loved their parents)*: Drypetina (75), Hypsipyle (16), Claudia (62), anonymous Roman woman (65).

12-29 *Examples of marital love*: Hypsicratea (78), Triaria (96), Arthemisia, Argia (29), Agrippina (90), Julia (81), Tertia Aemilia (74), Xanthippe, Pompeia Paulina (94), Sulpitia (85), Minyan women (31), Portia (82), Curia (83), Antonia, the wife of Alexander the Great.

30-35 *Examples of good which has come into the world thanks to women*: Thermutis, Judith, Esther, the Sabine women, Veturia (55), Queen Clotilda, Catulla.

36 *Arguments in favor of educating women*: Quintus Hortensius, father of Cornificia (86); Christine's father, Tommaso da Pizzano; Giovanni Andrea, father of Novella.

37-45 *Examples of chastity and the repugnance of women to rape*: Susanna, Sarah, Rebecca, Ruth, Penelope (40), Mariannes (87), Antonia, wife of Druso (89), Sulpitia (85), Lucretia (48), Queen of the Galatians (73), Hyppo (53), the Sicambrian women (80), Virginia (58).

46-53 *Examples of women's constancy; male fickleness compared to female steadfastness*: Nero (92-94), Galba, Otho, Vitellius, Griselda (Boccaccio's *Decameron*, Second Day, Ninth Tale).

54-60 *The faithfulness of women in love*: Dido (42), Medea (47), Thisbe (Christine used the version in Ovid's *Metamorphoses* instead of Boccaccio), Hero (Ovid is here again also the preferred source), Ghismonda (Boccaccio's

Decameron, Fourth Day, First Tale), Lisabetta (Boccaccio's *Decameron*, Fourth Day, Fifth Tale).

61 *Women famous by coincidence*: Deianeira (24), Juno (4), Europa (9), Jocasta (25), Medusa (22), Helen of Troy (37), Polyxena (33).

62-65 *Integrity and honesty as the basis for women's attractiveness*: Quinta Claudia (77), Lucretia (48), Queen Blanche.

66-69 *The generosity of woman*: Busa (59), Marguerite de la Rivière, Isabella of Bavaria, the Duchess of Orléans.

Part Three:
1 *Greeting to the Blessed Virgin*
2 *Mary Magdalene*
3 *Saint Catherine (example of a learned saint)*
4-9 *Martyred virgin saints*: Saint Margaret, Saint Lucy, Saint Martina, another Saint Lucy, Saint Justine, Saint Eulalia, Saint Marcianna, Saint Eufemia, Saint Theodosina, Saint Barbara, Saint Dorothy.
10 *Saint Christine, Christine's patron saint.*
11 *Women saints, who saw their children martyred before their own eyes, (i.e., the absorption of maternal love by the love of God)*
12-13 *Two women saints who lived disguised as monks:* Saint Marina, Saint Euphrosyne
14-17 *Other martyred women saints:* Anastasia, Theodata, Natalia, Afra
18 *Women who helped the Apostles:* Drusiana, Susanna, Maximilla, Ephigenia, Plautilla, Basilissa
19 *Conclusion.*

From such an overview one sees that it was one thing for Christine to have used Boccaccio's *De mulieribus claris* as her principal source and quite another for her to have so thoroughly reorganized it. Hitherto, source studies of *The Book of the City of Ladies* have failed to recognize how profoundly Christine remolded Boccaccio. The question of which version of the *De mulieribus claris* Christine used is secondary. She most likely had a French translation at hand, which does not exclude her having known the Latin original. The amazing feature of Christine's debt to Boccaccio is the extent of her borrowing and the thoroughgoing reorganization of this same material.

Although Christine frequently alludes to her own intellectual shortcomings,[30] the opening of *The Book of the City of Ladies* stresses Christine's cultivation of literature in a veritable hymn to literary study. It is precisely this *frequentacion d'estude de lettres* which sets the tone for Christine's argumentation. Christine confronts the allegations of women's inability to appreciate literary culture in an astonishingly learned and cultivated prose whose very difficulty serves simultaneously as the hallmark of her own culture. The irony here is patent. The language Christine uses casts the question of women's relationship to literary culture in an entirely different light, (indeed, the English translator of Christine's *Epistre d'Othea* thought *The Book of the City of Ladies* was written by a man commissioned by Christine!).

For Christine the touchstones of the dignity of her literary tools correspond to Dante's notion of an "illustrious vernacular" which combines the existential authenticity of the vernacular with the learnedness of Latin.[31] Christine's diction has long attracted considerable attention because of its cultivated learnedness: her neologism of learned words,[32] her preference for archaic Old French words, her use of learned, *i.e.* Latinate, spelling to make words resemble their respective Latin *etyma*. Moreover, her often criticized use of complicated periodic syntax, in imitation of Latin,[33] corresponds to her striving for the "defense and illustration" of the vernacular in tandem with her "defense and illustration" of femininity. Clément Marot, writing in his "Rondeau à Jeanne Gaillarde," recognized this essential trait in Christine's work: "D'avoir le prix en science et doctrine/Bien merita de Pisan la Christine." ("Christine de Pizan well deserved having the prize for knowledge and learnedness.") Christine envisaged her literary vocation in the vernacular in similar terms as Dante: that is, both viewed their poetic calling as emerging from a confrontation with Vergil, whose work they understood as the essential embodiment of poetry. In a long passage in the *Chemin de long estude*, which might be understood in part as a poetic self-portrayal, Christine recalls Dante's meeting Vergil in the first canto of *The Inferno*:

> Dant de Florence recorde
> En son livre qu'il composa
> Ou il moult beau stile posa
> Quante en la silve fu entrez
> Ou tout de paour ert oultrez.
> Lors que Virgile s'aparu
> A lui, dont il fu secouru,
> Adont lui dist par grant estude
> Ce mot: "Vaille moi lonc estude
> Qui m'a fait cercher tes volumes
> Par qui ensemble accointance eumes."
> Or cognois a cele parole
> Qui ne fu nice ne frivole
> Que le vaillant poete Dant,
> Qui a lonc estude ot la dent,
> Estoit en ce chemin entrez
> Quant Virgile y fu encontrez,
> Qui le mena par mi enfer
> Ou plus durs lieus vid que fer.
> Si dis que je n'oublieroie
> Celle parole: ains la diroie
> En lieu d'evvangile ou de croix
> Au passer de divers destrois
> Ou puis en maint peril me vis.
> (vv. 1120-1143, ed. Eargle)

("Dante of Florence tells in the book he wrote with such exquisite style how he entered the wood where he was overcome with fear. Vergil then appeared to him, by whom he was rescued and Dante eagerly told him, 'May that long study help me which made me search through your volumes, thanks to which we became acquainted.' I knew from this remark—which was neither silly nor frivolous—that the brave poet Dante, anxious for arduous study, had entered this path when he met Vergil there, who led him through Hell where he saw places harder than iron. So I said that I would not forget this motto but would repeat it in place of the Gospel or Cross when passing through the various straits where I found myself in great danger.")

This passage has usually been used by scholars to show that Christine imitated Dante's cosmic pilgrimage, that Dante's work had been diffused to France by the time Christine was writing (and that Christine was the first French writer to mention Dante, which, in fact, is not the case, for Philippe de Mezières mentions "le livre de Dante" in his *Songe du vieil pèlerin*, composed in 1382[34]). Its significance, however, is far greater, for the passage from *The Inferno* to which Christine alludes is Dante's invocation of Vergil to authorize his mission as a vernacular poet:

> O de li altri poeti onore e lume,
>   vagliami 'l lungo studio e 'l grande amore
>   che m'ha fatto cerca lo tuo volume.
> Tu se' lo mio maestro e 'l mio autore,
>   tu se' solo colui da cu' io tolsi
>   lo bello stile che m'ha fatto onore.
>
> (*Inf.* I, 82-87)

("O glory and light of other poets, may the long study and the great love that have made me search your volume avail me! You are my master and my author. You alone are he from whom I took the fair style that has done me honor." [edition and translation by Charles Singleton].)

Christine's *Chemin de long estude* is a calque of Dante's "lungo studio," that is, Christine explicitly conceives her literary career as a learned continuation in the vernacular of the poetic archievement of Vergil. This notion is her poetic Gospel, as she herself says. This is no small undertaking. It is indicative of the seriousness with which Christine viewed herself as a vernacular poet and corresponds well with the striking features of Christine's language, neologisms of learned words, cultivation of archaic Old French words, a complicated Latinate periodic syntax, and with the putative atmosphere in which Christine worked. While one cannot draw definite conclusions regarding the possible extent of Christine's personal acquaintance with Parisian humanists of the early fifteenth century (and Eric Hicks correctly warns against "conclusions hâtives"), Christine's extensive familiarity with contemporary French translation of Latin authors is a necessary corollary to her thematization of the learnedness and dignity of vernacular poetry which so informs *The Book of the City of Ladies*.

The Book of the City of Ladies is found in some twenty-five manuscripts[35] and several of these were executed during Christine's lifetime, most probably under her supervision. They include:

1. Paris, Bibliothèque Nationale, Fonds français 607, which was presented to John, Duke of Berry, and is dated 1407/1408.
2. Paris, Bibliothèque Nationale, Fonds français 1179, executed between November 1407 and 1410.
3. Brussels, Bibliothèque royale 9393, came from the library of the dukes of Burgundy and was probably copied for John the Fearless and his wife prior to 1410.
4. Paris, Bibliothèque Nationale, Fonds français 1178, dated between 1410 and 1418.
5. London, British Library, Harley 4431, dated between 1410 and 1415, belonged to Isabella of Bavaria.

The Harley 4431 manuscript is of most interest here because it probably represents the ultimate form of the work as intended by Christine[36] and because the possibility exists that Christine herself may have corrected it in her own hand.[37] For the present translation I have used a photocopy of Harley 4431 which is easily readable and compared it with the text offered by Curnow based on the Bibliothèque Nationale, Fonds français 607 codex. In all cases I have followed the text and paragraphing of the Harley manuscript except to indent for a new speaker. The five manuscripts listed above present almost identical versions of the text. My preference for the Harley manuscript stems from the philological arguments referred to, as well as from the principle that the text to be used, given the particular history of this work, should correspond to the final version Christine proposed. (A bilingual edition of *The Book of the City of Ladies* had been hoped for, but had to be abandoned in view of the exorbitant cost.) I have an additional, largely aesthetic reason for preferring the Harley manuscript: its orthography is more Latinate than that of the other manuscripts.[38] I would like to view the increased orthographic learnedness as an additional—albeit slight—argument on Christine's part for the affinity of women and learning.

The Book of the City of Ladies constitutes at once a moving *document humain* and a literary landmark. It represents the first work by a woman in praise of women. For the literary historian, it is important for the transmission and reception of Boccaccio's work in France. But as a literary composition it is more interesting for the dovetailing of its form and its content: the affinity of women and learning is both its vehicle and its message, and the one is inseparable from the other. Christine's first modern editor, Maurice Roy, noted in 1886 in his opening remarks to her *Œuvres poétiques* that a full accounting of Christine's life and works would have to await the complete publication of her works. Almost a century later this goal remains to be achieved. It is hoped this introduction and translation make this goal somewhat nearer.

I would like to take this occasion to recognize and thank Karen Braziller for her careful and friendly nurturing of this entire undertaking from its inception to its completion. Charity Cannon Willard was kind enough to read the introduction and notes and to suggest several revisions. My wife, Ingrid, also deserves special thanks for all her support and encouragement, and it is to her, *paohlbörger in Stientjes grote duorp för frauenlüe,* that I dedicate this translation.

EJR
Münster i.W., November 1981

NOTES

1. The chronology of Christine's life has been established largely from her own works. The biographical details here are from Suzanne Solente, "Christine de Pizan," *Histoire littéraire de la France* 40 (Paris, 1974), pp. 335-422, which is the most recent scholarly treatment of Christine. Earlier biographical treatments include: Gustav Gröber, *Grundriss der romanischen Philologie*, (Strasbourg, 1902), v. II, 1, pp. 1091-1099; Marie-Josèphe Pinet, *Christine de Pisan (1364-1430), Étude biographique et littéraire*, (Paris, 1927), and a popular biography by Enid McLeod, *The Order of the Rose, The Life and Ideas of Christine de Pisan*, (London, 1976).

2. The number of recent works treating the historical role of women in the Middle Ages is quite large. The following studies should be mentioned: E. Power, *Medieval Women*, (Cambridge, 1975); C. Erickson and K. Casey, "Women in the Middle Ages: A Working Bibliography," *Medieval Studies* 38 (1976); Barbara Beuys, *Familienleben in Deutschland, Neue Bilder aus der deutschen Vergangenheit*, (Reinbek bei Hamburg, 1980); Georges Duby, *Le chevalier, la femme et le prêtre; le mariage dans la France médiévale*, (Paris, 1981); and Shulamith Shahar, *Die Frau im Mittelalter*, (German translation of the Hebrew; Königstein, 1981).

3. Millard Meiss, *French Painting in the Time of Jean de Berry, The Late Fourteenth Century and the Patronage of the Duke* (London, 1968), pp. 1-13, and *ibid., The Limbourgs and Their Contemporaries* (New York, 1974), pp. 7-41.

4. Cf. My forthcoming article in the *Zeitschrift für romanische Philologie*, on "Reflections in Oiseuse's Mirror; Iconographic Tradition, Luxuria, and the *Roman de la Rose.*"

5. This list is deriving from Solente's list of Christine's works and her datings. I have up-dated and supplemented many entries.

6. Cf. Nadia Margolis, *The Poetics of History: An Analysis of Christine de Pizan's "Livre de la Mutacion de Fortune"* (Ph.D., Stanford University, 1977); DAI 38/06-A, p. 3544.

7. Josette Wisman has also edited this text as an appendix to her 1976 Ph.D. dissertation from the Catholic University of America, *L'Humanisme dans l'œuvre de Christine de Pisan*, DAI 37/02-A, p. 961.

8. Cf. Gianni Mombello, "Per un'edizione critica dell' *Epistre Othea* de Christine de Pizan," *Studi francesi* 8 (1964), pp. 402-408, 9 (1965) pp. 1-12; and, *ibid., La tradizione manoscritta dell'Epistre d'Othea di Christine di Pisan* (Turin, 1967).

9. Cf. *The Epistle of Othea*, translated from the French text by Stephen Scrope, edited by Curt F. Bühler, (London, 1970).

10. Charity Cannon Willard, "The Manuscript Tradition of the *Livre des Trois Vertus* and Christine de Pizan's Audience," *Journal of the History of Ideas 27* (1966), p. 440. The French text is not yet available in a critical edition.

11. *Le Livre du corps de policie,* critical edition by Robert H. Lucas, (Geneva, 1967). A facsimile edition of Scott's 1521 English translation appeared in New York in 1971. Cf. also Diane Borstein, *The Middle English Translation of Christine de Pisan's "Livre du corps de policie,"* (Heidelberg, 1977).

12. *"Les Sept psaumes allegorisés" of Christine de Pisan,* a critical edition by Ruth Ringland Rains, (Washington, D.C., 1965), reviewed by Charity Cannon Willard in *Romance Philology* 21:1 (1967), pp. 129-133.

13. There is no critical edition of the French text. The English translation made in 1489 by William Caxton was edited by A.T.P. Byles, *The Book of fayttes of armes and of chivalrye,* (London, 1932).

14. *Le Livre de la paix of Christine de Pisan,* edited by Charity Cannon Willard, (The Hague, 1958).

15. A partial edition was published by Suzanne Solente, "Un traité inédit de Christine de Pisan, *L'Epistre de la prison de vie humaine,"* *Bibliothèque de l'École des chartes* 85 (1924), pp. 263-301. The analogy to Vincent of Beauvais' *Consolatio* was suggested by Astrik L. Gabriel, "The Educational Ideas of Christine de Pisan," *Journal of the History of Ideas* 16 (1955), p. 6.

16. The best known statement of this topos in Old French Literature is found in the prologue to Chrétien de Troyes' *Cligés.* For its ramifications in Old French literature, cf. Michelle Freeman, "Problems in Romance Composition: Ovid, Chrétien de Troyes, and the *Romance of the Rose,"* *Romance Philology* 30 (1976-77) pp. 158-168.

17. Maureen Curnow, *The "Livre de la Cité des Dames": A Critical Edition,* (Ph.D., Vanderbilt University, 1975), pp. 138-155. Curnow failed to see that Christine's *The Book of the City of Ladies* is a refutation of Boccaccio's *De mulieribus claris.*

18. Dietmar Rieger, "Die französische Dichterin im Mittelalter: Marie de France—die 'trobairitz'—Christine de Pizan," *Die französische Autorin vom Mittelalter bis zur Gegenwart,* hrsg. von Renate Baader und Dietmar Fricke, (Wiesbaden, 1979), pp. 44-45.

19. Gianni Mombello, "Quelques aspects de la pensée politique de Christine de Pisan d'après ses œuvres publiées," *Culture et politique en France à l'epoque de l'humanisme et de la Renaissance,* ed. Franco Simone, (Turin, 1974), pp. 43-153.

20. Claude Gauvard, "Christine de Pisan a-t-elle eu une pensée politique?", *Revue historique* 250 (v. 97) (1973), pp. 417-430.
21. Pierre-Yves Badel, *Le Roman de la Rose au XIVe siècle, Étude de la réception de l'œuvre*, (Geneva, 1980).
22. F. Douglas Kelly, "Reflections on the Role of Christine de Pisan as a Feminist writer," *sub-stance* 2 (1972), p. 67.
23. Charity Cannon Willard, "A Fifteenth-Century View of Women's Role in Medieval Society: Christine de Pizan's *Livre des Trois Vertus*," in: *The Role of Women in the Middle Ages,* ed. by Rosemarie Thee Morewedge, (London, 1975), p. 100.
24. Angus F. Kennedy and Kenneth Varty, "Christine de Pisan's *Ditié de Jehanne d'Arc*, Part II," *Nottingham Medieval Studies,* 19 (1975), p. 60.
25. The French translation by Laurent de Premierfait was completed around 1401. For the purposes of the discussion here I have used the critical edition of the *De mulieribus claris* prepared by Vittorio Zaccaria, (Milan, 1967), and in my translation I have followed Zaccaria's orthography for proper names in most cases. I have also given chapter headings for stories from the Latin text of *De mulieribus claris* rather than the French translation to which Curnow refers. Obviously it would have been better to give the references in the translation but since the Latin original is available for comparison while the French translation exists only in manuscript, it seemed more practical to proceed in this manner. An English translation of Boccaccio's *De mulieribus claris* was published by Guido Guarino, *Concerning Famous Women* (New Brunswick, 1963).
26. Alfred Jeanroy, "Boccace et Christine de Pisan, Le *De claris mulieribus*, principale source du *Livre de la Cité des Dames*," *Romania* 48 (1922), pp. 92-105.
27. Carla Bozzolo, "Il *Decameron* come fonte del *Livre de la Cité des Dames* di Christine de Pisan; *Miscellanea di studi e ricerche sul Quattrocento francese,* ed. Franco Simone, (Turin, 1966), pp. 3-24.
28. Cf. Susan Groag Bell, "Christine de Pizan (1364-1430): Humanism and the Problems of a Studious Woman," *Feminist Studies* 3 (1975), pp. 173-184.
29. I have silently corrected mistaken references in Curnow's notes and on several occasions supplemented her remarks on sources.
30. In *The Book of the City of Ladies* (I.7) Christine calls herself "tabernacle troublé et obscur de la simple et ignorant estudiente." She excuses the simple prose of her letters on *The Romance of the Rose*. Curnow (p. 1044) gives three additional examples of Christine's invocation of the "modesty" *topos*: "moy, femme simple et ignorent en qui n'a science ne autre savoir ne mais

stille vulgal et rural en fait d'escripture" (*Livre de la paix*, p. 60);
"Comment sera ce possible/ A moy simple et pou sensible/
De proprement exprimer?" (*La Mutacion de Fortune*, vv. 1-3);
"Pour ce moy, Christine de Pizan, femme soubz les tenebres
d'ignorance an regart de cler entendement, mais douée de don
de Dieu et nature en tant comme desir se peut estendre en amour
d'estude," (*Le Livre des fais et bonnes meurs du sage Roy Charles* V,
v.I. p. 5). Perhaps Christine protests too much.

31. Cf. Karl Uitti's remarks on Dante's *De vulgari eloquentia* in his
Linguistics and Literary Theory, (New York, 1969), pp. 36-92.

32. Lucy M. Gay first studied Christine's diction, "On the Language
of Christine de Pisan," *Modern Philology 6* (July 1908, pp. 69-96).
She remarks (p. 72): "By Godefoy or by the authors of the
Dictionnaire générale de la langue française, she is credited with using
for the first time a large number of words: artiste, vindicatif,
compact, pertinent, circonspect, influer, invective, palpable,
stimulation, temporizer, investigation, preparatif, blandices,
transcendent, harangue etc." Since Gay wrote her article, a
great deal of etymological research has been done which somewhat modifies Gay's conclusion. After consulting Tobler/Lom-
matzsch's *Altfranzösisches Wörterbuch* and Warburg's *Französisches
Etymologisches Wörterbuch,* I have been able to update Gay's
claims: the first attributions for *circonspect, compact, invective,
investigation,* and *palpable* are found in Christine's works; *influer* is
an astrological term first dated to the fourteenth century, and
Christine probably learned this word from contact with her
astrologer father; *artiste* is a borrowing from medieval Latin and
while it cannot be determined when the word first became
"French" (competing with *artisan*), Christine might have been
influenced by the use of the word in Dante, Cino, and Boccaccio.
Nevertheless, the point remains that Christine's vocabulary is
extraordinarily learned.

33. Charity Cannon Willard in her edition of the *Livre de la paix*
noted (p. 50) "Christine's desire to imitate Latin sentence structure was most unfortunate when it led her to multiply subordinate clauses until the results were both involved and obscure." Gay noted how difficult Christine's prose is for a
modern French speaker: "Michaud and Poujoulat, who publish
in their collection of memoirs *Le Livre des fais et bonnes meurs du
sage Roy Charles V,* feel constrained to publish also a translation
of it in modern French, while it is not thought necessary to
publish a translation of the memoirs of Boucicaut, written by
one of Christine's contemporaries."

34. Giuseppe di Stefano, "Alain Chartier, ambassadeur à Venise,"

Culture et politique en France à l'époque de l'humanisme et de la Renaissance, ed. Franco Simone, (Turin, 1974), p. 166.

35. Solente lists twenty-seven manuscripts, one of which turns out to be a manuscript of the *Livre des trois vertus.* Curnow lists twenty-five codices, omitting the Leipzig manuscript mentioned by Solente.

36. Gianni Mombello, in *La tradizione manoscritta,* considers that the Harley manuscript provides the ultimate form of *L'Epistre d'Othea* (p. 210). The same may be argued for *The Book of the City of Ladies,* since the Harley manuscript is the last manuscript of the work copied during Christine's lifetime and under her supervision.

37. Charity Cannon Willard, "An Autograph Manuscript of Christine de Pizan?" *Studi francesi* 9 (1965), pp. 452–457.

38. For purposes of comparison one can cite a phrase from the opening of *The Book of the City of Ladies* where Christine writes in BN 607, "Mathéolus, qui entre les livres n'a aucune reputacion et qui *traitte* en manière de trufferie, mais generaument en tous *traittiez* philosophes, *pouettes,* tous orateurs..." In Harley 4431 the italicized words in the above passage are spelled *traicte, traictiez,* and *poetes;* that is, their orthography conforms more closely to their Latin roots, *tractare, tractus,* and *poeta.* This is perhaps a minor point, but since, as Aby Warburg said, "Der liebe Gott steckt im Detail" ("The good Lord lurks in details"), it is indicative of the care with which the Harley manuscript was written. Of course Harley 4431 is not flawless, but it represents an important stage in the transmission of the text. In his research on Christine's *Cent Ballades,* James Laidlaw has noted a similar evolution, "the preparation of a new collected manuscript was for Christine an opportunity to correct and revise her poems and other works," ("Christine de Pizan, the Earl of Salisbury and Henry IV," to appear in *French Studies*).

THE BOOK OF THE CITY OF LADIES

1. HERE BEGINS THE BOOK OF THE CITY OF LADIES,
WHOSE FIRST CHAPTER TELLS WHY AND FOR WHAT
PURPOSE THIS BOOK WAS WRITTEN.

One day as I was sitting alone in my study surrounded   *I.1.1*
by books on all kinds of subjects, devoting myself
to literary studies, my usual habit, my mind dwelt at
length on the weighty opinions of various authors whom I
had studied for a long time. I looked up from my book,
having decided to leave such subtle questions in peace and
to relax by reading some light poetry. With this in mind, I
searched for some small book. By chance a strange
volume came into my hands, not one of my own, but one
which had been given to me along with some others.
When I held it open and saw from its title page that it
was by Mathéolus, I smiled, for though I had never seen
it before, I had often heard that like other books it discussed respect for women. I thought I would browse
through it to amuse myself. I had not been reading for
very long when my good mother called me to refresh
myself with some supper, for it was evening. Intending
to look at it the next day, I put it down. The next
morning, again seated in my study as was my habit, I
remembered wanting to examine this book by Mathéolus.
I started to read it and went on for a little while. Because
the subject seemed to me not very pleasant for people
who do not enjoy lies, and of no use in developing virtue
or manners, given its lack of integrity in diction and
theme, and after browsing here and there and reading
the end, I put it down in order to turn my attention to
more elevated and useful study. But just the sight of this
book, even though it was of no authority, made me
wonder how it happened that so many different men—
and learned men among them—have been and are so
inclined to express both in speaking and in their treatises

3

and writings so many wicked insults about women and their behavior. Not only one or two and not even just this Mathéolus (for this book had a bad name anyway and was intended as a satire) but, more generally, judging from the treatises of all philosophers and poets and from all the orators—it would take too long to mention their names—it seems that they all speak from one and the same mouth. They all concur in one conclusion: that the behavior of women is inclined to and full of every vice. Thinking deeply about these matters, I began to examine my character and conduct as a natural woman and, similarly, I considered other women whose company I frequently kept, princesses, great ladies, women of the middle and lower classes, who had graciously told me of their most private and intimate thoughts, hoping that I could judge impartially and in good conscience whether the testimony of so many notable men could be true. To the best of my knowledge, no matter how long I confronted or dissected the problem, I could not see or realize how their claims could be true when compared to the natural behavior and character of women. Yet I still argued vehemently against women, saying that it would be impossible that so many famous men—such solemn scholars, possessed of such deep and great understanding, so clear-sighted in all things, as it seemed—could have spoken falsely on so many occasions that I could hardly find a book on morals where, even before I had read it in its entirety, I did not find several chapters or certain sections attacking women, no matter who the author was. This reason alone, in short, made me conclude that, although my intellect did not perceive my own great faults and, likewise, those of other women because of its simpleness and ignorance, it was however truly fitting that such was the case. And so I relied more on the judgment of others than on what I myself felt and knew. I was so transfixed in this line of thinking for such a long time that it seemed as if I were in a stupor. Like a gushing fountain, a series of authorities, whom I recalled one after another, came to mind, along with their opinions on this topic. And I finally decided that God formed a vile creature when He made woman, and I wondered how such a worthy artisan could have deigned to make such an abominable work which, from what they say, is the vessel as well as the refuge and abode of every evil and vice. As I was thinking this, a great unhappiness and sadness welled up in my heart, for I detested myself and the entire feminine sex, as though we were monstrosities in nature. And in my lament I spoke these words:

"Oh, God, how can this be? For unless I stray from *I.1.2* my faith, I must never doubt that Your infinite wisdom and most perfect goodness ever created anything which was not good. Did You yourself not create woman in a very special way and since that time did You not give her all those inclinations which it pleased You for her to have? And how could it be that You could go wrong in anything? Yet look at all these accusations which have been judged, decided, and concluded against women. I do not know how to understand this repugnance. If it is so, fair Lord God, that in fact so many abominations abound in the female sex, for You Yourself say that the testimony of two or three witnesses lends credence, why shall I not doubt that this is true? Alas, God, why did You not let me be born in the world as a man, so that all my inclinations would be to serve You better, and so that I would not stray in anything and would be as perfect as a man is said to be? But since Your kindness has not been extended to me, then forgive my negligence in Your service, most fair Lord God, and may it not displease You, for the servant who receives fewer gifts from his lord is less obliged in his service." I spoke these words to God in my lament and a great deal more for a very long time in sad reflection, and in my folly I considered myself most unfortunate because God had made me inhabit a female body in this world.

2. HERE CHRISTINE DESCRIBES HOW THREE LADIES APPEARED TO HER AND HOW THE ONE WHO WAS IN FRONT SPOKE FIRST AND COMFORTED HER IN HER PAIN.

I.2.1 So occupied with these painful thoughts, my head bowed in shame, my eyes filled with tears, leaning on the pommel of my chair's armrest, I suddenly saw a ray of light fall on my lap, as though it were the sun. I shuddered then, as if wakened from sleep, for I was sitting in a shadow where the sun could not have shone at that hour. And as I lifted my head to see where this light was coming from, I saw three crowned ladies standing before me, and the splendor of their bright faces shone on me and throughout the entire room. Now no one would ask whether I was surprised, for my doors were shut and they had still entered. Fearing that some phantom had come to tempt me and filled with great fright, I made the Sign of the Cross on my forehead.

I.2.2 Then she who was the first of the three smiled and began to speak, "Dear daughter, do not be afraid, for we have not come here to harm or trouble you but to console you, for we have taken pity on your distress, and we have come to bring you out of the ignorance which so blinds your own intellect that you shun what you know for a certainty and believe what you do not know or see or recognize except by virtue of many strange opinions. You resemble the fool in the prank who was dressed in women's clothes while he slept; because those who were making fun of him repeatedly told him he was a woman, he believed their false testimony more readily than the certainty of his own identity. Fair daughter, have you lost all sense? Have you forgotten that when fine gold is tested in the furnace, it does not change or vary in strength but becomes purer the more it is hammered and handled in different ways? Do you not know that the best things are the most debated and the most discussed? If you wish to consider the question of the highest form of reality, which consists in ideas or celestial substances, consider whether the greatest philosophers who have lived and whom you support against your own sex have ever resolved whether ideas are false and contrary to the truth. Notice how these same philosophers contradict and criticize one another, just as you have seen in the *Metaphysics* where Aristotle takes their opinions to task and speaks similarly of Plato and other philosophers. And note, moreover, how even Saint Augustine and the Doctors of the Church have criticized Aristotle in certain passages, although he is known as the prince of philosophers in whom both natural and moral philosophy attained their highest level. It also seems that you think that all the words of the philosophers are articles of faith, that they could never be wrong. As far as the poets of whom you speak are concerned, do you not know that they spoke on many subjects in a fictional way and that often they mean the contrary of what their words openly say? One can interpret them according to the grammatical figure of *antiphrasis*, which means, as you know, that if you call something bad, in fact, it is good, and also vice versa. Thus I advise you to profit from their works and to interpret them in the manner in which they are intended in those passages where they attack women. Perhaps this man, who called himself Mathéolus in his own book, intended it in such a way, for there are many things which, if taken literally, would be pure heresy. As for the attack against the estate of marriage—which is a holy estate, worthy and ordained by God—made not only by Mathéolus but also by others and even by the *Romance of the Rose* where greater credibility is averred because of the authority of its author, it is evident and proven by experience that the contrary of the evil which they posit and claim to be found in this estate through the obligation and fault of women is true. For where has the husband ever been found who would allow his wife to have authority to abuse and insult him as a matter of course, as these authorities maintain? I believe that, regardless of what you might have read, you will never see such a husband with your own eyes, so badly colored

7   *Christine de Pizan*

are these lies. Thus, in conclusion, I tell you, dear friend, that simplemindedness has prompted you to hold such an opinion. Come back to yourself, recover your senses, and do not trouble yourself anymore over such absurdities. For you know that any evil spoken of women so generally only hurts those who say it, not women themselves."

3. HERE CHRISTINE TELLS HOW THE LADY WHO HAD SAID THIS SHOWED HER WHO SHE WAS AND WHAT HER CHARACTER AND FUNCTION WERE AND TOLD HER HOW SHE WOULD CONSTRUCT A CITY WITH THE HELP OF THESE SAME THREE LADIES.

I.3.1   The famous lady spoke these words to me, in whose presence I do not know which one of my senses was more overwhelmed: my hearing from having listened to such worthy words or my sight from having seen her radiant beauty, her attire, her reverent comportment, and her most honored countenance. The same was true of the others, so that I did not know which one to look at, for the three ladies resembled each other so much that they could be told apart only with difficulty, except for the last one, for although she was of no less authority than the others, she had so fierce a visage that whoever, no matter how daring, looked in her eyes would be afraid to commit a crime, for it seemed that she threatened criminals unceasingly. Having stood up out of respect, I looked at them without saying a word, like someone too overwhelmed to utter a syllable. Reflecting on who these beings could be, I felt much admiration in my heart and, if I could have dared, I would have immediately asked their names and identities and what was the meaning of the different scepters which each one carried in her right hand, which were of fabulous richness, and why they had come here. But since I considered myself unworthy to address these questions to such high ladies as they appeared to me, I did not dare to, but continued to keep my gaze fixed on them, half-afraid and half-reassured by the words which I had heard, which had made me reject my first impression. But the most wise lady who had spoken to me and who knew in her mind what I was thinking, as one who has insight into everything, addressed my reflections, saying:

"Dear daughter, know that God's providence, which I.3.2 leaves nothing void or empty, has ordained that we, though celestial beings, remain and circulate among the people of the world here below, in order to bring order and maintain in balance those institutions we created according to the will of God in the fulfillment of various offices, that God whose daughters we three all are and from whom we were born. Thus it is my duty to straighten out men and women when they go astray and to put them back on the right path. And when they stray, if they have enough understanding to see me, I come to them quietly in spirit and preach to them, showing them their error and how they have failed, I assign them the causes, and then I teach them what to do and what to avoid. Since I serve to demonstrate clearly and to show both in thought and deed to each man and woman his or her own special qualities and faults, you see me holding this shiny mirror which I carry in my right hand in place of a scepter. I would thus have you know truly that no one can look into this mirror, no matter what kind of creature, without achieving clear self-knowledge. My mirror has such great dignity that not without reason is it surrounded by rich and precious gems, so that you see, thanks to this mirror, the essences, qualities, proportions, and measures of all things are known, nor can anything be done well without it. And because, similarly, you wish to know what are the offices of my other sisters whom you see here, each will reply in her own person about her name and character, and this way our testimony will be all the more certain to you. But now I myself will declare the reason for our coming. I must assure you, as we do nothing without good cause, that our appearance here is not at all in vain. For, although we are not common to many places and our knowledge does not come to all people, nevertheless you, for your great love of investigating the truth through long and continual study, for which you come here, solitary and separated from the world, you have deserved and deserve, our devoted friend, to be visited and consoled by us in your agitation and sadness, so that you might also see clearly, in the midst of the darkness of your thoughts, those things which taint and trouble your heart.

I.3.3   "There is another greater and even more special reason for our coming which you will learn from our speeches: in fact we have come to vanquish from the world the same error into which you had fallen, so that from now on, ladies and all valiant women may have a refuge and defense against the various assailants, those ladies who have been abandoned for so long, exposed like a field without a surrounding hedge, without finding a champion to afford them an adequate defense, notwithstanding those noble men who are required by order of law to protect them, who by negligence and apathy have allowed them to be mistreated. It is no wonder then that their jealous enemies, those outrageous villains who have assailed them with various weapons, have been victorious in a war in which women have had no defense. Where is there a city so strong which could not be taken immediately if no resistance were forthcoming, or the law case, no matter how unjust, which was not won through the obstinance of someone pleading without opposition? And the simple, noble ladies, following the example of suffering which God commands, have cheerfully suffered the great attacks which, both in the spoken and the written word, have been wrongfully and sinfully perpetrated against women by men who all the while appealed to God for the right to do so. Now it is time for their just cause to be taken from Pharaoh's hands, and for this reason, we three ladies whom you see here, moved by pity, have come to you to announce a particular edifice built like a city wall, strongly constructed and well founded, which has been predestined and established by our aid and counsel for you to build, where no one will reside except all ladies of fame and women worthy of praise, for the walls of the city will be closed to those women who lack virtue."

4. HERE THE LADY EXPLAINS TO CHRISTINE THE CITY WHICH SHE HAS BEEN COMMISSIONED TO BUILD AND HOW SHE WAS CHARGED TO HELP CHRISTINE BUILD THE WALL AND ENCLOSURE, AND THEN GIVES HER NAME.

"Thus, fair daughter, the prerogative among women *I.4.1* has been bestowed on you to establish and build the City of Ladies. For the foundation and completion of this City you will draw fresh waters from us as from clear fountains, and we will bring you sufficient building stone, stronger and more durable than any marble with cement could be. Thus your City will be extremely beautiful, without equal, and of perpetual duration in the world.

"Have you not read that King Tros founded the great *I.4.2* city of Troy with the aid of Apollo, Minerva, and Neptune, whom the people of that time considered gods, and also how Cadmus founded the city of Thebes with the admonition of the gods? And yet over time these cities fell and have fallen into ruin. But I prophesy to you, as a true sybil, that this City, which you will found with our help, will never be destroyed, nor will it ever fall, but will remain prosperous forever, regardless of all its jealous enemies. Although it will be stormed by numerous assaults, it will never be taken or conquered.

"Long ago the Amazon kingdom was begun through *I.4.3* the arrangement and enterprise of several ladies of great courage who despised servitude, just as history books have testified. For a long time afterward they maintained it under the rule of several queens, very noble ladies whom they elected themselves, who governed them well and maintained their dominion with great strength. Yet, although they were strong and powerful and had conquered a large part of the entire Orient in the course of their rule and terrified all the neighboring lands (even the Greeks, who were then the flower of all countries in the world, feared them), nevertheless, after a time, the power of this kingdom declined, so that as with all earthly kingdoms, nothing but its name has survived to the present. But the edifice erected by you in this City which you must construct will be far stronger, and for its founding I was commissioned, in the course of our common deliberation, to supply you with durable and pure mortar to lay the sturdy foundations and to raise the lofty walls all around, high and thick, with mighty towers and strong bastions, surrounded by moats with firm blockhouses, just as is fitting for a city with a strong and lasting defense. Following our plan, you will set the foundations deep to last all the longer, and then you will raise the walls so high that they will not fear anyone. Daughter, now that I have told you the reason for our coming and so that you will more certainly believe my words, I want you to learn my name, by whose sound alone you will be able to learn and know that, if you wish to follow my commands, you have in me an administrator so that you may do your work flawlessly. I am called Lady Reason; you see that you are in good hands. For the time being then, I will say no more."

5. HERE CHRISTINE TELLS HOW THE SECOND LADY TOLD HER NAME AND WHAT SHE SERVED AS AND HOW SHE WOULD AID HER IN BUILDING THE CITY OF LADIES.

I.5.1   When the lady above finished her speech, before I could resume, the second lady began as follows: "I am called Rectitude and reside more in Heaven than on Earth, but as the radiance and splendor of God and messenger of His goodness, I often visit the just and exhort them to do what is right, to give to each person what is his according to his capacity, to say and uphold the truth, to defend the rights of the poor and the innocent, not to hurt anyone through usurpation, to uphold the reputation of those unjustly accused. I am the shield

and defense of the servants
and might of evil-doers. I
reward those who act well. Tl
His friends His secrets; I am tl
This shining ruler which you se
hand instead of a scepter is the str
rates right from wrong and shows
good and evil: who follows it doe
the rod of peace which reconciles
they find support and which beats an
What should I tell you about this? All t
by this ruler, for its powers are infinite.
to measure the edifice of the City whic
commissioned to build, and you will n
structing the façade, for erecting the hig
measuring the palaces, houses, and all pul
the streets and squares, and all things pr
populate the City. I have come as your assist
will be my duty. Do not be uneasy about t
and long circuit of the walls, for with God's
our assistance you will build fair and sturdy man
inns without leaving anything vague, and you wil
the City with no trouble."

6. HERE CHRISTINE TELLS HOW THE THIRD LADY HER WHO SHE WAS AND HER FUNCTION AND HOW WOULD HELP BUILD THE HIGH ROOFS OF THE TOW AND PALACES AND WOULD BRING TO HER THE QUEI ACCOMPANIED BY NOBLE LADIES.

Afterward, the third lady spoke and said, "My frienc
Christine, I am Justice, the most singular daughter of
God, and my nature proceeds purely from His person.
My residence is found in Heaven, on Earth, or in Hell:
in Heaven, for the glory of the saints and blessed souls;
on Earth, for the apportionment to each man of the good
or evil which he has deserved; in Hell, for the punishment
of the evil. I do not bend anywhere, for I have not friend
nor enemy nor changeable will; pity cannot persuade me

cruelty move me. My duty is only to judge, to decide,
to dispense according to each man's just deserts. I
tain all things in their condition, nothing could be
ble without me. I am in God and God is in me, and we
e as one and the same. Who follows me cannot fail, and
ıy way is sure. I teach men and women of sound mind
who want to believe in me to chastise, know, and correct
hemselves, and to do to others what they wish to have
done to themselves, to distribute wealth without favor,
to speak the truth, to flee and hate lies, to reject all
viciousness. This vessel of fine gold which you see me
hold in my right hand, made like a generous measure,
God, my Father, gave me, and it serves to measure out to
each his rightful portion. It carries the sign of the fleur-
de-lis of the Trinity, and in all portions it measures true,
nor can any man complain about my measure. Yet the
men of the Earth have other measures which they claim
depend upon and derive from mine, but they are mistaken. Often they measure in my shadow, and their
measure is not always true but sometimes too much for
some and too little for others. I could give a rather long
account of the duties of my office, but, put briefly, I
have a special place among the Virtues, for they are all
based on me. And of the three noble ladies whom you
see here, we are as one and the same, we could not
exist without one another; and what the first disposes, the
second orders and initiates, and then I, the third, finish
and terminate it. Thus I have been appointed by the will
of us three ladies to perfect and complete your City, and
my job will be to construct the high roofs of the towers
and of the lofty mansions and inns which will all be made
of fine shining gold. Then I will populate the City for
you with worthy ladies and the mighty Queen whom I
will bring to you. Hers will be the honor and prerogative
among all other women, as well as among the most
excellent women. And in this condition I will turn the
City over to you, completed with your help, fortified
and closed off with strong gates which I will search for
in Heaven, and then I will place the keys in your hands."

7. HERE CHRISTINE TELLS HOW SHE SPOKE TO THE THREE LADIES.

I.7.1

When the speeches of all three ladies were over—to which I had listened intently and which had completely taken away the unhappiness which I had felt before their coming—I threw myself at their feet, not just on my knees but completely prostrate because of their great excellence. Kissing the earth around their feet, adoring them as goddesses of glory, I began my prayer to them:

"Oh ladies of supreme dignity, radiance of the heavens and light of the earth, fountains of Paradise and joy of the blessed, where did such humility come from to Your Highnesses that you have deigned to come down from your pontifical seats and shining thrones to visit the troubled and dark tabernacle of this simple and ignorant student? Who could give fitting thanks for such a boon? With the rain and dew of your sweet words, you have penetrated and moistened the dryness of my mind, so that it now feels ready to germinate and send forth new branches capable of bearing fruits of profitable virtue and sweet savor. How will such grace be bestowed on me that I will receive the boon, as you have said, to build and construct in the world from now on a new city? I am not Saint Thomas the Apostle, who through divine grace built a rich palace in Heaven for the king of India, and my feeble sense does not know the craft, or the measures, or the study, or the science, or the practice of construction. And if, thanks to learning, these things were within my ken, where would I find enough physical strength in my weak feminine body to realize such an enormous task? But nevertheless, my most respected ladies, although the awesomeness of this news seems strange to me, I know well that nothing is impossible for God. Nor do I doubt that anything undertaken with your counsel and help will not be completed well. Thus, with all my strength, I praise God and you, my ladies, who have so honored me by assigning me such a noble commission, which I most happily accept. Behold your handmaiden ready to serve. Command and I will obey, and may it be unto me according to your words."

8. HERE CHRISTINE TELLS HOW, UNDER REASON'S COMMAND AND ASSISTANCE, SHE BEGAN TO EXCAVATE THE EARTH AND LAY THE FOUNDATION.

I.8.1   Then Lady Reason responded and said, "Get up, daughter! Without waiting any longer, let us go to the Field of Letters. There the City of Ladies will be founded on a flat and fertile plain, where all fruits and freshwater rivers are found and where the earth abounds in all good things. Take the pick of your understanding and dig and clear out a great ditch wherever you see the marks of my ruler, and I will help you carry away the earth on my own shoulders."

I.8.2   I immediately stood up to obey her commands and, thanks to these three ladies, I felt stronger and lighter than before. She went ahead, and I followed behind, and after we had arrived at this field I began to excavate and dig, following her marks with the pick of cross-examination. And this was my first work:

I.8.3   "Lady, I remember well what you told me before, dealing with the subject of how so many men have attacked and continue to attack the behavior of women, that gold becomes more refined the longer it stays in the furnace, which means the more women have been wrongfully attacked, the greater waxes the merit of their glory. But please tell me why and for what reason different authors have spoken against women in their books, since I already know from you that this is wrong; tell me if Nature makes man so inclined or whether they do it out of hatred and where does this behavior come from?"

Then she replied, "Daughter, to give you a way of entering into the question more deeply, I will carry away this first basketful of dirt. This behavior most certainly does not come from Nature, but rather is contrary to Nature, for no connection in the world is as great or as strong as the great love which, through the will of God, Nature places between a man and a woman. The causes which have moved and which still move men to attack women, even those authors in those books, are diverse and varied, just as you have discovered. For some have attacked women with good intentions, that is, in order to draw men who have gone astray away from the company of vicious and dissolute women, with whom they might be infatuated, or in order to keep these men from going mad on account of such women, and also so that every man might avoid an obscene and lustful life. They have attacked all women in general because they believe that women are made up of every abomination."

"My lady," I said then, "excuse me for interrupting you here, but have such authors acted well, since they were prompted by a laudable intention? For intention, the saying goes, judges the man."

"That is a misleading position, my good daughter," she said, "for such sweeping ignorance never provides an excuse. If someone killed you with good intention but out of foolishness, would this then be justified? Rather, those who did this, whoever they might be, would have invoked the wrong law; causing any damage or harm to one party in order to help another party is not justice, and likewise attacking all feminine conduct is contrary to the truth, just as I will show you with a hypothetical case. Let us suppose they did this intending to draw fools away from foolishness. It would be as if I attacked fire—a very good and necessary element nevertheless—because some people burnt themselves, or water because someone drowned. The same can be said of all good things which can be used well or used badly. But one must not attack them if fools abuse them, and you have yourself touched on this point quite well elsewhere in your writings. But those who have spoken like this so abundantly—whatever their intentions might be— have formulated their arguments rather loosely only to make their point. Just like someone who has a long and wide robe cut from a very large piece of cloth when the material costs him nothing and when no one opposes him, they exploit the rights of others. But just as you have said elsewhere, if these writers had only looked for the ways in which men can be led away from foolishness and could have been kept from tiring themselves in attacking the life and behavior of immoral and dissolute women—for to tell the straight truth, there is nothing which should be avoided more than an evil, dissolute, and perverted woman, who is like a monster in nature, a counterfeit estranged from her natural condition, which must be simple, tranquil, and upright—then I would grant you that they would have built a supremely excellent work. But I can assure you that these attacks on all women—when in fact there are so many excellent women—have never originated with me, Reason, and that all who subscribe to them have failed totally and will continue to fail. So now throw aside these black, dirty, and uneven stones from your work, for they will never be fitted into the fair edifice of your City.

I.8.4   "Other men have attacked women for other reasons: such reproach has occurred to some men because of their own vices and others have been moved by the defects of their own bodies, others through pure jealousy, still others by the pleasure they derive in their own personalities from slander. Others, in order to show they have read many authors, base their own writings on what they have found in books and repeat what other writers have said and cite different authors.

I.8.5   "Those who attack women because of their own vices are men who spent their youths in dissolution and enjoyed the love of many different women, used deception in many of their encounters, and have grown old in their sins without repenting, and now regret their past follies and the dissolute life they led. But Nature, which allows the will of the heart to put into effect what the powerful appetite desires, has grown cold in them. Therefore they are pained when they see that their 'good times' have now passed them by, and it seems to them that the young, who are now what they once were, are on top of the world. They do not know how to overcome their sadness except by attacking women, hoping to make women less attractive to other men. Everywhere one sees such old men speak obscenely and dishonestly, just as you can fully see with Mathéolus, who himself confesses that he was an impotent old man filled with desire. You can thereby convincingly prove, with this one example, how what I tell you is true, and you can assuredly believe that it is the same with many others.

"But these corrupt old men, like an incurable leprosy,   *I.8.6* are not the upstanding men of old whom I made perfect in virtue and wisdom—for not all men share in such corrupt desire, and it would be a real shame if it were so. The mouths of these good men, following their hearts, are all filled with exemplary, honest, and discreet words. These same men detest misdeeds and slander, and neither attack nor defame men and women, and they counsel the avoidance of evil and the pursuit of virtue and the straight path.

"Those men who are moved by the defect of their own   *I.8.7* bodies have impotent and deformed limbs but sharp and malicious minds. They have found no other way to avenge the pain of their impotence except by attacking women who bring joy to many. Thus they have thought to divert others away from the pleasure which they cannot personally enjoy.

"Those men who have attacked women out of jealousy   *I.8.8* are those wicked ones who have seen and realized that many women have greater understanding and are more noble in conduct than they themselves, and thus they are pained and disdainful. Because of this, their overweening jealousy has prompted them to attack all women, intending to demean and diminish the glory and praise of such women, just like the man—I cannot remember which one—who tries to prove in his work, *De philosophia*, that it is not fitting that some men have revered women and says that those men who have made so much of women pervert the title of his book: they transform 'philosophy,' the love of wisdom, into 'philofolly,' the love of folly. But I promise and swear to you that he himself, all throughout the lie-filled deductions of his argument, transformed the content of his book into a true philofolly.

I.8.9   "As for those men who are naturally given to slander, it is not surprising that they slander women since they attack everyone anyway. Nevertheless, I assure you that any man who freely slanders does so out of a great wickedness of heart, for he is acting contrary to reason and contrary to Nature: contrary to reason insofar as he is most ungrateful and fails to recognize the good deeds which women have done for him, so great that he could never make up for them, no matter how much he try, and which he continuously needs women to perform for him; and contrary to Nature in that there is no naked beast anywhere, nor bird, which does not naturally love its female counterpart. It is thus quite unnatural when a reasonable man does the contrary.

I.8.10   "And just as there has never been any work so worthy, so skilled is the craftsman who made it, that there were not people who wanted, and want, to counterfeit it, there are many who wish to get involved in writing poetry. They believe they cannot go wrong, since others have written in books what they take the situation to be, or rather, *mis*-take the situation—as I well know! Some of them undertake to express themselves by writing poems of water without salt, such as these, or ballads without feeling, discussing the behavior of women or of princes or of other people, while they themselves do not know how to recognize or to correct their own servile conduct and inclinations. But simple people, as ignorant as they are, declare that such writing is the best in the world."

9. HERE CHRISTINE TELLS HOW SHE DUG IN THE GROUND, BY WHICH SHOULD BE UNDERSTOOD THE QUESTIONS

WHICH SHE PUT TO REASON, AND HOW REASON RE-
PLIED TO HER.

"Now I have prepared for you and commanded from   *I.9.1*
you a great work. Consider how you can continue to
excavate the ground following my marks." And so, in
order to obey her command, I struck with all my force
in the following way:

"My lady, how does it happen that Ovid, who is   *I.9.2*
thought to be one of the best poets—although many
believe, and I would agree with them, thanks to your
correcting me, that Vergil is much more praiseworthy—
that Ovid attacks women so much and so frequently,
as in the book he calls *Ars amatoria*, as well as in the
Remedia amoris and other of his volumes?"

She replied, "Ovid was a man skilled in the learned
craft of poetry, and he possessed great wit and understanding in his work. However, he dissipated his body in
every vanity and pleasure of the flesh, not just in one
romance, but he abandoned himself to all the women he
could, nor did he show restraint or loyalty, and so he
stayed with no single woman. In his youth he led this
kind of life as much as he could, for which in the end
he received the fitting reward—dishonor and loss of
possessions and limbs—for so much did he advise others
through his own acts and words to lead a life like the
one he led that he was finally exiled for his excessive
promiscuity. Similarly, when afterward, thanks to the
influence of several young, powerful Romans who were
his supporters, he was called back from exile and failed
to refrain from the misdeeds for which his guilt had
already punished him, he was castrated and disfigured
because of his faults. This is precisely the point I was
telling you about before, for when he saw that he could
no longer lead the life in which he was used to taking
his pleasure, he began to attack women with his subtle
reasonings, and through this effort he tried to make
women unattractive to others."

"My lady, you are right, and I know a book by another Italian author, from the Tuscan marches, I think, called Cecco d'Ascoli, who wrote in one chapter such astounding abominations that a reasonable person ought not to repeat them."

She replied, "If Cecco d'Ascoli spoke badly about all women, my daughter, do not be amazed, for he detested all women and held them in hatred and disfavor; and similarly, on account of his horrible wickedness, he wanted all men to hate and detest women. He received the just reward for it: in his shame he was burned to death at the stake."

"I know another small book in Latin, my lady, called the *Secreta mulierum*, *The Secrets of Women*, which discusses the constitution of their natural bodies and especially their great defects."

She replied, "You can see for yourself without further proof, this book was written carelessly and colored by hypocrisy, for if you have looked at it, you know that it is obviously a treatise composed of lies. Although some say that it was written by Aristotle, it is not believable that such a philosopher could be charged with such contrived lies. For since women can clearly know with proof that certain things which he treats are not at all true, but pure fabrications, they can also conclude that the other details which he handles are outright lies. But don't you remember that he says in the beginning that some pope— I don't know which one— excommunicated every man who read the work to a woman or gave it to a woman to read?"

"My lady, I remember it well."

"Do you know the malicious reason why this lie was presented as credible to bestial and ignorant men at the beginning of the book?"

"No, my lady, not unless you tell me."

"It was done so that women would not know about the book and its contents, because the man who wrote it knew that if women read it or heard it read aloud, they would know it was lies, would contradict it, and make fun of it. With this pretense the author wanted to trick and deceive the men who read it."

"My lady, I recall that among other things, after he has discussed the impotence and weakness which cause the formation of a feminine body in the womb of the mother, he says that Nature is completely ashamed when she sees that she has formed such a body, as though it were something imperfect."

"But, sweet friend, don't you see the overweening madness, the irrational blindness which prompt such observations? Is Nature, the chambermaid of God, a greater mistress than her master, almighty God from whom comes such authority, who, when He willed, took the form of man and women from His thought when it came to His holy will to form Adam from the mud of the ground in the field of Damascus and, once created, brought him into the Terrestrial Paradise which was and is the most worthy place in this world here below? There Adam slept, and God formed the body of woman from one of his ribs, signifying that she should stand at his side as a companion and never lie at his feet like a slave, and also that he should love her as his own flesh. If the Supreme Craftsman was not ashamed to create and form the feminine body, would Nature then have been ashamed? It is the height of folly to say this! Indeed, how was she formed? I don't know if you have already noted this: she was created in the image of God. How can any mouth dare to slander the vessel which bears such a noble imprint? But some men are foolish enough to think, when they hear that God made man in His image, that this refers to the material body. This was not the case, for God had not yet taken a human body. The soul is meant, the intellectual spirit which lasts eternally just like the Deity. God created the soul and placed wholly similar souls, equally good and noble in the feminine and in the masculine bodies. Now, to turn to the question of the creation of the body, woman was made by the Supreme

Craftsman. In what place was she created? In the Terrestrial Paradise. From what substance? Was it vile matter? No, it was the noblest substance which had ever been created: it was from the body of man from which God made woman."

I.9.3   "My lady, according to what I understand from you, woman is a most noble creature. But even so, Cicero says that a man should never serve any woman and that he who does so debases himself, for no man should ever serve anyone lower than him."

She replied, "The man or the woman in whom resides greater virtue is the higher; neither the loftiness nor the lowliness of a person lies in the body according to the sex, but in the perfection of conduct and virtues. And surely he is happy who serves the Virgin, who is above all the angels."

"My lady, one of the Catos—who was such a great orator—said, nevertheless, that if this world were without women, we would converse with the gods."

She replied, "You can now see the foolishness of the man who is considered wise, because, thanks to a woman, man reigns with God. And if anyone would say that man was banished because of Lady Eve, I tell you that he gained more through Mary than he lost through Eve when humanity was conjoined to the Godhead, which would never have taken place if Eve's misdeed had not occurred. Thus man and woman should be glad for this sin, through which such an honor has come about. For as low as human nature fell through this creature woman, was human nature lifted higher by this same creature. And as for conversing with the gods, as this Cato has said, if there had been no woman, he spoke truer than he knew, for he was a pagan, and among those of this belief, gods were thought to reside in Hell as well as in Heaven, that is, the devils whom they called the gods of Hell—so that it is no lie that these gods would have conversed with men, if Mary had not lived."

10. MORE ARGUMENTS AND ANSWERS ON THIS SAME SUBJECT.

"This same Cato Uticensis also said that women who I.10.1
are pleasing to men naturally resemble the rose, which
is pleasant to look at but whose thorn always lurks
beneath to prick."

She answered, "Again this Cato spoke truer than he
knew, for every good and honest woman of virtuous life
ought to be, and is, one of the most pleasant things to
look at which exist. And, nevertheless, there remains the
thorn of fear of sinning and of contrition in the heart
of such a woman, who cannot separate herself from what
makes her remain tranquil, composed, and respectful, and
it is this which saves her."

"My lady, is it true that some authors have testified
that women are naturally lecherous and gluttonous?"

"My daughter, you have many times heard the proverb
repeated which says 'What Nature gives, no one can take
away.' Thus it would be surprising if women were so
much inclined that way and yet were *rarely* or *never* found
in those places ordained to this purpose. They are, however, scarce there, and if anyone would respond that
shame keeps women away, I say that this is not at all true,
that nothing keeps them away except their nature, which
is not inclined this way at all. But let us suppose that
they were so inclined and that shame made them resist
their natural inclination, then this virtue and constancy
should redound to their credit. Furthermore, recall that
not long ago, during a holiday, as you were standing in
the doorway of your residence conversing with the
honorable young lady who is your neighbor, you spied a
man coming out of a tavern who was telling another
man, 'I spent so much in the tavern, my wife will not
drink any wine today,' and then you asked why she would
not drink any wine that day, and he answered, 'Because,
my lady, every time I come back from the tavern, my
wife always asks me how much I spent, and if it is more

than twelve pennies, she makes up for what I have spent with her own sobriety and says that if we both wanted to spend so much, we could not afford it.'"

"My lady," I said then, "I remember this well."

And she to me, "Thus you have plenty of examples that women are by nature sober, and that women who are not go against their own nature. There is no uglier vice in a woman than gluttony, for this vice, wherever it might be, attracts many others. And you can see them quite well in big crowds and groups near churches during sermons and at confession, reciting the Our Father and the Offices."

"This is obvious, my lady," I said, "but these men say that women go there all dressed up to show off their beauty and to attract men to their love."

She responded, "This would be believable if you saw only young and pretty women there. But if you watch carefully, for every young woman whom you see, you will see twenty or thirty old women dressed simply and honestly as they pray in these holy places. And if women possess such piety, they also possess charity, for who is it who visits and comforts the sick, helps the poor, takes care of the hospitals, and buries the dead? It seems to me that these are all women's works and that these same works are the supreme footprints which God commands us to follow."

I.10.2 "My lady, you are only too right, but another author has said that women by nature have a servile heart and that they are like infants, and because of this, infants love to speak to them and they love to speak to infants."

She answered, "My daughter, if you observe closely an infant's condition, you know that infants naturally love tenderness and gentleness. And what is more tender and gentle than a well ordered woman? Indeed! They are evil, diabolical people who wish to twist the good as well as the virtue of kindness naturally found in women into evil and reproach. For if women love infants, such affection does not spring from the vice of ignorance but comes from the sweetness of their character. And if women resemble infants in kindness, then they are superbly well advised to be so, for as the Gospel recalls, did not our Lord tell His Apostles, when they were arguing among themselves who was the greatest among them and He called a child and placed His hand on the child's head, 'I tell you that whoever humbles himself like this child shall be the most rewarded, for whoever humbles himself is raised up and whoever raises himself up is humbled.'"

"My lady, men have burdened me with a heavy charge taken from a Latin proverb, which runs, 'God made women to speak, weep, and sew,' which they use to attack women." *I.10.3*

"Indeed, sweet friend," she replied, "this proverb is so true that it cannot be held against whoever believes or says it. Early on, God placed these qualities in those women who have saved themselves by speaking, weeping, and sewing. And in answer to those who attack women for their habit of weeping, I tell you that if our Lord Jesus Christ—from whom no thought is hidden and who sees and knows every heart—had believed that women's tears come only from weakness and simplemindedness, the dignity of His most great Highness would never have been so inclined through compassion to shed tears Himself from the eyes of His worthy and glorious body when He saw Mary Magdalene and her sister Martha weep for their dead brother Lazarus the leper and then to resurrect him. What special favors has God bestowed on women because of their tears! He did not despise the tears of Mary Magdalene, but accepted them and forgave her sins, and through the merits of those tears she is in glory in Heaven.

"Similarly, He did not reject the tears of the widow who wept as she followed the corpse of her only son as it was being carried away for burial. And our Lord, the fountain of all pity, moved to compassion by her tears as He saw her weep, asked her, 'Woman, why do you weep?' and then brought her child back to life. God has *I.10.4* performed other miracles, which are found in the Holy Scriptures and would take too long to relate, on behalf of many women because of their tears, and continues to do so, for I believe that many women, as well as others for whom they pray, are saved by the tears of their devotion. Was not Saint Augustine, the glorious Doctor of the Church, converted to the Faith by his mother's tears? For the good woman wept continuously, praying to God that it would please Him to illuminate the heart of her pagan, unbelieving son with the light of faith. Saint Ambrose, to whom the holy lady often went to ask that he pray to God on behalf of her son, told her for this reason, 'Woman, I believe it is impossible that so many tears could be shed in vain.' O blessed Ambrose who did not think that women's tears were frivolous! And this might answer those men who attack women so much, because thanks to a woman's tears does this holy luminary, Saint Augustine, stand at the fore of the Holy Church which he completely brightens and illuminates. Therefore, let men stop talking about this question.

I.10.5   "Similarly, God endowed women with the faculty of speech—may He be praised for it—for had He not done so, they would be speechless. But in refutation of what this proverb says, (which someone, I don't know whom, invented deliberately to attack them), if women's language had been so blameworthy and of such small authority, as some men argue, our Lord Jesus Christ would never have deigned to wish that so worthy a mystery as His most gracious resurrection be first announced by a woman, just as He commanded the blessed Magdalene, to whom He first appeared on Easter, to report and announce it to His apostles and to Peter. Blessed God, may you be praised, who, among the other infinite boons and favors which You have bestowed upon the feminine sex, desired that woman carry such lofty and worthy news."

"All those who are jealous of me would do best to be silent if they had any real insight, my lady," I said, "but I smile at the folly which some men have expressed and

I even remember that I heard some foolish preachers teach that God first appeared to a woman because He knew well that she did not know how to keep quiet so that this way the news of His resurrection would be spread more rapidly."

She answered, "My daughter, you have spoken well when you call them fools who said this. It is not enough for them to attack women. They impute even to Jesus Christ such blasphemy, as if to say that He wished to reveal this great perfection and dignity through a vice. I do not know how a man could dare to say this, even in jest, as God should not be brought in on such joking matters. But as for the first question, regarding talking —in fact it was fortunate for the woman from Canaan who was so great a talker and who would not stop yelling and howling after Jesus Christ as she followed Him through the streets of Jerusalem, crying, 'Have mercy on me, Lord, for my daughter is sick.' And what did the good Lord do? He in whom all mercy abounded and abounds and from whom a single word from the heart sufficed for Him to show mercy! He seemed to take pleasure in the many words pouring from the mouth of this woman ever perseverant in her prayer. But why did He act like this? In order to test her constancy, for when He compared her to the dogs— which seemed a little harsh because she followed a foreign cult and not that of God— she was not ashamed to speak both well and wisely when she replied, 'Sire, that is most true, but the little dogs live from the crumbs from their master's table.' 'O most wise woman, who taught you to speak this way? You have won your cause through your prudent language which stems from your good will.' And one could clearly see this, for our Lord, turning to His Apostles, testified from His mouth that He had never found such faith in all of Israel and granted her request. Who could sufficiently sum up this honor paid to the feminine sex which the jealous despise, considering that in the heart of this little bit of a pagan woman God found more faith than in all the bishops, princes, priests, and all the people of the Jews, who called themselves the worthy people of God? In this manner, at equal length and with great eloquence, the Samaritan woman spoke well on her own behalf when she went to the well to draw water and met Jesus Christ sitting there completely exhausted. O blessed Godhead conjoined to this worthy body! How could You allow Your holy mouth to speak at such length for the sake of this little bit of a woman and a sinner who did not even live under Your Law? You truly demonstrated that You did not in the least disdain the pious sex of women. God, how often would our contemporary pontiffs deign to discuss anything with some simple little woman, let alone her own salvation?"

I.10.6 "Nor did the woman who sat through Christ's sermon speak less wisely. For she was so fired up by His holy words that—as they say, women can never keep quiet—she then fortunately spoke the words which are solemnly recorded in the Gospel, which she loudly pronounced after having stood up through great force of will, 'Blessed is the womb which bore You and the breasts which You sucked.'

I.10.7 "Thus you can understand, fair sweet friend, God has demonstrated that He has truly placed language in women's mouths so that He might be thereby served. They should not be blamed for that from which issues so much good and so little evil, for one rarely observes that great harm comes from their language.

I.10.8 "As for sewing, truly has God desired that this be natural for women, for it is an occupation necessary for divine service and for the benefit of every reasonable creature. Without this work, the world's estates would be maintained in great chaos. Therefore it is a great wickedness to reproach women for what should redound to their great credit, honor, and praise."

11. CHRISTINE ASKS REASON WHY WOMEN ARE NOT IN THE SEATS OF LEGAL COUNSEL; AND REASON'S RESPONSE.

I.11.1 "Most high and honored lady, your fair words amply

satisfy my thinking. But tell me still, if you please, why women do not plead law cases in the courts of justice, are unfamiliar with legal disputes, and do not hand down judgments? For these men say that it is because of some woman (whom I don't know) who governed unwisely from the seat of justice."

"My daughter, everything told about this woman is frivolous and contrived out of deception. But whoever would ask the causes and reasons of all things would have to answer for too much in this question, nor would Aristotle be at all sufficient, in spite of all the many reasons which he gives in his *Problemata* and *Categoriae*. Now, as to this particular question, dear friend, one could just as well ask why God did not ordain that men fulfill the offices of women, and women the offices of men. So I must answer this question by saying that just as a wise and well ordered lord organizes his domain so that one servant accomplishes one task and another servant another task, and that what the one does the other does not do, God has similarly ordained man and woman to serve Him in different offices and also to aid and comfort one another, each in their ordained task, and to each sex has given a fitting and appropriate nature and inclination to fulfill their offices. Inasmuch as the human species often errs in what it is supposed to do, God gives men strong and hardy bodies for coming and going as well as for speaking boldly. And for this reason, men with this nature learn the laws—and must do so—in order to keep the world under the rule of justice and, in case anyone does not wish to obey the statutes which have been ordained and established by reason of law, are required to make them obey with physical constraint and force of arms, a task which women could never accomplish. Nevertheless, though God has given women great understanding—and there are many such women—because of the integrity to which women are inclined, it would not be at all appropriate for them to go and appear so brazenly in the court like men, for there are enough men who do so. What would be accomplished by sending

31 *Christine de Pizan*

three men to lift a burden which two can carry easily? But if anyone maintained that women do not possess enough understanding to learn the laws, the opposite is obvious from the proof afforded by experience, which is manifest and has been manifested in many women—just as I will soon tell—who have been very great philosophers and have mastered fields far more complicated, subtle, and lofty than written laws and man-made institutions. Moreover, in case anyone says that women do not have a natural sense for politics and government, I will give you examples of several great women rulers who have lived in past times. And so that you will better know my truth, I will remind you of some women of your own time who remained widows and whose skill governing—both past and present—in all their affairs following the deaths of their husbands provides obvious demonstration that a woman with a mind is fit for all tasks."

12. HERE SHE TELLS OF NICAULA, EMPRESS OF ETHIOPIA.

I.12.1   "Please tell me where there was ever a king endowed with greater skill in politics, government, and sovereign justice, and even with such lofty and magnificent style as one can read about the most noble Empress Nicaula. For though there had been many kings of great fame called pharaohs in the vast, wide, and varied lands which she governed, and from whom she was descended, during her rule this lady was the first to begin to live according to laws and coordinated policies, and she destroyed and abolished the crude customs found in the territories over which she was lord and reformed the rude manners of the savage Ethiopians. This lady accomplished even more praiseworthy deeds than reforming the rough manners of others, according to the authors who speak of her. She remained the heiress of these pharaohs, and not just of a small land but of the kingdom of Arabia, Ethiopia, Egypt, and the island of Meroë (which is very long and wide and filled with all kinds of goods and is near to the Nile), which she governed with wonderful prudence.

What more should I tell you about this lady? She was so wise and so capable a ruler that even the Holy Scriptures speak of her great virtue. She herself instituted laws of far-reaching justice for governing her people. She enjoyed great nobility and vast wealth—almost as much as all the men who have ever lived. She was profoundly learned in the Scriptures and all fields of knowledge, and she had so lofty a heart that she did not deign to marry, nor did she desire that any man be at her side."

13. HERE REASON SPEAKS OF A QUEEN OF FRANCE, NAMED FREDEGUND, AND ALSO OF SEVERAL QUEENS AND PRINCESSES OF FRANCE.

"I could tell you a great deal about ladies who governed wisely in ancient times, just as what I will presently tell you will deal with this question. In France there was once a queen, Fredegund, who was the wife of King Chilperic. Although she was cruel, contrary to the natural disposition of women, nevertheless, following her husband's death, with great skill this lady governed the kingdom of France which found itself at this time in very great unrest and danger, and she was left with nothing else besides Chilperic's heir, a small son named Clotaire. There was great division among the barons regarding the government, and already a great civil war had broken out in the kingdom. Having assembled the barons in council, she addressed them, all the while holding her child in her arms: 'My lords, here is your king. Do not forget the loyalty which has always been present among the French, and do not scorn him because he is a child, for with God's help he will grow up, and when he comes of age he will recognize his good friends and reward them according to their deserts, unless you desire to disinherit him wrongfully and sinfully. As for me, I assure you that I will reward those who act well and loyally with such generosity that no other reward could be better.' Thus did this queen satisfy the barons, and through her wise government, she delivered her son from the hands of his enemies. She herself nourished him until he was grown, and he was invested by her with the crown and honor of the kingdom, which never would have happened if she had not been so prudent.

I.13.2   "Similarly, the same can be said of the most wise and in every instance virtuous and noble Queen Blanche, mother of Saint Louis, who governed the kingdom of France while her son was a minor so nobly and so prudently that it was never better ruled by any man. Even when he was grown, she was still the head of his council because of her experience of wise government, nor was anything done without her, and she even followed her son to war.

I.13.3   "I could tell you countless other examples which I will omit for brevity's sake. But since we have started speaking about the ladies of France, we do not need to go any further to seek examples from history: you yourself saw in childhood Queen Jeanne, widow of King Charles, the fourth of that name. As you recall her, remember this lady's good deeds to which her fame attests, as much in the noble arrangement of her court as in both customs and the maintenance of sovereign justice. Never has any prince been as renowned as this lady for having so upheld justice and preserved her land's prerogatives.

I.13.4   "Her noble daughter who married the duke of Orléans, son of King Philip, resembled her a great deal. During her widowhood which lasted a long time, she maintained justice in her country with such righteousness that more could not have been done.

I.13.5   "Likewise Blanche, queen of France, late wife of King John, ruled and governed her land with great order of law and justice.

I.13.6   "What can one say of the valiant and wise duchess of Anjou, late daughter of Saint Charles of Blois, duke of Brittany, and late wife of the second oldest brother of the wise King Charles of France, who was then king of Sicily? How well did this lady hold her lands and countries under the firm rod of justice—as much in Provence as elsewhere—which she governed and kept in hand on behalf of her most noble children as long as they were minors! How greatly is this lady to be praised in all virtues! During her youth she was of such supreme beauty that she surpassed all other ladies, and of most perfect chastity and wisdom, and in her maturity, of most great government and sovereign prudence and force and constancy of heart, as became apparent when, for a short time after her lord's death in Italy, his entire fief of Provence rebelled against her and her noble children. But this noble lady worked and strove so hard that either through force or negotiation she restored the entire land to obedience and allegiance. So well did she maintain the order of law in that country that a single outcry or complaint of the slightest injustice which she might have committed was never heard.

"I could tell you much about other ladies of France $I.13.7$ who, as widows, governed themselves and their jurisdictions with fairness and justice. The countess of La Marche, lady and countess of Vendôme and of Castres, and a most great landowner, who is still alive—what can one say of her government? Does she not wish to know how and in what way her own justice is upheld? And she herself, as a good and wise ruler, takes an avid interest in this whole question. What should I tell you? I assure you that the same can be said of a great many women, whether from the upper, middle, or lower class, who, as anyone who wishes to pay attention can clearly see, have maintained and maintain their dominions in as good condition as did their husbands during their lifetime and who are as well-loved by their subjects. There are better examples, too, for there can be no doubt—no offense to men, certainly—that although there are ignorant women, there are many women who have better minds and a more active sense of prudence and judgment than most men—isn't it so?—and if their husbands would believe them or would have equal sense, it would be a great boon and profit for them.

I.13.8   "All the same, it makes no difference if women are not usually involved in handing down decisions or pleading cases: for they have that fewer burdens on their souls and bodies. Although it is necessary to punish criminals and to secure justice for everyone, there are enough men in these offices who must wish that they never knew any more than their mothers, for if they follow the right path, when a crime is committed, if God knows of it, the punishment is not small."

14. MORE EXCHANGES BETWEEN CHRISTINE AND REASON.

I.14.1   "Certainly you speak well, my lady, and your words are most harmonious in my heart. But though such is the case as far as women's minds are concerned, it is a proven fact that women have weak bodies, tender and feeble in deeds of strength, and are cowards by nature. These things, in men's judgment, substantially reduce the degree and authority of the feminine sex, for men contend that the more imperfect a body, the lesser is its virtue and, consequently, the less praiseworthy."

She answered, "My dear daughter, such a deduction is totally invalid and unsupported, for invariably one often sees that when Nature does not give to one body which she has formed as much perfection as she has given to another and thereby makes some things imperfect, whether in shape or beauty or with some impotence or weakness of limbs, she makes up the difference with an even greater boon than she has taken away. For example, just as is said, the great philosopher Aristotle had a very ugly body, with one eye lower than the other and with a strange face, but although he had some physical deformity, truly Nature made this up to him spectacularly by giving him a retentive mind and great sense, just as he appears in his authentic writings. This recompense of such a fine mind was thus worth more to him than if he had had the very body of Absalom or a similar body.

I.14.2   "The same might be said of the great emperor Alexander, who was quite ugly, little, and had a sickly build. Nevertheless, it seems that he possessed great virtue in his heart. It is the same situation for many others. Fair friend, I assure you that a large and strong body never makes a strong and virtuous heart but comes from a natural and virtuous vigor which is a boon from God, which He allows Nature to imprint in one reasonable creature more than in another, and thus a malady is transformed into understanding or courage and not at all into the strength of the body or its limbs. We have observed this often, having seen many large men with strong bodies who are cowardly and recreant and others with small and weak bodies who are bold and vigorous, and the same holds true for other virtues. But as for boldness and physical strength, God and Nature have done a great deal for women by giving them such weakness, because, at least, thanks to this agreeable defect, they are excused from committing the horrible cruelties, the murders, and the terrible and serious crimes which have been perpetrated through force and still continuously take place in the world. Thus women will never receive the punishment which such cases demand, and it would be better, or would have been better, for the souls of several of the strongest men, if they had spent their pilgrimage in this world in weak feminine bodies. And truly I tell you, and here I come back to my major point, that if Nature did not give great strength of limb to women's bodies, she has made up for it by placing there that most virtuous inclination to love one's God and to fear sinning against His commandments. Women who act otherwise go against their own nature.

"But recall, nevertheless, dear friend, how it seems *I.14.3* that God has deliberately wished to show men that even if women do not possess the great strength and physical daring which men usually have, they should not say nor should they believe that this is because strength and physical daring are excluded from the feminine sex: this is obvious, because in many women God has made manifest enormous courage, strength, and boldness to undertake and execute all kinds of hard tasks, just like those great men—solemn and valorous conquerors—have accomplished, which different writings frequently mention, and presently I will give you several examples.

I.14.4 "Fair daughter and dear friend, now I have prepared for you a large and wide ditch, completely cleared of earth, which I have carried out in large basketfuls on my shoulders. Now it is time that you lay down the heavy and sturdy stones for the foundation of the walls of the City of Ladies. Take the trowel of your pen and ready yourself to lay down bricks and to labor diligently, for you can see here a great and large stone which I want to place as the first in the first row of stones in the foundation of your City. I want you to know that Nature herself has foretold in the signs of the zodiac that it be placed and situated in this work. So I shall draw you back a little and I will throw it down for you."

15. HERE SHE SPEAKS OF THE QUEEN SEMIRAMIS.

I.15.1 "Semiramis was a woman of very great strength—in fact, of strong and powerful courage in enterprises and undertakings in deeds of arms—and was so outstanding that the people of that time who were pagans used to say, because of her enormous strength on land and on sea, that she was a sister of the great god Jupiter and daughter of the ancient god Saturn who, they believed, were the gods of the earth and the sea. This lady was the wife of King Ninus, who named the city of Nineveh after his own name and who was such a forceful conqueror that, with the help of his wife Semiramis (who, like him, would campaign in arms), he subjugated mighty Babylon and all the strong land of Assyria and many other countries. When the lady was still quite young, Ninus her husband was killed by an arrow, during the assault of a city. Once the funeral rites had been solemnly celebrated, as befitted Ninus, the lady did not give up the exercise of arms, but, with greater courage than before, vigorously undertook to govern and rule the kingdoms and lands over which her husband and she had held power on their own to begin with, as well as those which they had conquered with the sword and which she memorably and valorously controlled. She undertook and accomplished so many notable works that no man could surpass her in vigor and strength. This lady, with her great courage, feared no pain and was frightened by no danger, and so bravely exposed herself to every peril that she vanquished all her enemies who had thought to expel her during her widowhood from the countries she had conquered. Because of this, she was so feared and revered in arms that, finally, she not only controlled the lands already in her power, but also marched with a very large army to Ethiopia, with which she subjugated Ethiopia and annexed it to her empire, and from there she moved in force against India. She attacked the Indians in force, whom no man had ever approached before with the intention of making war on them, and subdued and vanquished them, and then advanced against other countries so that, in brief, she had soon conquered the entire Orient and placed it under her rule. Along with these great and mighty conquests, this lady, Semiramis, reinforced and rebuilt the strong and cruel city of Babylon, which had been founded by Nimrod and the giants and was located on the plain of Shinar. This lady strengthened the city even more with many defenses and had wide and deep moats dug around it. Once, when Semiramis was in her chamber surrounded by her maidens who were braiding her hair, news came that one of her kingdoms had revolted against her. She stood up immediately and swore by her power that the other lock of her hair which remained to be braided would not be braided until she had avenged this injustice and brought this land back under her dominion. She had her massed troops quickly armed and advanced on the rebels and, thanks to great force and strength, brought them back under her authority. She so frightened these rebels and all her other subjects that ever after no one dared revolt. A large and richly gilt cast-bronze statue on a high pillar in Babylon which portrayed a princess holding a sword, with one side of her hair braided, the other not, bore witness to this noble and courageous deed for a long time. This queen founded and built several new cities and fortifications and performed many other outstanding deeds and accomplished so much that greater courage and more marvelous and memorable deeds have never been recorded about any man.

I.15.2   "It is quite true that many people reproach her—and if she had lived under our law, rightfully so—because she took as husband a son she had had with Ninus her lord. But here are the two principal reasons which prompted her to do this: first, she wanted no other crowned lady in her empire besides herself, which would have happened if her son had married another lady; and second, it seemed to her that no other man was worthy to have her as wife except her own son. But this lady did nothing to excuse herself for this great mistake because at this time there was still no written law, and people lived according to the law of Nature, where all people were allowed to do whatever came into their hearts without sinning, for there can be no doubt that if she thought this was evil or that she would incur the slightest reproach, she would never have done this, since she had such a great and noble heart and so deeply loved honor. And now the first stone is set in the foundation of our City. Now we must lay many more stones to advance our edifice."

16. CONCERNING THE AMAZONS.

I.16.1   "A country called Scythia lies along the borders of Europe near the great ocean which surrounds the entire world. A long time ago it happened that this land lost all the important men living there through war. When the women of the place saw that they had all lost their husbands and brothers and male relatives, and only old

men and children were left them, they courageously
assembled and took counsel among themselves and decided
finally that thenceforth they would maintain their dominion by themselves without being subject to men, and
they promulgated an edict whereby no man was allowed
to enter into their jurisdiction. In order to maintain a
succession, they would go into neighboring lands during
certain times of the year and then return; if they then
gave birth to males, they would send them to their
fathers, but if their offspring were females, they would
raise them. To carry out this ordinance, they selected
two of the most noble ladies from among them and
crowned them queens, the first of whom was named
Lampheto and the second Marpasia. Once this was
accomplished, they banished all the remaining males from
their land, and afterward they armed themselves and in
large battalions constituted solely of ladies and maidens,
they advanced on their enemies and laid waste to their
lands with fire and the sword, and no one could resist
them. In short, they exacted a most fine revenge for their
husbands' deaths. And in this way the women of Scythia
began to carry arms and were then called Amazons,
which actually means the 'breastless ones,' because they
had a custom whereby the nobles among them, when they
were little girls, burned off their left breast through
some technique so that it would not hinder them from
carrying a shield, and they removed the right breast of
commoners to make it easier for them to shoot a bow.
They so delighted in the vocation of arms that through
force they greatly increased their country and their
dominion, and their high fame spread everywhere. Just
as I mentioned before, these two queens, Lampheto and
Marpasia, extended their rule into various countries, each
leading a very great army, and they finally conquered a
great portion of Europe and of Asia, subjugating and
adding many kingdoms to their dominion, founding many
cities and towns, and, in Asia itself, they founded the
city of Ephesus, which has long been very famous. Of

these queens, Marpasia died first, in battle, and in her place the Amazons crowned one of her fair and noble virgin daughters, who was called Synoppe. She had such a great and lofty heart that not for a day in her life did she deign to couple with a man, but remained a virgin her entire lifetime. Her only love and care was the exercise of arms. Here she so ardently cultivated all her pleasure that she could never be sated in the attacking and conquering of different lands. She soundly revenged her mother by having all the inhabitants of the country where her mother was killed put to the sword, and she devastated the entire land, and along with this country, she conquered many others."

17. CONCERNING THAMIRIS, THE QUEEN OF AMAZONIA.

I.17.1 "Just as you heard, for a long time the Amazons strongly maintained their dominion, over which ruled queens in succession, one after another, all valiant ladies, and to name all of them one by one could bore readers, so it will suffice to name a few important ones.

I.17.2 "The brave, valiant, and wise Thamiris was once queen of this land. Thanks to her sense, prudence, and strength, the Amazons captured and conquered Cyrus, the strong and powerful king of Persia who had wrought so many marvels and had conquered mighty Babylon and much of the world. After so many other conquests, Cyrus wanted to proceed against the kingdom of Amazonia, in the hope of placing it too under his lordship, like the other lands he had conquered. Thus, when this wise queen learned from her spies that Cyrus was moving against her with a force great enough to conquer the entire world, she realized that it would be impossible to defeat such an army through force of arms, so it occurred to her to employ a ruse. Then, like a valiant sovereign, when she found out that Cyrus had already, much earlier, entered her land (which she had deliberately allowed to take place without his having met any resistance), she had all her maidens armed and, in an extremely clever move, positioned them in different ambushes in the mountains and woods where Cyrus would have to pass. Then Thamiris very quietly deployed all her forces, so that Cyrus and his entire army were caught in the passes and dark narrows between rocks and in the dense forests through which they had to travel. Upon seeing his front guard, the lady had her war trumpet loudly sounded. Since Cyrus had taken no precautions, he was completely dumbstruck when he saw himself under attack from every direction, for the ladies standing above on the high mountains were throwing down huge rocks which crushed his army all together. They could not advance or move forward because the terrain was so rough. An ambush lay ahead in which the ladies killed Cyrus' troops as fast as they escaped from the passes, nor could they retreat because of the ambush lying in wait behind them for a similar purpose. Thus, they were all killed or crushed, and Cyrus was captured and, by the queen's command, kept alive, as were his barons whom she had brought before her, after their defeat, into a tent which she had had pitched there. Out of anger over the death of one of her beloved sons, whom she had sent to Cyrus, she did not wish to take pity on him. First, she had all his barons beheaded in front of him, and then she told him, 'Cyrus, because of your cruelty, you were never sated with men's blood. Now you can drink all you want.' And then she had his head severed and thrown into a bucket in which she had had collected the blood of his barons.

"Fair daughter and my dear friend, I recall these things *I.17.3* to you because they are appropriate to the subject of which I was speaking to you, although you know them well and have recited them before in your *Livre de la Mutacion de Fortune* and also in your *Epistre d'Othea*. Now I will relate other examples to you."

18. HOW THE STRONG HERCULES AND THESEUS, HIS COMPANION, WENT FROM GREECE WITH A LARGE ARMY AND FLEET TO THE AMAZONS, AND HOW THE TWO

MAIDENS, MENALIPPE AND HIPPOLYTA, BEAT THEM,
HORSES AND ALL, INTO A HEAP.

I.18.1   "What should I tell you? The ladies of Amazonia
had already accomplished so much through the strength
of their bodies that they were feared and respected by
all countries. The news of their power reached the land
of Greece, which was quite distant, as well as the report
of how these ladies never stopped invading and conquering but went everywhere, laying waste lands and
countries if they did not immediately surrender, and of
how there was no force which could resist them. The
Greeks were frightened by this news, fearing that the
power of these women might at the same time extend
even to their own land.

I.18.2   "At this time, in Greece, the marvelous and strong
Hercules was in the flower of his youth; in his time he
performed more wonders of physical strength than men
born of women who are mentioned in historical accounts
had ever accomplished, for he fought with giants, lions,
serpents, and fabulous monsters, and he was victorious
over all. In short, he was so strong that no man ever
equaled him in strength except the mighty Samson. This
Hercules said that it would not be wise to wait until
the Amazons came to them, and that therefore it was by
far the best thing to invade them first. In order to accomplish this, he had a fleet armed and he assembled a large
mass of noble youths to go there in great strength. When
the valiant and brave Theseus, who was king of Athens,
learned this news, he said that Hercules would never go
without him and so assembled his army with that of
Hercules, and thus they put to sea in large numbers,
heading for the land of Amazonia. When, after a short
while, they had approached Amazonia, Hercules, notwithstanding his fabulous strength and boldness and his
large army of such valiant soldiers, did not dare to come
into port nor to land during the day, so much did he fear
the great power and daring of these women. This would
be fantastic to repeat and hard to believe if so many

historical writings did not attest to it, that a man who could not be conquered by the power of any creature feared the strength of women. So Hercules, as well as his army, waited until dark night had come, and then, at the hour when all mortal creatures should rest and sleep, these men streamed out of the ships and entered the country and began to put different cities to the torch and to slay all those women who were caught off-guard, unarmed. Within a short time, the alarm was great, and the women ran to arms as fast as they could, and with their best effort they began most courageously to rush in great troops toward the ocean, against their enemies.

"At this time the queen, Orithyia, a lady of most   *I.18.3*
outstanding valor who had conquered many lands, ruled over the Amazons. She was the mother of the brave queen Penthesilea, of whom mention will be made hereafterward. This Orithyia had been crowned after the valiant queen Antiope, who had upheld and governed the Amazons with a great discipline of valor and had been most brave in her time. Orithyia heard the news that the Greeks, without provocation, had fallen upon their land at night and were slaying all whom they met. No one need ask whether she was angered with them. She resolved that they would pay dearly for her displeasure, and, immediately, with strong threats against these men whom she did not fear in the least, she commanded all her battalions to be armed. You would have seen how urgently the ladies rushed to arms and assembled around their queen, who, by daybreak, had all her troops ready.

"But while this assembly was forming and the queen   *I.18.4*
was preparing to put her armies and battalions in order, two valiant maidens of supreme strength and valor, bold and brave over all others— the one called Menalippe and the other Hippolyta, both close relatives of the queen— could not wait for the troops of their lady. As soon as they were able to arm themselves, with lances in hand, shields of strong elephant hide hanging from their necks, mounted on swift chargers, they left for the port at the

45   *Christine de Pizan*

fastest possible gallop, and with great ardor, as though seized with wrath and displeasure, they charged with lowered lances against the most prominent warriors of the Greeks, that is, Menalippe toward Hercules and Hippolyta toward Theseus. It was clear how angered they were, for regardless of the great strength, boldness, and courage of these men, so forcefully did these maidens attack them that each maiden struck down her knight, horse and all, in one heap. The maidens themselves fell down on the other side, but as quickly as possible got up and with drawn swords rushed the two knights. What an honor these maidens must have enjoyed, for they had unhorsed the two most valiant knights in the world! This deed would be unbelievable without the testimony of so many credible authors. These same authorities, themselves astounded by this adventure, make special excuse for Hercules, since, considering his unlimited strength, they say it could have been his horse's fault (who was upset by the great force of the blow) and they maintain that had he been on foot, he would not have been brought down. The two knights were ashamed at having been unhorsed by two maidens. Nevertheless, these women fought them with their swords; with great strength and for a long time they carried on the battle, but at last— and this was indeed a marvel, since there had never been such a pair—the maidens were taken captive.

I.18.5   "Hercules and Theseus considered themselves so greatly honored by this capture that they would not have preferred the captured wealth of an entire city, and so they then went back to their ships to refresh themselves and to take off their armor, certain that they had performed superbly. They greatly honored the ladies, and when they saw that without their armor on they were so beautiful and comely, then their joy doubled; they had never captured prey which pleased them so much, and they looked at them with great satisfaction.

I.18.6   "The queen had already advanced on the Greeks with her army when the news came that the two maidens had been captured, and she was terribly grieved by this. But out of fear that they would do worse to the maidens whom they held captive if she should attack them, she halted and sent two of her baronesses with word to the Greeks, that if they would release the two maidens, she would send to them as much ransom as they wanted. Hercules and Theseus received the messengers with great honor and replied in a most courtly manner that if the queen would make peace with them and promise that she and her baronesses would never take up arms against the Greeks, but would be their good friends, that, in turn, the Greeks would promise to free the maidens with no other ransom except for their armor, for the Greeks wanted very much to have this in honor and in perpetual memory of this victory which they had won over the maidens. The queen, because she wished to have her two highly esteemed maidens returned, was constrained to make peace with the Greeks. The matter was discussed, and it was agreed among them that the queen, completely unarmed, accompanied by ladies and maidens dressed in such rich costumes whose equal the Greeks had never seen, would come to celebrate and to solemnize the peace with them, whereupon there was great rejoicing. But, nevertheless, it greatly bothered Theseus to give up Hippolyta, because he loved her with a great devotion. So much did Hercules ask and petition the queen that she granted that Theseus could take her into his own country. The wedding was solemnly celebrated, and then the Greeks departed. Thus did Theseus marry Hippolyta, who later bore a son by him called Hippolytus, a highly picked knight of great fame. And when it became known in Greece that they would have peace with the Amazons, never had there been greater joy, for there was nothing they feared as much as the Amazons."

19. CONCERNING THE QUEEN PENTHESILEA AND HOW SHE CAME TO THE AID OF TROY.

"The queen Orithyia lived for a long time, and she   *I.19.1*

47   *Christine de Pizan*

kept the kingdom of Amazonia in great prosperity and was already quite advanced in years when she died. After Orithyia's death, the Amazons crowned her noble daughter, the brave Penthesilea, who, beyond all others, wore the crown of wisdom, esteem, valor, and bravery. She never tired of bearing arms and fighting, and through her their dominion was increased more than ever before, for she never rested and was so feared by her enemies that none dared to lie in wait for her. This lady was so high-minded that she never condescended to couple with a man, remaining a virgin her whole life. During her time, the great war of the Greeks on the Trojans took place. Because of the great reputation, which then flourished throughout the entire world, of Hector of Troy as one of the bravest men in the world and the one who most excelled in all graces, and as it is normal for someone to love one's peer freely, Penthesilea, who was sovereign of all ladies of the world and who had constantly heard so much of the great deeds of the brave Hector, loved him honorably with a great love and, above all else, wished to see him. And to fulfill this wish, she left her kingdom, with a great army and with a most noble company of ladies and maidens of great prowess and most richly armed, and made her way to distant Troy. But nothing seems long nor burdensome to a heart which loves well, when great desire carries it along. The noble Penthesilea arrived in Troy, but it was too late, for she found Hector already dead. He had been killed in battle by Achilles through ruse, and shortly afterward, all the flower of Trojan knighthood had perished. Penthesilea was honorably received in Troy by King Priam and Queen Hecuba and by all the barons. But her heart was so grieved at not finding Hector alive that nothing could cheer her. But the king and queen, who unceasingly mourned the death of their son Hector, said to her that since they could not show him to her alive, they would show him to her dead. So they led her to the temple where they had constructed his tomb as the richest and noblest which had ever been built, of which there is mention in historical writings. There, sitting in a chair inside a rich chapel all of gold and precious stones, in front of the high altar of their gods, was the body of Hector which had been so well embalmed and richly dressed that it clearly seemed as though he were completely alive, holding an unsheathed sword in his hand, and his proud countenance still seemed to threaten the Greeks. There he was, clothed with a large and wide garment woven entirely from fine gold, surrounded and bordered with precious stones, and which dragged on the ground covering his legs which were rubbed with a fine balm, giving off a marvelous scent. There, in the light of a great wax lamp of remarkable brightness, the Trojans revered this body with the same honor reserved for one of their gods, nor could anyone sum up the wealth to be found there. They led Queen Penthesilea there, who, as soon as the chapel was open and she saw the body, knelt down and saluted him just as though he were alive. Then she approached and, looking him intently in the face, began to speak these words, all the while in tears:

" 'O, flower and excellence of the world's knighthood, *I.19.2* summit, height, and consumation of all valor, who can now, after you, ever boast of prowess or put on a sword, now that the light and model of such highness has been extinguished? Alas! When was the cursed and damned arm born which outrageously dared to despoil the world of so great a treasure? O most noble prince, why was Fate so contrary to me that I was not near you when the traitor who did this to you lay waiting in ambush? This would never have happened, for I would have protected you well against it. If he is still alive, I will avenge your death on him and vent the great anger and sorrow which my heart feels seeing you thus, lifeless and powerless to speak to me, something which I so desired. But since Fate has willed this, and it cannot be otherwise, I swear by all the high gods in whom we believe, and promise and affirm to you, my dear lord, that as long as life remains in my body, your death will be avenged by me on the Greeks.' So kneeling before the body, Penthesilea spoke loudly enough for the large crowd of barons, ladies, and knights who were there to be able to hear her, and they all wept from pity, and she could not move herself from that place. Nevertheless, at last, kissing the hand with which he held his sword, she departed, saying, 'O dignity and excellence of knighthood, what you must have been in your lifetime to judge from the nobility to which the countenance of your dead body still bears witness!'

"And then she left, weeping softly, and, as quickly as she could, she armed herself and with her army she departed the city in the company of a noble troop of retainers against the besieging Greeks. And in short, without a doubt did she and her troops fight so splendidly that if she had lived longer, few Greeks would have ever returned to Greece. She attacked Pyrrhus, the son of Achilles and a most valiant knight in his own right, and struck him so hard that he was nearly killed, and he was rescued by his people in very great pain and carried away as though he were dead, nor did the Greeks think he would escape this fate, and they mourned greatly since he was their entire hope. Penthesilea certainly demonstrated to the son, without much room for doubt, that she hated his father. Nevertheless, to shorten the story, although her deeds were marvelous, at last, after the brave Penthesilea had fought there for several days with her troops and the fortunes of the Greeks had ebbed quite low, Pyrrhus, recovered from his wounds and terribly upset and ashamed at having been struck down and wounded by her, ordered the valiant soldiers of his army to concentrate during the battle on nothing else but surrounding Penthesilea and drawing her away from her own troops, for he wanted to kill her with his own hand, and he promised them a large reward if they were able to do this. In their fear to approach her because of the many blows she was dealing out, Pyrrhus's soldiers had to struggle for a long time before even getting close to her. However, finally, one day they fought so resolutely that they surrounded and separated her from the rest of the battle, driving off the ladies so that they could not help her. She had fought so much that a single day would hardly have been long enough for Hector to match her, and she was understandably exhausted. And there, although she defended herself boldly, they smashed through all her armor and struck off a large quarter of her helmet. Pyrrhus was there, and seeing her bare head with its blond hair, dealt her such a great blow that he split open her head and brain. So died the brave Penthesilea, a terrible loss to the Trojans and a profound sorrow for all her land which went into deep mourning, and rightly so, for afterward a woman of her caliber never again ruled over the Amazons. Filled with great sadness, they brought her body back to her country.

"And thus, as you can hear, this kingdom of women, *I.19.3* founded and powerfully upheld, lasted more than eight hundred years, and you yourself can see from the various epochs given in charts in different history books how much time elapsed from their founding until after the conquest of Alexander the Great, who conquered the world, during which the kingdom and dominion of the Amazons apparently still existed. For the historical accounts about him tell how he went to this kingdom and was received there by the queen and the ladies. Alexander lived long after the destruction of Troy and more than four hundred years after the founding of Rome, which also occurred long after the destruction of Troy. Therefore, if you wish to take the occasion to synchronize different historical accounts and calculate the periods and epochs, you will find this kingdom and dominion of women lasted for quite a long time, and you will be able to note that, in all the dominions which have existed in the world and which have lasted as long, one will not find more notable princes in greater numbers nor as many people who accomplished such noteworthy deeds than among the queens and ladies of this kingdom."

20. HERE SHE SPEAKS OF ZENOBIA, QUEEN OF THE PALMYRENES.

I.20.1   "The women of Amazonia were not the only valorous women, for no less celebrated is Zenobia, queen of the Palmyrenes, a lady of noble blood and offspring of the Ptolemies, kings of Egypt. The great courage of this lady and the chivalrous inclination she possessed were obvious throughout her childhood. As soon as she was even slightly strong, no one could keep her from leaving the residence of walled cities, palaces, and royal chambers in order to live in the woods and forests, where, armed with sword and spear, she eagerly hunted wild game. After stags and hinds, she began to fight with lions and bears and all other wild beasts which she would attack fearlessly and conquer marvelously. This lady did not consider it a hardship to sleep in the woods, on the hard ground, in cold and in heat, for she feared nothing, nor did she mind traveling through forest passes, climbing mountains, going down into villages as she pursued the various beasts. This maiden despised all physical love and refused to marry for a long time, for she was a woman who wished to keep her virginity for life. In the end, under pressure from her parents, she took as husband the king of the Palmyrenes, who had a handsome face and body. The noble Zenobia was always possessed of supreme self-control and paid little attention to her own beauty, and Fortune was extremely favorable to Zenobia's inclinations by allowing her to have a husband who corresponded so well to her own mores. This king, who was quite brave, desired to conquer by force all the Orient and nearby empires. In this time Valerianus, the ruler of the Roman Empire, was captured by Sapor, the king of the Persians. The king of the Palmyrenes assembled his great army; whereupon Zenobia, who did not give any thought to preserving the freshness of her beauty, resolved to suffer the exercise of arms with her husband, to arm herself and to participate with him in all the labors of the exercise of chivalry. The king, who was named

Odenatus, appointed a son, named Herod, whom he had had by another woman, to lead a part of his army in the advance guard against the Persian king Sapor, who then occupied Mesopotamia. He then ordered Zenobia his wife to advance from the one flank, in all boldness; he would then advance from the other flank with a third of his army; and they set out under these orders. But what should I tell you? The end of this affair, just as you can read in history books, was as follows: this lady Zenobia conducted herself so bravely and courageously and with such boldness and strength that she won several battles against this Persian king, and so decisively, thanks to her prowess, that she placed Mesopotamia under her husband's rule. In the end she lay siege to Sapor in his city and captured him with his concubines and great treasure. After this victory it happened that her husband was killed by one of his own relatives out of jealousy, but it did not help the relative at all because this noble-hearted lady kept him out of power; she bravely and valiantly took possession of the empire on behalf of her children, who were still small. She placed herself on the royal throne as empress, took over the government, exercised great strength and care, and, to tell the entire story, governed so well, so wisely, and with so much chivalric discipline that Gallienus, and after him, Claudius, emperors of Rome, although they occupied a large part of the Orient on behalf of Rome, never dared to undertake anything against her. The same was true for the Egyptians, the Arabians, and the Armenians: they so feared her power and bravery that they were all happy to maintain the boundaries of their lands. So wisely did this lady govern that she was honored by her princes, obeyed and loved by her people, and feared and respected by her knights. When she rode out in arms, which happened frequently, she did not speak to the members of her army unless she was in armor, with her helmet on her head, nor did she ever have herself carried in a litter, although the kings of that time all had themselves transported in this manner, but she was always mounted on a war-charger, and sometimes, to spy on her enemies, she would ride incognito in front of her troops. Just as she surpassed in discipline and chivalry all the knights of her time in the world, this noble lady Zenobia surpassed all other ladies in her noble and upright conduct and integrity of living. In her entire life-style she was extraordinarily sober. But, notwithstanding this, she often held great assemblies and feasts with her barons and with foreigners, and on these occasions she spared nothing in magnificence and royal generosity and bestowed large and beautiful gifts, for she knew well how to attract beautiful people to her love and benevolence. This woman was supremely chaste. Not only did she avoid other men, but she also slept with her husband only to have children, and demonstrated this clearly by not sleeping with her husband when she was pregnant. And to make certain that her entire outward appearance corresponded and joined with her inner character, she refused to allow any lecherous man or man of vile morals to frequent her court and insisted that all who wished to have her favor were virtuous and well-bred. She bestowed honor upon people according to their goodness, bravery, and strength and never on account of their wealth or noble birth, and she loved men with rough-hewn manners who were, nevertheless, proven in chivalry. She lived in the magnificent and lavish royal custom of an empress, in the Persian manner, which was the most stately ever to have prevailed among kings. She was served in vessels of gold and precious stones, adorned with every decoration. She amassed great treasures from her revenues and her own goods without extorting wealth from any of her subjects, and so generously did she give, when it was reasonable, that there was never seen a prince of greater generosity nor of greater magnificence.

I.20.2   "With all this having been said, the high point of her virtues which I have to tell you was, in summary, her profound learnedness in letters, both in those of the Egyptians and in those of her own language. When she rested, she diligently applied herself to study and wished to be instructed by Longinus the philosopher, who was her master and introduced her to philosophy. She knew Latin as well as Greek, through the aid of which she organized and arranged all historical works in concise and very careful form. Similarly, she desired that her children, whom she raised with strict discipline, be introduced to learning. Therefore, my dear friend, note and recall if you have ever seen or read of any prince or knight more complete in every virtue."

21. CONCERNING THE NOBLE QUEEN ARTEMISIA.

"Could we say less about the most noble and excellent Artemisia, queen of Caria, than about other brave ladies? I.21.1 Little remained in her heart when she was left widowed by her husband, King Mausolus, because she loved him so deeply. Moreover, as was then apparent and as will be recounted to you presently, this lady was left with an extremely large country to govern. Nor was she frightened to rule, for she possessed strong virtue, moral wisdom, and political prudence. In addition to all this, she had such great boldness in acts of chivalry and so well did she maintain discipline that, thanks to the numerous victories which she had, she raised the majesty of her name very high through its wide renown, for during her widowhood, in addition to governing her land in a most noteworthy manner, she frequently took up arms, particularly on two very notable occasions, the one to protect her country, the other to uphold the loyalty of friendship and promised faith. The first occasion was after this king Mausolus, her husband, had died, and the Rhodians, whose country bordered closely upon this lady's kingdom, became very jealous and disdainful that a woman had dominion over the kingdom of Caria. For this reason, in hopes of driving her out and winning the land, they advanced against her with a large army and a great fleet and headed for the city of Halicarnassus, which was located near the sea on high ground called Icaria, a strongly fortified place. This city has two ports, one of which lay inside the city, practically hidden and out of sight, with a very narrow entry so that one could enter or leave the palace without being seen by people outside or inside the city. The other common port was located next to the walls of the city. When the wise and brave Artemisia learned from her spies that her enemies were coming, she summoned a large number of troops and had them armed. But before she left, she arranged with the city inhabitants and with several good and faithful servants whom she trusted and had left behind for this mission that, when she gave them the signal, they should show the Rhodians signs of peace and call down from the walls and tell them that they would surrender the city to them, and that they, the Rhodians, should come boldly and that then her servants should do their utmost to get the Rhodians to leave their ships and come into the city marketplace. Once these preparations had been arranged, the lady departed from the small port with all her army and in a roundabout way they headed for the high seas without her enemies taking notice. When she had given her signal and learned from the counter-signal of the city inhabitants that their enemies had entered the city, she immediately returned by the large port and captured their fleet, re-entered the city and had her ambushes attack the Rhodians in full strength from all sides while she and her army were in front of them. In this way they conquered or killed them all and secured the victory. Artemisia performed even greater bravery, for afterward she traveled in her enemies' ships with her army to Rhodes and had the flag of victory raised high, as though the Rhodian army were returning victorious, and the people of the country, seeing this sign and believing these ships were their own, were overjoyed and left their port open. Then Artemisia came in, arranged for her troops to hold the port under control, and went straight to the palace. There she captured and killed all the princes. All the Rhodians who had not been on their guard were captured, and the lady took possession of the city for herself, and immediately afterward the entire island of Rhodes surrendered to her. After she had placed the whole island under her control and under tribute to her, she left it garrisoned with able guards and returned home. But before she left, she had two brass statues erected in the city, the one representing Artemisia herself as a conqueror and the other the city of Rhodes as conquered.

"The other notable deed, among others, which this *I.21.2* lady performed occurred when Xerxes, king of Persia, moved against the Spartans. All the countryside was already filled with his cavalry, foot soldiers, and his whole army, and the shore occupied by his ships and vessels as would be expected from someone who intended to destroy all of Greece. Then the Greeks, who had a friendship treaty with the queen Artemisia, sent to her for help. She did not send this aid, but rather, as she was most chivalrous, went in person with an enormous army and immediately engaged Xerxes in battle and defeated him. After beating him on land, she returned to her ships, and at the head of her navy, near the city of Salamis, she gave him battle. In the midst of this intense fighting, the valiant Artemisia stood among the barons and captains at the front of her army and encouraged them and gave them heart, thanks to her own considerable courage, saying, 'Onward, my brothers and good knights, strive hard so that honor will be ours. You will earn praise and glory, and my great treasures will not be spared from you!' Then, to tell the whole story, she acted so energetically that, just as on land, she defeated Xerxes at sea. He fled shamefully, along with his countless troops, for, as several historians attest, he commanded such a large army that wherever they passed, the shores of the rivers and fountains dried up. So this valiant lady obtained this noble victory and returned gloriously with the entire crown of honor to her own land.

22. SHE SPEAKS TO HER OF LILIA, MOTHER OF THE BRAVE KNIGHT THEODORIC.

I.22.1   "Although the noble lady Lilia was not personally present at the battle, should she not be greatly praised for her bravery in admonishing Theodoric her son, the valiant knight, to return to the battle, as you will hear? In his time, Theodoric was one of the greatest princes in the palace of the emperor of Constantinople; he was very handsome and proven in the valor of chivalry and extremely well-bred. It happened that a prince named Odoacre attacked the Romans, intending to destroy them and all of Italy if he could. When the Romans sought help from the emperor of Constantinople, he sent them this Theodoric, as the best representative of his knighthood, accompanied by quite a large army of troops. It happened that while he was fighting in ordered battle against this Odoacre the fortune of battle turned against him, so that out of fear he was forced to flee toward the city of Ravenna. When the brave and wise mother, who had been paying close attention to the battle, saw her son flee, she was terribly pained, considering that there could be no greater reproach for a knight than having fled in battle. Then her noble heart made her forget all maternal pity, and she would have preferred to see her son die honorably than to incur such shame. She immediately ran in front of him and implored him not to dishonor himself with such a flight but to regroup his troops and return to the battle. But as he did not pay much attention to words, the lady, overcome with great anger, lifted up the front of her dress and said to him, 'Truly, dear son, you have nowhere to flee unless you return to the womb from which you came.' Then Theodoric was so ashamed that he abandoned his flight, regrouped his troops, and returned to the battle in which, because of the incitement stemming from his shame at his mother's words, he fought so bravely that he defeated his enemies and killed Odoacre. Thus all of Italy, which had been in danger of being completely lost, was delivered by the sense of this lady. Therefore it seems to me that the honor of this victory should be credited to the mother rather than the son."

23. SHE SPEAKS AGAIN OF THE QUEEN FREDEGUND.

"As for this queen of France, Fredegund, of whom I spoke to you before, the boldness of her deeds in battle was equally great, for, as I have already mentioned, when she was widowed by King Chilperic her husband, with Clotaire her son at her breast and the kingdom beset by war, she told the barons, 'My lords, do not be afraid of all the enemies who have come upon us, for I have thought up a ruse by which we will conquer, provided you believe me. I will abandon all feminine fear and arm my heart with a man's boldness in order to increase your courage and that of the soldiers in the army, out of pity for your young prince. I will walk ahead of everyone, holding him in my arms, and you will follow me. You will do exactly as I have ordered our high constable to do.' The barons replied that she should command and that they would willingly obey her in everything. She cleverly deployed her army and then rode out in front of them, her son in her arms, with the barons and battalions of knights following after. They rode in this formation toward their enemies until nightfall when they entered a forest. The high constable cut off a high branch from a tree and the others did the same. They covered their horses with may boughs and hung little bells on several of them just as one does with horses who go out to pasture. In this way, tightly grouped together, they rode close to their enemies' tents and held the leafy may boughs high in their hands. The queen courageously kept moving ahead, exhorting her troops with promises and sweet words of encouragement to fight well, all the while holding the little king in her arms, with the barons behind her, all of whom felt great pity for the baby and waxed all the braver in order to protect his rights. When they seemed quite close to their enemies, they stopped and

I.23.1

stood still. When the dawn began to break, the enemy sentries who saw them began to say to one another, 'Here is a great wonder, because last night there was no wood or forest near us, and now there is a large and thick wood.' The others who saw this said the wood had to have been there already, for it could not be otherwise, unless they had been too foolish not to notice it, and the bells of the horses and cows who were at pasture should reassure them that it was truly a forest. Just as they were talking, never suspecting any trickery, the soldiers of the army suddenly threw down their branches. Then what had seemed to their enemies to be a wood suddenly appeared as armed knights. The soldiers rushed upon them and it was such a sudden attack that the enemy did not have a chance to take up arms, for they were all in their beds. They went from tent to tent and attacked their unarmed foe, killing or capturing all of them. Thanks to Fredegund's cleverness they were victorious."

24. SHE SPEAKS OF THE VIRGIN CAMILLA.

I.24.1   "I could tell you a lot about brave and valiant women: the virgin Camilla was no less valiant than any of the women whom I have told you about. This Camilla was the daughter of the ancient king of the Volscians named Metabus. Her mother died when she was born, and soon after her father was overthrown by his own people, who rebelled and threatened him so much that he was forced to flee for his life. He could carry away nothing except Camilla, whom he loved deeply. When he came to a large river which he would have to cross by swimming, he was at a loss because he could not figure out how to get his little daughter across. But after thinking about it a great deal, he tore off great patches of bark from the trees and fashioned a vessel which looked like a little boat. He placed the child inside and tied the little boat to his arm with strong vines of ivy. Then he plunged into the river and swam, drawing the boat after him, and in this way he and his daughter crossed the river. The king lived in the woods because he could go nowhere else for fear of his enemies' ambushes. He fed his daughter with the milk of wild hinds until she was stronger and somewhat bigger, and he clothed himself and the maiden with the skins of beasts which he killed. They had no other bed or blankets. When she was grown, she began to hunt down the beasts and kill them with slingshots and stones and she ran so swiftly after her quarry that no greyhound could have done better. She lived like this until she reached maturity, when she possessed an astonishing capacity for swiftness and boldness. After learning from her father of the wrong done to him by his subjects, she departed and took up arms. Put briefly, she struggled and fought so hard that, with the help of a few relatives, she managed through force of arms to reconquer her land, personally taking part in the fierce battles. Afterward she continued to perform deeds of chivalry so that she gained quite a reputation. She was so high-minded that she did not deign to take a husband or to couple with a man. This Camilla was the virgin who went to the aid of Turnus against Aeneas when he descended on Italy, just as the histories mention."

25. SHE SPEAKS OF THE QUEEN BERENICE OF CAPPADOCIA.

"There was a queen in Cappadocia who was called I.25.1
Berenice, of noble blood and heart, as would be expected from a daughter of the mighty king Mithridates (who ruled over a large part of the Orient) and from the wife of King Ariaractus of Cappadocia. While this lady was a widow, a brother of her late husband made war on her to disown her and her children. When, during a battle in the course of this struggle, the uncle killed two of his nephews, that is, this lady's sons, she was so grieved that her anger purged her of all feminine fear. She took up arms herself and with a great army advanced against her brother-in-law and fought so hard that in the end she

killed him with her own hands, had her chariot driven over him, and won the battle."

26. SHE SPEAKS OF THE BRAVERY OF CLOELIA.

I.26.1   "The noble Cloelia was a brave and wise woman, even though she never participated in a war or battle. It happened once that the Romans agreed to guarantee various treaties by sending the noble maiden Cloelia and other Roman virgins of noble lineage to a king who had been their enemy. After Cloelia had been held hostage for a while, she considered it dishonorable for the city of Rome that so many noble virgins were being held as prisoners by a foreign king. Cloelia therefore armed her heart with great boldness and cleverly managed with fair words and promises to deceive the guards and so escaped by night, leading her companions away until they came to the river Tiber. In a meadow nearby Cloelia found a horse at pasture, and though she had never before ridden a horse, she got on and, not fearing the deep water, placed one of her companions behind her and crossed the river, and then returned for the others and in this way ferried them all, one by one, across, safe and sound, and then took them to Rome and returned them to their parents.

I.26.2   "This virgin's bravery was much prized by the Romans and even the king who had held her hostage esteemed her for it and was in fact quite amused. The Romans, in permanent memory of this deed, had a statue of Cloelia sculpted which portrayed a maiden mounted on a horse, and they set this statue in a prominent location along the road to the temple, where it remained for a long time.

I.26.3   "Now the foundations of our City are complete: we must now build the high wall to surround it."

27. CHRISTINE ASKS REASON WHETHER GOD HAS EVER WISHED TO ENNOBLE THE MIND OF WOMAN WITH THE LOFTINESS OF THE SCIENCES; AND REASON'S ANSWER.

I.27.1   After hearing these things, I replied to the lady who spoke infallibly: "My lady, truly has God revealed great wonders in the strength of these women whom you describe. But please enlighten me again, whether it has ever pleased this God, who has bestowed so many favors on women, to honor the feminine sex with the privilege of the virtue of high understanding and great learning, and whether women ever have a clever enough mind for this. I wish very much to know this because men maintain that the mind of women can learn only a little."

She answered, "My daughter, since I told you before, you know quite well that the opposite of their opinion is true, and to show you this even more clearly, I will give you proof through examples. I tell you again—and don't doubt the contrary—if it were customary to send daughters to school like sons, and if they were then taught the natural sciences, they would learn as thoroughly and understand the subtleties of all the arts and sciences as well as sons. And by chance there happen to be such women, for, as I touched on before, just as women have more delicate bodies than men, weaker and less able to perform many tasks, so do they have minds that are freer and sharper whenever they apply themselves."

"My lady, what are you saying? With all due respect, could you dwell longer on this point, please. Certainly men would never admit this answer is true, unless it is explained more plainly, for they believe that one normally sees that men know more than women do."

She answered, "Do you know why women know less?"

"Not unless you tell me, my lady."

"Without the slightest doubt, it is because they are not involved in many different things, but stay at home, where it is enough for them to run the household, and there is nothing which so instructs a reasonable creature as the exercise and experience of many different things."

"My lady, since they have minds skilled in conceptualizing and learning, just like men, why don't women learn more?"

She replied, "Because, my daughter, the public does not require them to get involved in the affairs which men are commissioned to execute, just as I told you before.

It is enough for women to perform the usual duties to which they are ordained. As for judging from experience, since one sees that women usually know less than men, that therefore their capacity for understanding is less, look at men who farm the flatlands or who live in the mountains. You will find that in many countries they seem completely savage because they are so simpleminded. All the same, there is no doubt that Nature provided them with the qualities of body and mind found in the wisest and most learned men. All of this stems from a failure to learn, though, just as I told you, among men and women, some possess better minds than others. Let me tell you about women who have possessed great learning and profound understanding and treat the question of the similarity of women's minds to men's."

28. SHE BEGINS TO DISCUSS SEVERAL LADIES WHO WERE ENLIGHTENED WITH GREAT LEARNING, AND FIRST SPEAKS ABOUT THE NOBLE MAIDEN CORNIFICIA.

I.28.1   "Cornificia, the noble maiden, was sent to school by her parents along with her brother Cornificius when they were both children, thanks to deception and trickery. This little girl so devoted herself to study and with such marvelous intelligence that she began to savor the sweet taste of knowledge acquired through study. Nor was it easy to take her away from this joy to which she more and more applied herself, neglecting all other feminine activities. She occupied herself with this for such a long period of time that she became a consummate poet, and she was not only extremely brilliant and expert in the learnedness and craft of poetry but also seemed to have been nourished with the very milk and teaching of perfect philosophy, for she wanted to hear and know about every branch of learning, which she then mastered so thoroughly that she surpassed her brother, who was also a very great poet, and excelled in every field of learning. Knowledge was not enough for her unless she could put her mind to work and her pen to paper in the compilation of several very famous books. These works, as well as her poems, were much prized during the time of Saint Gregory and he himself mentions them. The Italian, Boccaccio, who was a great poet, discusses this fact in his work and at the same time praises this woman: 'O most great honor for a woman who abandoned all feminine activities and applied and devoted her mind to the study of the greatest scholars!' As further proof of what I am telling you, Boccaccio also talks about the attitude of women who despise themselves and their own minds, and who, as though they were born in the mountains totally ignorant of virtue and honor, turn disconsolate and say that they are good and useful only for embracing men and carrying and feeding children. God has given them such beautiful minds to apply themselves, if they want to, in any of the fields where glorious and excellent men are active, which are neither more nor less accessible to them as compared to men if they wished to study them, and they can thereby acquire a lasting name, whose possession is fitting for most excellent men. My dear daughter, you can see how this author Boccaccio testifies to what I have told you and how he praises and approves learning in women."

29. HERE SHE TELLS OF PROBA THE ROMAN.

"The Roman woman, Proba, wife of Adelphus, was equally outstanding and was a Christian. She had such a noble mind and so loved and devoted herself to study that she mastered all seven liberal arts and was an excellent poet and delved so deeply into the books of the poets, particularly Vergil's poems, that she knew them all by heart. After she had read these books and poems with profound insight and intelligence and had taken pains in her mind to understand them, it occurred to her that one could describe the Scriptures and the stories found in the Old and New Testament with pleasant verses filled with substance taken from these same works. 'Which in itself,' Boccaccio remarked, 'is not just admirable, that such a noble idea would come into a woman's

I.29.1

brain, but it is even more marvelous that she could actually execute it.' For then this woman, quite eager to bring her thinking to fruition, set to work: now she would run through the *Eclogues*, then the *Georgics*, and the *Aeneid* of Vergil—that is, she would skim as she read—and in one part she would take several entire verses unchanged and in another borrow small snatches of verse and, through marvelous craftsmanship and conceptual subtlety, she was able to construct entire lines of orderly verse. She would put small pieces together, coupling and joining them, all the while respecting the metrical rules, art and measure in the individual feet, as well as in the conjoining of verses, and without making any mistakes she arranged her verses so masterfully that no man could do better. In this way, starting from the creation of the world, she composed the opening of her book, and following all the stories of the Old and New Testament she came as far as the sending of the Holy Spirit to the Apostles, adapting Vergil's works to fit all this in so orderly a way that someone who only knew this work would have thought that Vergil had been both a prophet and evangelist. For these reasons, Boccaccio himself says that this woman merits great recognition and praise, for it is obvious that she possessed a sound and exhaustive knowledge of the sacred books and volumes of Holy Scripture, as do many great scholars and theologians of our time. This most noble lady wished that this said work, drawn up and composed through her labor, be called the *Cento*. Although the labor demanded by this work, because of its grandeur, would have been enough for one man's lifetime, she spent much less time in devoting herself to its execution, and was also able to compose several other excellent books. One, among others, she composed in verse, also called *Cento* because it contained one hundred lines of verse. She also made use of the poems and verses of the poet Homer, so that in praising her one can conclude that she knew not only Latin literature but also Greek literature perfectly. Boccaccio observes that it should be a great pleasure for women to hear about her and these things."

30. HERE SHE SPEAKS OF SAPPHO, THAT MOST SUBTLE WOMAN, POET, AND PHILOSOPHER.

"The wise Sappho, who was from the city of Mytilene, *I.30.1* was no less learned than Proba. This Sappho had a beautiful body and face and was agreeable and pleasant in appearance, conduct, and speech. But the charm of her profound understanding surpassed all the other charms with which she was endowed, for she was expert and learned in several arts and sciences, and she was not only well-educated in the works and writings composed by others but also discovered many new things herself and wrote many books and poems. Concerning her, Boccaccio has offered these fair words couched in the sweetness of poetic language: 'Sappho, possessed of sharp wit and burning desire for constant study in the midst of bestial and ignorant men, frequented the heights of Mount Parnassus, that is, of perfect study. Thanks to her fortunate boldness and daring, she kept company with the Muses, that is, the arts and sciences, without being turned away. She entered the forest of laurel trees filled with may boughs, greenery, and different colored flowers, soft fragrances and various aromatic spices, where Grammar, Logic, noble Rhetoric, Geometry, and Arithmetic live and take their leisure. She went on her way until she came to the deep grotto of Apollo, god of learning, and found the brook and conduit of the fountain of Castalia, and took up the plectrum and quill of the harp and played sweet melodies, with the nymphs all the while leading the dance, that is, following the rules of harmony and musical accord.' From what Boccaccio says about her, it should be inferred that the profundity of both her understanding and of her learned books can only be known and understood by men of great perception and learning, according to the testimony of the ancients. Her writings and poems have survived to this day, most remarkably constructed and composed, and they serve as illumination and models of consummate poetic craft and composition to those who have come afterward. She invented different genres of lyric and poetry, short narratives, tearful laments and strange lamentations about love and other emotions, and these were so well made and so well ordered that they were named 'Sapphic' after her. Horace recounts, concerning her poems, that when Plato, the great philosopher who was Aristotle's teacher, died, a book of Sappho's poems was found under his pillow.

I.30.2   "In brief this lady was so outstanding in learning that in the city where she resided a statue of bronze in her image was dedicated in her name and erected in a prominent place so that she would be honored by all and be remembered forever. This lady was placed and counted among the greatest and most famous poets, and, according to Boccaccio, the honors of the diadems and crowns of kings and the miters of bishops are not any greater, nor are the crowns of laurel and victor's palm.

I.30.3   "I could tell you a great deal about women of great learning. Leontium was a Greek woman and also such a great philosopher that she dared, for impartial and serious reasons, to correct and attack the philosopher Theophrastus, who was quite famous in her time."

31. HERE SHE DISCUSSES THE MAIDEN MANTO.

I.31.1   "If women are able to apprehend and fit to learn literary and scientific subjects, I want you to know for certain that the arts likewise are not forbidden to women, just as you will hear. In the ancient cult of the pagans long ago, people would divine the future from the flight of birds, the flames of fire, and the entrails of dead animals. This was an art or science in itself which they held in great respect. The supreme mistress of the art was a maiden, the daughter of Tiresias, who was the high priest of the city of Thebes (or what we would call the bishop, for in other religions priests could marry). This woman, who was named Manto and flourished in the time of Oedipus, king of Thebes, possessed such a brilliant and wide-ranging mind that she was well-versed in the art of pyromancy, that is, divination by fire. The Chaldaeans who invented this art made use of it in very ancient times, though others say that the giant Nimrod discovered it. There was no man in her time who could better discern the movements and colors of flames or the sounds which came out of fire, and who could so brilliantly read the veins of animals, the throats of bulls, and the entrails of beasts; and it was believed that with her arts she often forced spirits to speak in answer to her inquiries. During the lifetime of this lady, Thebes was destroyed as a result of the struggle between the sons of Oedipus the king, so she went to live in Asia and there built a temple to Apollo, which subsequently became quite famous. She ended her life in Italy, and because of her authority a city of that country was, and still is, named after this lady, Mantua, where Vergil was born."

32. SHE SPEAKS HERE OF MEDEA AND OF ANOTHER QUEEN, NAMED CIRCE.

"Medea, whom many historical works mention, was *I.32.1* no less familiar with science and art than Manto. She was the daughter of Aetes, king of Colchis, and of Persa, and was very beautiful, with a noble and upright heart and a pleasant face. In learning, however, she surpassed and exceeded all women; she knew the powers of every herb and all the potions which could be concocted, and she was ignorant of no art which can be known. With her spells she knew how to make the air become cloudy or dark, how to move winds from the grottoes and caverns of the earth, and how to provoke other storms in the air, as well as how to stop the flow of rivers, confect poisons, create fire to burn up effortlessly whatever object she chose, and all such similar arts. It was thanks to the art of her enchantments that Jason won the Golden Fleece.

"Circe, similarly, was queen of a country on a sea *I.32.2* which lay at the entrance to Italy. This lady knew so much about the art of enchantments that there was nothing which she might want to do that she could not accomplish by virtue of the strength of her spells. She knew how to metamorphose the bodies of men into those of wild beasts and animals through the power of a drink which she would administer. In testifying to this power, the story of Ulysses recounts that when he was returning home after the destruction of Troy, intending to go back to his own land in Greece, Fortune and stormy weather drove his ships in all directions, through many tempests, so that they finally arrived in the port of the city of this queen Circe. Since the clever Ulysses did not wish to disembark without the leave and permission of that country's queen, he sent his knights to her in order to find out whether it would please her for them to land. But this lady, thinking they were her enemies, gave the ten knights a drink of her concoction, which immediately changed them into swine. Ulysses quickly went to her, and the men were subsequently changed back to their proper form. Likewise, some say that when Diomedes, another prince of Greece, arrived in the port of Circe, she had his knights changed into birds, which they still remain. These birds are quite large and have a different shape from other birds. The natives are quite proud of them and call them 'Diomedius birds.'"

33. CHRISTINE ASKS REASON WHETHER THERE WAS EVER A WOMAN WHO DISCOVERED HITHERTO UNKNOWN KNOWLEDGE.

I.33.1   I, Christine, concentrating on these explanations of Lady Reason, replied to her regarding this passage: "My lady, I realize that you are able to cite numerous and frequent cases of women learned in the sciences and the arts. But I would then ask you whether you know of any women who, through the strength of emotion and of subtlety of mind and comprehension, have themselves discovered any new arts and sciences which are necessary, good, and profitable, and which had hitherto not been discovered or known. For it is not such a great feat of mastery to study and learn some field of knowledge already discovered by someone else as it is to discover by oneself some new and unknown thing."

She replied, "Rest assured, dear friend, that many noteworthy and great sciences and arts have been discovered through the understanding and subtlety of women, both in cognitive speculation, demonstrated in writing, and in the arts, manifested in manual works of labor. I will give you plenty of examples.

"First I will tell you of the noble Nicostrata whom the *I.33.2* Italians call Carmentis. This lady was the daughter of a king of Arcadia, named Pallas. She had a marvelous mind, endowed by God with special gifts of knowledge: she was a great scholar in Greek literature and had such fair and wise speech and venerable eloquence that the contemporary poets who wrote about her imagined she was beloved of the god Mercury. They claimed that a son whom she had with her husband, and who was in his time most learned, was in fact the offspring of this god. Because of certain changes which came about in the land where she lived, this lady left her country in a large boat for the land of Italy, and in her company were her son and a great many people who followed her; she arrived at the river Tiber. Landing there, she proceeded to climb a high hill which she named the Palentine, after her father, where the city of Rome was later founded. There, this lady and her son and all those who had followed her built a fortress. After discovering that the men of that country were all savages, she wrote certain laws, enjoining them to live in accord with right and reason, following justice. She was the first to institute laws in that country which subsequently became so renowned and from which all the statutes of law derive. This lady knew through divine inspiration and the spirit of prophecy (in which she was remarkably distinguished, in addition to the other graces she possessed) how in time to come this land would be ennobled by excellence and famous over all the countries of the world. Therefore it seemed to her that once the grandeur of the Roman Empire, which would rule the entire world, had been established, it would not be right for the Romans to use the strange and inferior letters and characters of another country. Moreover, in order to show forth her wisdom and the excellence of her mind to the centuries to come, she worked and studied so hard that she invented her own letters, which were completely different from those of other nations, that is, she established the Latin alphabet and syntax, spelling, the difference between vowels and consonants, as well as a complete introduction to the science of grammar. She gave and taught these letters to the people and wished that they be widely known. This was hardly a minor or unprofitable contribution to learning which this woman invented, nor one for which she merits slight gratitude, for thanks to the subtlety of this teaching and to the great utility and profit which have since accrued to the world, one can say that nothing more worthy in the world was ever invented. The Italians were not ungrateful for this benefit, and rightly so, since for them this discovery was so fantastic that they not only deemed this woman to be greater than any man, but they also considered her a goddess and even honored her during her lifetime with divine honors. After her death they erected a temple to her, built at the foot of the hill where she had resided. To ensure eternal remembrance of this lady, they used many names taken from the science she had discovered and gave her name to many other things, so that the people of this country even called themselves Latins in honor of the science of Latin developed by this lady. Moreover, because *ita*, which means *oui* in French, is the strongest affirmation in Latin, they were not satisfied calling this country the 'Latin land,' but rather they wished that all the country beyond the mountains, which is quite large and contains many diverse countries and dominions, be called *Italy*. Poems were named *carmen* in Latin, after this lady, Carmentis, and even the Romans who lived long afterward, called one of the gates of the city of Rome the *Carmentalis*. Regardless of the prosperity which the Romans enjoyed and the majesty of some of their emperors, the Romans did not change these names, just as it is apparent in the present-day since they still survive.

"What more do you want, fair daughter? Can one say *I.33.3*
anything more solemn about any man born of woman? And do not think for a minute that she was the only woman in the world by whom numerous and varied branches of learning have been discovered!"

34. HERE SHE SPEAKS OF MINERVA, WHO INVENTED MANY SCIENCES AND THE TECHNIQUE OF MAKING ARMOR FROM IRON AND STEEL.

"Minerva, just as you have written elsewhere, was a *I.34.1*
maiden of Greece and surnamed Pallas. This maiden was of such excellence of mind that the foolish people of that time, because they did not know who her parents were and saw her doing things which had never been done before, said she was a goddess descended from Heaven; for the less they knew about her ancestry, the more marvelous her great knowledge seemed to them, when compared to that of the women of her time. She had a subtle mind, of profound understanding, not only in one subject but also generally, in every subject. Through her ingenuity she invented a shorthand Greek script in which a long written narrative could be transcribed with far fewer letters, and which is still used by the Greeks today, a fine invention whose discovery demanded great subtlety. She invented numbers and a means of quickly counting and adding sums. Her mind was so enlightened with general knowledge that she devised various skills and designs which had never before been discovered. She developed the entire technique of gathering wool and making cloth and was the first who ever thought to shear sheep of their wool and then to pick, comb, and card it with iron spindles and finally to spin it with a distaff, and then she

invented the tools needed to make the cloth and also the method by which the wool should finally be woven.

I.34.2   "Similarly she initiated the custom of extracting oil from different fruits of the earth, also from olives, and of squeezing and pressing juice from other fruits. At the same time she discovered how to make wagons and carts to transport things easily from one place to another.

I.34.3   "This lady, in a similar manner, did even more, and it seems all the more remarkable because it is far removed from a woman's nature to conceive of such things; for she invented the art and technique of making harnesses and armor from iron and steel, which knights and armed soldiers employ in battle and with which they cover their bodies, and which she first gave to the Athenians whom she taught how to deploy an army and battalions and how to fight in organized ranks.

I.34.4   "Similarly she was the first to invent flutes and fifes, trumpets and wind instruments. With her considerable force of mind, this lady remained a virgin her entire life. Because of her outstanding chastity, the poets claimed in their fictions that Vulcan, the god of fire, wrestled with her for a long time and that finally she won and overcame him, which is to say that she overcame the ardor and lusts of the flesh which so strongly assail the young. The Athenians held this maiden in such high reverence that they worshiped her as a goddess and called her the goddess of arms and chivalry because she was the first to devise their use, and they also called her the goddess of knowledge because of her learnedness.

I.34.5   "After her death they erected a temple in Athens dedicated to her, and there they placed a statue of her, portraying a maiden, as a representation of wisdom and chivalry. This statue had terrible and cruel eyes because chivalry has been instituted to carry out rigorous justice; they also signified that one seldom knows toward what end the meditation of the wise man tends. She wore a helmet on her head which signified that a knight must have strength, endurance, and constant courage in the deeds of arms, and further signified that the counsels of the wise are concealed, secret, and hidden. She was dressed in a coat of mail which stood for the power of the estate of chivalry and also taught that the wise man is always armed against the whims of Fortune, whether good or bad. She held some kind of spear or very long lance, which meant that the knight must be the rod of justice and also signified that the wise man casts his spears from great distances. A buckler or shield of crystal hung at her neck, which meant that the knight must always be alert and oversee everywhere the defense of his country and people and further signified that things are open and evident to the wise man. She had portrayed in the middle of this shield the head of a serpent called Gorgon, which teaches that the knight must always be wary and watchful over his enemies like the serpent, and furthermore, that the wise man is aware of all the malice which can hurt him. Next to this image they also placed a bird that flies by night, named the owl, as if to watch over her, which signified that the knight must be ready by night as well as by day for civil defense, when necessary, and also that the wise man should take care at all times to do what is profitable and fitting for him. For a long time this lady was held in such high regard and her great fame spread so far that in many places temples were founded to praise her. Even long afterward, when the Romans were at the height of their power, they included her image among their gods."

35. SHE DISCUSSES QUEEN CERES, WHO DISCOVERED THE ART OF CULTIVATING THE EARTH AND MANY OTHER ARTS.

"Ceres, who was in ancient times queen of the kingdom of the Sicilians, enjoys the privilege of being the first to discover cultivation and to invent the necessary tools. She taught her subjects to master and tame oxen as well as to train them to the yoke. She also invented the plow and showed her subjects how to plow the earth   *I.35.1* with plowshares tipped in iron and how to carry out all the accompanying tasks. Afterward she taught them how to cast seed on this ground and cover it over, and later, after the seed had grown and multiplied, she showed them how to reap the grains and how to sift out the ears by beating them with flails. Then she cleverly taught them how to grind the grain between hard stones and in mills and then how to mix the ingredients to make bread. Thus this woman taught and instructed men who had been accustomed, like beasts, to live on acorns, wild grains, and haws, to make use of more convenient foods. This lady did even more: for she had the people of that time gather together in communities. They had traditionally lived scattered here and there in the forest and wilderness, wandering like animals. She taught them to build cities and towns of permanent construction where they could reside together. Thus, thanks to this woman, the world was led away from bestial living conditions to a rational, human life. Poets dreamed up the fable that Ceres' daughter was carried off by Pluto, the god of Hell. And because of the authority of her knowledge and the great good she brought about for the world, the people of that time worshiped her and called her the goddess of grain."

36. HERE SHE SPEAKS OF ISIS, WHO DISCOVERED THE ART OF CONSTRUCTING GARDENS AND OF PLANTING.

I.36.1   "Isis, likewise, was a woman of such great learning acquired through labor that she was not only named the queen of Egypt but also the most singular and special goddess of the Egyptians. The tale has it that Jupiter loved Isis and changed her into a cow and that then she reassumed her original form, all of which signifies her vast knowledge, just as you yourself have touched upon in your *Epistre d'Othea*. She invented a form of shorthand which she taught to the Egyptians and provided them a way to abridge their excessively involved script. She was the daughter of Inachos, king of the Greeks, and sister of the wise Phoroneus. For some reason this lady went from Greece to Egypt with this brother of hers. There, among other things, she taught the Egyptians how to set up vegetable gardens and how to make plantings and grafts from different stalks. She handed down and instituted several good and upright laws; she instructed the people of Egypt, who had, until then, lived like savages without law, justice, or order, to live according to the rule of the law. And to put it briefly, she did so much there that both in her lifetime and after her death they held her in the greatest reverence. Her fame spread everywhere in the world so that temples and chapels were established everywhere. Even at the height of their power, the Romans had a temple in Rome erected in her name where they instituted sacrifices, offerings, and solemn rights in conformity to the custom observed in Egypt.

"The husband of this noble lady was called Apis, who, *I.36.2* according to the error of the pagans, was supposed to be the son of the god Jupiter and of Niobe, daughter of Phoroneus, who is mentioned frequently in ancient histories and in the work of ancient poets."

37. CONCERNING THE GREAT GOOD ACCRUED TO THE WORLD THROUGH THESE WOMEN.

"My lady, I greatly admire what I have heard you say, *I.37.1* that so much good has come into the world by virtue of the understanding of women. These men usually say that women's knowledge is worthless. In fact when someone says something foolish, the widely voiced insult is that this is women's knowledge. In brief, the typical opinions and comments of men claim that women have been and are useful in the world only for bearing children and sewing."

She answered, "Now you can recognize the massive ingratitude of the men who say such things; they are like people who live off the goods of others without knowing their source and without thanking anyone. You can also clearly see how God, who does nothing without a reason, wished to show men that He does not despise the feminine sex nor their own, because it so pleased Him to place such great understanding in women's brains that they are intelligent enough not only to learn and retain the sciences but also to discover new sciences themselves, indeed sciences of such great utility and profit for the world that nothing has been more necessary. You can therefore see from this Carmentis, whom I just mentioned to you and who invented the Latin alphabet, toward which God has been so favorable and which has spread the skill developed by this lady so that it has even effaced some of the glory of the Hebrew and Greek alphabets, which once enjoyed such great esteem, that all of Europe (which contains a very large part of the world) uses this script, in which practically an endless number of books and volumes have been written and composed, where the deeds of man and the noble and excellent glories of God, as well as the sciences and the arts, have been placed and held in perpetual memory. And let no one say that I am telling you these things just to be pleasant: they are Boccaccio's own words, and his credibility is well-known and evident. Thus you can conclude that the benefits realized by this woman are endless, for, thanks to her, men have been brought out of ignorance and led to knowledge, even if they do not recognize it; thanks to her, they possess the means to send the secrets and meditations of their minds as far away as they want, to announce and to report whatever they wish anywhere, and, by the same token, the means to know the past, present, and future. Moreover, because of this one woman's learning, men can conclude agreements and maintain friendships with distant people and, through the exchange of responses, they can know one another without having seen one another. In short, all the good which comes from the alphabet and thus from books cannot be told; for books describe and facilitate the understanding and knowledge of God, celestial things, the sea, the earth, all people, and all things. Where was there ever a man who did more good?"

38. ON THE SAME TOPIC.

"Similarly, where was there ever a man thanks to whom more good came into the world than thanks to this noble queen Ceres whom I have just discussed with you? How could anyone ever acquire a more praise-worthy name than by leading wandering and savage men, living in the woods like cruel beasts without the rule of justice, to reside in cities and towns and by teaching them to make use of law and by securing better provisions for them than acorns and wild apples, that is, grains and cereals? Because of this food, men have more beautiful and more radiant bodies and stronger and more flexible limbs, for this food is more beneficial and useful for humans. And who will ever win more praise for teaching men to beautify the land, which had been overgrown with thistles, thorns, poorly arranged shrubs, and wild trees, to clear it through labor and to sow seed, so that the savage land, thanks to cultivation, became domesti-cated and ennobled for the common profit of all? Because of this lady, humanity benefited from the transformation of the harsh and untamed world into a civilized and urban place. She transformed the minds of vagabond and lazy men by drawing them to herself and leading them from the caverns of ignorance to the heights of contemplation and proper behavior. By organizing certain men to per-form field work, she made it possible for so many cities and towns to be populated and for their residents, who perform the other works necessary for life, to be sup-ported. *I.38.1*

"The same holds true for Isis and gardening. Who could sum up the great good which she procured for the world by developing a method for taking grafts from trees which bear so many good fruits and spices so useful for human nourishment? *I.38.2*

"Minerva, too, from her knowledge provided human- *I.38.3*

ity with so many necessary objects, like woolen clothing for men who had previously worn only animal skins, and solved the problems they had transporting necessities in their arms from one place to another by inventing wagons and carts to help them. For nobles and knights she devised a means of making armor to cover their bodies for greater protection in war and developed better-looking, stronger, and more practical armor than they had had before, which had only consisted of leather from animals."

I.38.4   Then I said to her, "Now, my lady, I indeed understand more than before why you spoke of the enormous ingratitude, not to say ignorance, of these men who malign women, for although it seems to me that the fact that the mother of every man is a woman is reason enough not to attack them, not to mention the other good deeds which one can clearly see that women do for men, truly, one can see here the many benefits afforded by women with the greatest generosity to men which they have accepted and continue to accept. Henceforth, let all writers be silent who speak badly of women, let all of them be silent— those who have attacked women and who still attack them in their books and poems, and all their accomplices and supporters too— let them lower their eyes, ashamed for having dared to speak so badly, in view of the truth which runs counter to their poems; this noble lady, Carmentis, through the profundity of her understanding taught them like a school-mistress— nor can they deny it— the lesson thanks to which they consider themselves so lofty and honored, that is, she taught them the Latin alphabet!

I.38.5   "But what did all the many nobles and knights say, who generally slander women with such false remarks? From now on let them keep their mouths shut and remember that the customs of bearing arms, of dividing armies into battalions, and of fighting in ordered ranks— a vocation upon which they so pride themselves and for which they consider themselves so great— came to them from a woman and were given to them by a woman. Would men who live on bread, or who live civilly in cities following the order of law, or who cultivate the fields, have any good reason to slander and rebuff women so much, as many do, if they only thought of all the benefits? Certainly not, because thanks to women, that is, Minerva, Ceres, and Isis, so many beneficial things have come to men, through which they can lead honorable lives and from which they live and will live always. Ought not these things be considered?"

"Doubtless, my lady. It seems to me that neither in the teaching of Aristotle, which has been of great profit to human intelligence and which is so highly esteemed and with good reason, nor in that of all the other philosophers who have ever lived, could an equal benefit for the world be found as that which has been accrued and still accrues through the works accomplished by virtue of the knowledge possessed by these ladies."

And she said to me, "They were not alone, but there are many others and I will tell you about a few of them."

39. HERE SHE SPEAKS OF THE MAIDEN ARACHNE, WHO INVENTED THE ART OF DYEING WOOL AND OF MAKING TAPESTRIES OF EXQUISITELY WORKED CLOTH WITH FINE THREADS AND ALSO DISCOVERED THE ART OF CULTIVATING FLAX AND MAKING LINEN.

"In fact, God has wished to provide the world with *I.39.1* many necessary and profitable things not only through these women but also through many other women, as, for example, a maiden from the land of Asia who was named Arachne, daughter of Idmonius of Colophon, who had a marvelously subtle mind. Thanks to all her reflections she was the first to invent the art of dyeing woolens in various colors and of weaving art works into cloth, like a painter, according to the 'fine thread' technique of weaving tapestry. She was marvelously skilled in all kinds of weaving. Moreover, she is mentioned in the fable which says she was the one who competed with Pallas who changed her into a spider.

I.39.2   "This woman discovered an even more necessary science, for she was the first to invent a way of cultivating flax and hemp, along with harvesting and breaking them, as well as steeping and hackling the flax, spinning it with a distaff, and weaving linen. It seems to me that this technique was quite necessary for the world, although many men have reproached women for practicing it. This Arachne also invented the art of making nets, snares, and traps for catching birds and fishes, and she invented the art of fishing and of trapping strong and cruel wild beasts with snares and nets, as well as rabbits and hares, and birds too; no one knew anything about these techniques before her. This woman, as far as I can tell, performed no small service for the world, which has since derived and derives much ease and profit from it.

I.39.3   "Nevertheless, several authors, and even the poet Boccaccio who relates those things, have argued that this world was better off when people lived only from haws and acorns and wore nothing more than animal skins than it is now that they have been taught to live in greater refinement. But with all due respect for him and for those who argue that it was unfortunate for the world that such things were discovered for the ease and nourishment of the human body, I would maintain that the more goods, favors, and boons the human creature receives from God, the better he is required to serve God, and if he makes poor use of the goods which his Creator has promised and granted to him to use profitably and which his Creator ordained for the use of man and woman, then this abuse comes from the mischief and perversity of those who misuse them, and not because the things in themselves are not excellent and profitable when used or employed lawfully. Jesus Christ himself showed us this in His own person, for He used bread and wine, fish, colored robes, and all these things which have thus become necessary, which He would not have done if He could have made better use of acorns and haws. He paid a great honor to the science which Ceres invented, that is, bread-making, when it pleased Him to give to man and woman such a worthy body in the form of bread which they have made use of."

40. HERE SHE DISCUSSES PAMPHILE, WHO INVENTED THE ART OF REMOVING SILK FROM WORMS AND OF DYEING AND WEARING CLOTH FROM SILK.

"Among all the good and useful and profitable sciences I.40.1 invented by women, one ought not to forget the one which the noble Pamphile from the land of Greece discovered. This lady had a mind skilled in various crafts, and she so enjoyed researching and examining strange things that she was the first to invent the art of weaving silk, for with her speculative and imaginative mind, she used to watch the worms who naturally make silk on the tree branches in the country where she resided. She took the cocoons which these worms had made and which she saw were quite beautiful and assembled the threads from several of them. Then she experimented to see whether this thread would take a good dye of various colors, and when she had tried all of these things and seen that the results were gratifying, she began to weave silk cloth. Thanks to the techniques developed by this woman, great beauty and profit have come into the world and spread to all lands, for God is honored and served by different vestments; silk is used for the noble robes and vestments of prelates as well as of emperors, kings, and princes, and also for garments for people of those lands which make use of no other kind of clothing because they do not have woolens but do have an abundance of silk-worms."

41. HERE SHE SPEAKS OF THAMARIS, WHO WAS THE SUPREME MISTRESS OF THE ART OF PAINTING, AND LIKEWISE OF ANOTHER WOMAN, CALLED IRENE, AND OF THE ROMAN, MARCIA.

"Should I also tell you whether a woman's nature is I.41.1 clever and quick enough to learn speculative sciences as well as to discover them, and likewise the manual arts? I assure you that women are equally well-suited and skilled to carry them out and to put them to sophisticated use once they have learned them, just as is written concerning a woman named Thamaris who possessed such great subtlety in the art and science of painting that during her lifetime she was the most supreme painter known. According to Boccaccio, she was the daughter of the painter Mycon and was born during the ninetieth Olympiad. The Olympiad was a day of great solemnity, instituted for holding different games, and whoever won these was granted whatever he wanted, within reason. This festival and these games were held in honor of the god Jupiter and were celebrated every four years. Hercules first established this festival, and the Greeks reckon their calendar from its founding, just as the Christians reckon their dates from the birth of Jesus Christ. This Thamaris, having abandoned all the usual tasks of women, pursued her father's art with subtlety of mind. On this account she earned such singular praise during Archelaos' reign over the Macedonians that the Ephesians, who worshiped the goddess Diana, had Thamaris carefully paint the image of their goddess on a tablet, which they revered long afterward as an object wrought with consummate excellence and skill. They exhibited this image only during the festival and rites of the goddess. This painting, since it survived a long time, bore such great witness to the subtlety of this woman that even today her genius is still discussed.

I.41.2   "Similarly, another woman, named Irene, also from Greece, was supremely skilled in the science of painting and surpassed all others in the world, during her time. She was a disciple of the painter Cratinus, a consummate artisan, but she was so sophisticated and had learned so much of this science that she marvelously surpassed and exceeded her master. This accomplishment seemed such a great wonder to the people of that time that in her memory they had her likeness sculpted as a maiden who was painting, and, to honor her, they placed it among the sculptures representing the great artists of various masterpieces who had lived before her. The ancients customarily honored all those who surpassed others in any outstanding achievements, whether in knowledge, strength, beauty, or some other grace, and, in order to ensure their perpetual memory in the world, they had sculptures of them erected in high and honorable places.

"How equally outstanding in the art of painting was   *I.41.3* Marcia the Roman, a virtuous virgin of noble bearing! She practiced this art with great skill and so masterfully that she excelled all men, including Dyonisius and Sopolis, then considered to be the best painters in the world. In fact, she reached and surpassed the acme of all that can be known in this science, according to the opinion of the masters. Among her noteworthy works was such a realistic self-portrait (which she skillfully painted by looking at herself in a mirror in order that her memory survive her) that every man who saw it would swear it was alive. Afterward, this portrait was carefully guarded and shown to artists as a solemn treasure."

Then I said to her, "My lady, through these examples   *I.41.4* it can be seen that long ago the wise were honored considerably more than they are today and that the sciences were held in much greater esteem. Regarding what you say about women expert in the art of painting, I know a woman today, named Anastasia, who is so learned and skilled in painting manuscript borders and miniature backgrounds that one cannot find an artisan in all the city of Paris—where the best in the world are found—who can surpass her, nor who can paint flowers and details as delicately as she does, nor whose work is more highly esteemed, no matter how rich or precious the book is. People cannot stop talking about her. And I know this from experience, for she has executed several things for me which stand out among the ornamental borders of the great masters."

She replied, "I can readily believe you, for whoever wants to look for intellectually sophisticated women can find many in the world. And I will tell you about another Roman woman as further illustration of this argument."

42. SHE SPEAKS OF SEMPRONIA THE ROMAN.

I.42.1   "This Sempronia from Rome was a woman of great beauty. But although the beauty of her body and face surpassed that of practically all other women in her time, even more so did the excellence and subtlety of her mind surpass and exceed those of all others. Her intellect was so remarkable that there was nothing too subtle in word or in deed which she could not recall completely and flawlessly. She could do whatever she wanted because of her body's skill and could repeat everything she had heard, no matter how long a story it was! She knew not only Latin but also Greek perfectly, and she wrote Greek so ingeniously that it was an admirable feat.

I.42.2   "She was also so beautiful, comely, and graceful in speech, in eloquence, and in conduct that she could make everyone do what she wanted. For is she wished to have people play, there was no one too sad whom she could not move to mirth and joy, or if she wanted, to anger or tears or sadness. Likewise, she could make any man act boldly or forcefully or perform any possible task. She could make all those who heard her speak follow her, if she wished. Moreover, the way she spoke and held her body was so full of gentleness and sweetness that no one could look at her or listen to her enough. She sang so melodiously and played all string instruments so skillfully that she won every contest. In short, she was extremely clever and ingenious at doing all those things which the human mind can comprehend."

43. CHRISTINE ASKS REASON WHERE PRUDENCE IS FOUND IN THE NATURAL SENSIBILITY OF WOMEN; AND REASON'S ANSWER TO HER.

I.43.1   Then I, Christine, said to her, "My lady, I can truly and clearly see that God—may He be praised for it—has granted that the mind of an intelligent woman can conceive, know, and retain all perceptible things. Even though there are so many people who have such subtle minds that they understand and learn everything which they are shown and who are so ingenious and quick to conceptualize everything that every field of learning is open to them, with the result that they have acquired extraordinary knowledge through devotion to study, I am baffled when eminent scholars—including some of the most famous and learned—exhibit so little prudence in their morals and conduct in the world. Certainly scholarship teaches and provides an introduction to morals. If you please, my lady, I would gladly learn from you whether a woman's mind (which, as it seems to me from your proofs as well as from what I myself see, is quite understanding and retentive in subtle questions of scholarship and other subjects) is equally prompt and clever in those matters which prudence teaches, that is, whether women can reflect on what is best to do and what is better to be avoided, and whether they remember past events and become learned from the examples they have seen, and, as a result, are wise in managing current affairs, and whether they have foresight into the future. Prudence, it seems to me, teaches those lessons."

"You speak correctly, my daughter," she replied, "but this prudence of which you speak is bestowed by Nature upon men and women, and some possess more, others less. But Nature does not impart knowledge of everything, as much as it simultaneously perfects in those who are naturally prudent, for you realize that two forces together are stronger and more resistant than one force alone. For this reason I say that the person who, from Nature, possesses prudence (which is called 'natural sense'), as well as acquired knowledge along with this prudence, deserves special praise for remarkable excellence. Yet just as you yourself have said, some who possess the one do not possess the other, for the one is the gift of God thanks to the influence of Nature, and the other is acquired through long study, though both are good. But some people prefer natural sense without acquired knowledge rather than a great deal of acquired knowledge with little natural sense. All the same, many opinions can be based upon this proposition, from which many questions can arise. For one could say that one achieves more good by choosing what is more useful for the profit and the utility of the general public. Therefore, one person's knowing the different fields of learning is more profitable for everyone than all the natural sense which he might possess which he could demonstrate to all: for this natural sense can only last as long as the lifetime of the person who has it, and when he dies, his sense dies with him. Acquired learning, on the other hand, lasts forever for those who have it, because of their fame, and it is useful for many people insofar as it can be taught to others and recorded in books for the sake of future generations. In this way their learning does not die with them, and therefore I can show you, using the example of Aristotle and others through whom learning has been transmitted to the world, that their acquired knowledge was more useful to the world than all the prudence without acquired knowledge possessed by all men, past and present, although thanks to the prudence of many, several kingdoms and empires have been well-governed and directed. All of these things are transitory, however, and disappear with time, while learning endures forever.

I.43.2   "Nevertheless, I will leave these questions unanswered and for others to solve, for they do not pertain to the problem of building our City, and I will come back to the question you raised, that is, whether women possess natural prudence. Of course they do. You know this already from what I have said to you before, just as, in general, you can see from women's conduct in those duties assigned to them to perform. But be careful if you find this good, for you will see that all women, or the vast majority, are so very attentive, careful, and diligent in governing their households and in providing everything for them, according to their capacities, that sometimes some of their negligent husbands are annoyed; they think their wives are pushing and pressuring them too much to do what they are supposed to and they say their wives want to run everything and be smarter than they are. In this way, what many women tell their husbands with good intentions turns out to their disadvantage. The proverbs of Solomon discuss such prudent women and what follows gives you the gist of this book for the purposes of our argument here."

44. THE EPISTLE OF SOLOMON, OR THE BOOK OF PROVERBS.

"'Who can find a virtuous, a prudent woman? Her   *I.44.1*
husband will never lack anything. She is renowned throughout the whole land, and her husband is proud of her because she always gives him every good and rich thing. She seeks out and buys woolens, which should be understood as work to occupy her household in profitable activity, and she fits out her household and lends a hand to the tasks. She is like the merchant's ship which brings all kinds of goods and which supplies bread. And there is plenty of meat, even for her servants. She considers the value of a manor before buying it, and thanks to her own common sense, she has planted the vineyard which provides for her household. She girds her loins with the strength of her constant solicitude, and her arms are hardened in continual good works. No matter how dark it is, the light from her labor will never go out. She occupies herself even with difficult tasks and does not despise feminine chores but applies herself to them. She stretches out her hand to the poor and needy to help them. Because of her foresight, her house is protected against the cold and snow, and those over whom she rules are clothed in double robes. She makes herself clothes from silk and purple, with honor and fame, and her husband is honored when he sits among the leaders of the world's elders. She makes fabrics and fine linens, which

she sells, and her own clothes are strength and honor, and for this reason, her joy shall be perpetual. Her mouth always speaks words of wisdom and the law of kindness is on her tongue. She takes thought for the provisions of her household everywhere throughout her house, nor does she ever eat the bread of idleness. The behavior of her children shows that she is their mother and their works preach blessedness. The fair adornment of her husband brings her praise. She is the mistress of her daughters in all things, even though they are grown. She despises false glory and vain beauty. Such a woman fears our Lord, she shall be commended, and He will reward her according to her works which praise her everywhere.'"

45. HERE SHE SPEAKS OF GAIA CIRILLA.

I.45.1   "Regarding what the Epistle of Solomon says about the prudent woman, one might well recall the noble queen Gaia Cirilla. This lady was either from Rome or Tuscany and was married to the king of the Romans named Tarquin. She showed the greatest prudence in governing and was very virtuous, given her sensibility, loyalty, and goodness. She reputedly surpassed all women in her skill at being an excellent housewife with noteworthy foresight. Although she was the queen and could well avoid working with her hands, she was always so inclined to profit from everything and never to be idle that she was always working at some task and, likewise, had her ladies and maidens who attended her, at work. This noble lady was famed, honored, esteemed, and renowned throughout the world for these actions. Because of her fame and in her memory, the Romans, who subsequently became a far greater power than they were in her time, established and maintained the custom at their daughters' marriages of having the bride answer 'Gaia' when she was asked her name upon entering the groom's house for the first time. This indicated her desire to imitate this lady in works and deeds as far as she could."

46. HERE REASON SPEAKS OF THE PRUDENCE AND ATTENTIVENESS OF QUEEN DIDO.

"Just as you yourself said before, prudence means I.46.1 taking pains to be able to finish those tasks which one wishes to undertake. I will give more examples of other powerful ladies to show you that women are attentive in this matter, even in questions of great importance, and the first example is Dido, originally called Elissa. In her works she clearly demonstrated her prudence and erudition, just as I will tell. She founded and built a city called Carthage, in the land of Africa, where she was lady and queen. The way in which she founded her city and acquired and took possession of her land demonstrated her exceptional constancy, nobility, and strength, and without these graces true prudence is impossible. This lady was descended from the Phoenicians, who came from the hinterlands of Egypt to the land of Syria where they founded and built several noble cities and towns. Among these people was a king named Agenor, of whom Dido's father, who was named Belus, was a direct descendant, and he was the king of Phoenicia and conquered the kingdom of Cyprus. This king had only one son, named Pygmalion, along with this maiden Dido, and no other children. As he lay dying, he charged his barons to bear love and loyalty to his two children. He even made them promise to do so. After the king had died, they crowned Pygmalion, his son, and married Elissa, who was quite beautiful, to a duke who was the most powerful man in the country after the king, whose name was Acerbas Sychaeon or Sychaeus. And this Sychaeus was a high priest in the temple of Hercules, according to their law, and was fantastically rich. Sychaeus and Elissa loved each other very much, and they led a good life. But King Pygmalion was evil, cruel, and extraordinarily greedy: he could not have enough without coveting even more. Elissa, his sister, well acquainted with his greed and realizing that her husband had great wealth and that his wealth was quite famous, counseled and advised her husband to protect himself against the king and to hide his treasure in a secret place so that the king could not take it away from him. Sychaeus believed this advice but neglected to protect his person against the king's ambushes, as she had advised him. One day this king had him killed in order to have his great treasures. Elissa was so grieved at this death that she too nearly died, and for a long time she wept and moaned, piteously lamenting her beloved and her lord while cursing her cruel brother who had had him put to death. But this criminal king, who felt robbed of his expectations because he found little or nothing of Sychaeus' wealth, bore great malice toward his sister, for he thought that she had hidden her husband's treasures. Realizing that her life was in great danger, Elissa's own prudence prompted her to leave her homeland and to go into exile. Having considered this question, she courageously reflected on what she should do and armed herself with strength and constancy to put her intended undertaking into effect. This lady knew very well that the king was not at all loved by the barons nor by the people because of the atrocities and crimes he had perpetrated. Therefore, she took with her several princes and citizens, as well as some common people, and after she had sworn them to secrecy, she began to eloquently explain her plans, as long as they agreed to go with her and swear to her that they would be good and faithful subjects. This lady secretly had her ship readied as quickly as possible and left at night with all her great treasures, accompanied by many people, and she ordered her sailors to hurry to depart. This lady was even more clever, for she knew very well that her brother would have her followed as soon as he knew of her departure, and for this reason she had large trunks, coffers, and bundles secretly filled with heavy, worthless objects, as though these were her treasure, so that by turning these trunks and bundles over to her brother's envoys, they would let her go and not impede her voyage. And so it happened: for they had not yet traveled very far when a great number of the king's henchmen came rushing in pursuit to stop her. But the lady spoke well and wisely to them and said she was going on a pilgrimage of her own, unless they cared to prevent her. Seeing that this excuse was worthless, she declared that she knew well that her brother the king had no use for her, but that, in fact, if he wanted to have her treasure, she would willingly send it back to him. The king's henchmen, knowing well that he was aiming at nothing else but this, said that she should give the treasure to them immediately, for with this they would try to satisfy the king and reconcile him to her. The lady, therefore, with a sad face as though it pained her, had all of these trunks and chests delivered to them and loaded on their ships. And they left immediately, thinking that they had acted well and were bringing the king good news. The queen, without even slightly seeming to do so, turned her thoughts to her voyage as quickly as she could. They kept on traveling, by day and by night, until they arrived at the island of Cyprus. There they rested a little. Then, after offering sacrifices to the gods, she returned to her ship and brought along with her the priest of Jupiter and his household. This same priest had prophesied that a lady from the lands of Phoenicia would come, on whose behalf he would leave his country in order to accompany her. So, leaving the land of Crete behind them, they proceeded, with Sicily to their right, sailing along the coast of Massylia, until they arrived in Africa, where they landed. The people in that country immediately came to look at the ship and its passengers. After they saw the lady and realized that her followers were men of peace, they brought them many provisions. And the lady spoke to them graciously and told them that, because of the good she had heard recounted about this country, they had come to live there, provided that the natives were agreed, who thereupon indicated their willingness. Pretending that she did not wish to make a very large settlement on foreign land, the lady asked them to sell her only as much land on the beach which a cow-hide would enclose for building a lodging there for herself and her people. This request was granted to her, and, once the conditions of the sale were drawn up and sworn between them, the lady then demonstrated her cleverness and prudence: she took out a cowhide and cut it into the thinnest possible strips and then connected them together in a kind of belt, which she spread out on the ground around the port and which enclosed a marvelously large piece of land. The sellers were very surprised at this and amazed by the ruse and cleverness of this woman, but, nevertheless, they had to keep their part of the bargain.

I.46.2   "In such a manner this lady acquired land in Africa, and within this enclosure a horse's head was found. According to their divinations, they interpreted this horse's head, along with the flight and cry of birds, to mean that a warrior people, exceptionally valorous at arms, would inhabit the city to be founded there. This lady then summoned workers from everywhere and unpacked her treasure. She had a marvelously beautiful, large, and strong city constructed, which she named Carthage; she called the tower and citadel 'Byrsa,' which means 'cowhide.'

I.46.3   "And just as she was beginning to construct her city, she received news that her brother was threatening her and all those who had accompanied her because she had mocked him and duped him of the treasure. But she told all his envoys that the treasure had been perfectly intact when she had given it up to be taken to her brother, and that it could be that those who had received it had stolen it and replaced it with counterfeits, or that, by chance, because of the sin committed by the king in having her husband murdered, the gods had not wanted him to enjoy her husband's treasure and so had transmuted it. As far as his threat was concerned, she thought that with the help of the gods she could defend herself well against her brother. She summoned all those whom she had led and told them that she did not wish them to stay with her unwillingly or reluctantly nor to endure the slightest trouble on her account. For these reasons, if they wished to return, all or any of them, she would compensate them for their labor and send them away. And they all responded unanimously that they would live and die with her, without leaving her for a single day of their lives. These messengers left, and the lady hurried to complete the city as fast as possible. After it was finished, she instituted statutes and ordinances so that the people would live according to the rule of law and justice. So remarkably and prudently did she govern that her reputation spread to all lands. She was spoken of only in terms of her outstanding strength, courage, and her bold undertaking. Because of her prudent government, they changed her name and called her Dido, which is the equivalent of saying *virago* in Latin, which means 'the woman who has the strength and force of a man.' Thus she lived for a long time in glory and would have lived so the rest of her life if Fortune had not been unfavorable to her, but Fortune, often envious of the prosperous, mixed too harsh a brew for her in the end, just as I will tell you afterward, at the right time and place."

47. HERE SHE SPEAKS OF OPS, QUEEN OF CRETE.

"Ops, or Opis, who was called both goddess and *I.47.1* mother of the gods, was considered in the most ancient times to be prudent because, according to what the ancient historians relate, she knew how to conduct herself most prudently and steadfastly among the prosperities and adversities which befell her during her lifetime. This lady was the daughter of Uranus, an extremely powerful man in Greece, and of his wife, Vesta. The world was still quite rough and ignorant. At this time she had Saturn, the king of Crete, as her husband, who was also her brother. Now, this king of Crete dreamt that his wife would bear a son who would kill him, so that, to escape this fate, he ordered that all of the queen's male offspring be killed. Either with her wits or through ruse, she succeeded in saving her three sons, Jupiter, Neptune, and Pluto, from death, and for her prudence was greatly honored and praised. During her lifetime she acquired such a great reputation through the knowledge and authority of her children that foolish people called her a goddess and mother of the gods, for her sons were reputed gods even during their lifetimes, because they surpassed other men, who were all bestial, in their learnedness. Therefore, temples and sacrifices to this lady were ordered. Like fools they maintained this belief for a long time, and even at the height of Rome's prosperity, this folly endured and she was held in the highest esteem to be a goddess."

48. CONCERNING LAVINIA, DAUGHTER OF KING LATINUS.

I.48.1   "Lavinia, queen of the Laurentines, also enjoyed a reputation for prudence. This noble lady was also descended from this king of Crete, Saturn, of whom we have spoken, and was the daughter of King Latinus and afterward married to Aeneas. Before her marriage, Turnus, king of the Rutulians, desired to have her. However, her father had heard in an omen from the gods that she must be given to a duke of Troy and kept postponing her marriage, even though his wife, the queen, pressured him a great deal. After Aeneas had arrived in Italy, he sought permission from King Latinus to land in his country, and not only did Latinus grant him permission but also immediately gave him his daughter Lavinia in marriage. For this reason Turnus waged war against Aeneas, in which he did much killing and was himself killed. Aeneas was victorious and married Lavinia, who later bore his son, with whom she was pregnant when Aeneas died. When her time came to give birth, fearing that Ascanius, Aeneas' son by another woman, would have the child she was about to bear put to death in his desire to rule, she fled to the woods, and she named the child Julius Silvius. This lady did not wish to marry ever again, and during her widowhood she acted most prudently and ruled the kingdom with her considerable intelligence. She knew how to cherish her stepson so that he harbored no evil against her nor against his half-brother; therefore, after building the city of Alba, he went there to live. Lavinia governed very wisely with her son until he was grown. From this child descended Romulus and Remus who founded Rome, as well as the great Roman princes who came later. What more do you want me to tell you, my dear daughter? It seems to me that I have brought sufficient proof of my intention, which was to show you, through reasoning and example, that God has never held, nor now holds, the feminine sex—nor that of men—in reproach, just as you realize, and just as has become evident and will appear even more so in the depositions of my two sisters who are here. For it seems to me that, for now, the walls I have built for you to enclose the City of Ladies must suffice, and they are all finished and plastered. Let my other sisters come forward, and with their aid and counsel may you complete the remainder of the edifice!"

HERE ENDS THE FIRST PART OF THE BOOK OF THE CITY OF LADIES.

HERE BEGINS THE SECOND PART OF THE BOOK OF THE CITY
OF LADIES, WHICH TELLS HOW AND BY WHOM THE CITY
INSIDE THE WALLS WAS CONSTRUCTED, BUILT, AND PEOPLED.

1. THE FIRST CHAPTER TELLS ABOUT THE TEN SIBYLS.

After the remarks of the first lady, who was called *II.1.1*
Reason, the second lady, who was called Rectitude,
drew toward me and spoke, "Dear friend, with your help,
I will not hesitate to continue to build along the circuit
and enclosure and the wall already built by my sister
Reason for the City of Ladies. Now take your tools and
come with me, and go ahead, mix the mortar in your ink
bottle so that you can fortify the City with your tempered
pen, for I will supply you with plenty of mortar, and,
thanks to divine virtue, we will soon finish building the
lofty royal palaces and noble mansions for the excellent
ladies of great glory and fame who will be lodged in this
City and who will remain here perpetually, forever
more."

Then I, Christine, after hearing the word of this *II.1.2*
honored lady, spoke, "Most excellent lady, you see me
here ready. Command, for my desire is to obey."

And she replied to me, "Friend, look at the beautiful
shining stones more precious than any others which I have
assembled together and prepared to be placed in this
masonry. Was I idle while you and Reason were so busy
building? Come, arrange the stones along my line which
you see here, following the instructions which I will
give you.

"Foremost among the ladies of sovereign dignity are *II.1.3*
the wise sibyls, most filled with wisdom, who, just as
the most credible authors note in their manuals, were ten
in number. Pay attention here, dear friend. What greater
honor in revelation did God ever bestow upon any single

prophet, regardless of how much God loved him, than He gave and granted to these most noble ladies whom I am describing to you? Did He not place in them such a profound and advanced prophecy that what they said did not seem to be prognostications of the future but rather chronicles of past events which had already taken place, so clear and intelligible were their pronouncements and writings? They even spoke more clearly and farther in advance of the coming of Jesus Christ, who came long afterward, than all the prophets did, just as can be seen from their writings. They were all called sibyls, but it should not be taken that this was their own name, for saying 'sibyl' means 'knowing the thinking of God.' Thus they were so called because they prophesied such marvelous things that what they said must have come to them from the pure thinking of God. Thus 'sibyl' is a title of office rather than a proper name. They were born in different countries of the world and not all at one time, and all foretold a great many things to come, and in particular they prophesied quite clearly Jesus Christ and His coming, just as has been said. And yet they were all pagans and did not follow the law of the Jews. The first was from the land of Persia and so was named Persia. The second was from Libya and was called Libica. The third came from Delphi, was born in the Temple of Apollo, and thus was called Delphica. She foretold long in advance the destruction of Troy—Ovid even placed several of her verses in his works. The fourth was from Italy and was named Cimeria. The fifth was born in Babylon and named Eriphile; she replied to the Greeks when they asked her whether Troy and Ilium, its citadel, would be destroyed by them, a subject which Homer wrote about with so many lies. She was called Erythrea because she lived on this island, and there her books were written. The sixth was from the island of Samos and was called Samia. The seventh was named Cumana and was from Italy, born in the city of Cumae in the land of Campania. The eighth was named Hellespontina and was born on the Hellespont in the country of Troy, and she flourished in the time of the noble author Solon and of Cyrus. The ninth was from Phrygia and so was called Phrygica; she spoke a great deal about the fall of several dominions and she also spoke quite pertinently about the false prophet Antichrist. The tenth was called Tiburtina, and also by another name, Albunia, and her statements were greatly revered because she wrote the most clearly about Jesus Christ. Even though these sibyls were all born pagans and lived among pagans, they all attacked pagan religion and assailed the pagans for worshiping many gods, declaring that there was only one God and that the idols were useless."

2. SHE SPEAKS OF THE SIBYL ERYTHREA.

"It should be noted that, among the sibyls, Erythrea *II.2.1* had the greatest prerogative of wisdom, for hers was so great a virtue, thanks to a unique and special gift from God, that she described and prophesied several events to come so clearly that it seemed to be Gospel more than prophecy. And, at the Greeks' request, she described their struggles and battles and the destruction of Troy so clearly in her poems that this last story was no more clear after the fact than it had been before. Likewise, in very few words—nevertheless true—she wrote about the Roman Empire and the dominion of the Romans and their different adventures long before they took place as if it were a brief history of past events rather than an account of events which had yet to take place.

"And she prophesied an even more important and *II.2.2* more wonderful event, for she foretold and clearly revealed the secret of God's powers which had not been revealed by the prophets except in figures and in obscure and secret words, which is to say, the profound mysteries of the Holy Spirit of the Incarnation of the Son of God in the Virgin. In her book she had written, ' Ἰησοῦς Χριστὸς Θεοῦ υἱὸς σωτήρ,' that is, 'Jesus Christ, son of God, Savior,' as well as all about His life and works, the betrayal, the capture, His being mocked, His death, resurrection, victory, and ascension, the coming of the Holy Spirit to the Apostles, His coming on the Day of Judgment. In this way she seemed to have expressed and composed in brief the mysteries of the Christian faith, and not to have predicted things yet to happen.

II.2.3   "Concerning the Day of Judgment, she pronounced the following words, 'On that day, Earth, shaking with fear, will sweat blood as a sign of judgment. The King who will judge the whole world will descend, from the sky, and the good and the evil alike will behold Him. Each soul will take on its body again and each soul will be rewarded according to its merits. Then riches and false idols shall fail. Fire will appear and every living thing shall perish. Then shall there be tears and grief, and people will gnash their teeth in their distress. The sun, moon, and stars will lose their brightness; mountains and valleys will be leveled and all things here below will be made equal. Heaven's trumpet will call the human race to judgment. Then madness will be great and everyone will bewail his folly. And then a New Earth will be created. Kings, princes, and all people will stand before the Judge who will reward each soul according to its merits. Fire and brimstone from Heaven will descend on Hell.' And these things are contained in the twenty-seven poems which this sibyl wrote. Because of her merits, Boccaccio says—and all the other wise authors who have written about her concur—it is believed that she was much beloved of God and that, after the holy Christian women of Paradise, she ought to be honored more than any other woman. Because of her lifelong virginity, she should be presumed to have been elect in every purity, for in a heart tainted and soiled with vices these could not have been such a great light and knowledge of things to come."

3. HERE SHE SPEAKS OF THE SIBYL ALMATHEA.

II.3.1   "The sibyl Almathea was born, as has been said, in the land of Campania, which lies near Rome. She possessed, it appears, the most special grace of the spirit of prophecy. She was born, just as several histories observe, in the time of the destruction of Troy and lived until the time of Tarquin the Proud. Some called her Deiphebe. This lady, who lived to a wonderful old age, nevertheless remained a virgin all her life, and because of her great wisdom, several poets claimed that she was loved by Phoebus (whom they called the god of wisdom) and that, through this same Phoebus's gift, she acquired such great learning and lived so long. This should be taken to mean that because of her virginity and purity she was loved by God, the sun of wisdom, who illuminated her with the prophetic brilliance through which she predicted and wrote of many things to come. Moreover, it is written that while standing on the shore of the lake of Avernus near Baiae she received a noble and wonderful response and divine revelation, written and preserved in her name and composed in rhymed verses. And although this example is extremely old, it still elicits admiration for this woman's grandeur and excellence from all who consider and examine her. Several fictions claim that she led Aeneas to Hell and back. She brought nine books with her to Rome, which she presented to King Tarquin for sale. But when he refused to pay the price which she was asking for them, she burnt three of them in his presence. And when on the next day she demanded this same price for the six other remaining books which she had demanded for the nine and said that if he did not pay the price she was asking, she would immediately burn three more books and on the following day the last three, King Tarquin paid the price which she had first demanded. The books were well preserved, and so it was discovered that they declared in full the future of the Romans. All the great events which subsequently were to befall them were predicted in these books, which were specially guarded in the treasury of the emperors so that they could consult them as though they were consulting a divine oracle.

II.3.2   "Now, pay attention here, dear friend, and consider
how God bestowed such great favor on a single woman
who possessed the insight to counsel and advise not only
one emperor during his lifetime but also, as it were, all
those who were to come in Rome as long as the world
lasts, as well as to comment upon all the affairs of the
empire. Tell me then, please, where was there ever a
man who did this? A short while ago, like a fool, you
considered yourself unlucky to be a member of the sex of
such creatures, thinking that God held this sex in repro-
bation.

II.3.3   "Vergil speaks in verse about this sibyl in his book.
She ended her days in Sicily and for a long time afterward
her tomb was shown to visitors."

4. CONCERNING SEVERAL WOMEN PROPHETS.

II.4.1   "But these ten ladies were not the only ladies in the
world prophesying thanks to a remarkable gift from God,
rather there were a great many others indeed, in all the
religions that have been followed. For if you seek in the
Jewish religion, you will find many of them, like Deborah, who was a woman prophet during the time when
judges ruled over Israel. The people of God were delivered from servitude to the king of Canaan, who had
held them as slaves for twenty years, by this Deborah
and by her intelligence. Likewise, was not the blessed
Elizabeth, cousin of our Lady, a prophet when she declared to the glorious Virgin who had come to see her,
'How does it happen that the Mother of God has come
to me?' Yet without the spirit of prophecy Elizabeth
would not have known that Mary had conceived of the
Holy Spirit, just like Simeon the prophet, to whom our
Lady presented Jesus Christ at the altar of the temple
during the Feast of Lights. And the holy prophet knew
that this was the Savior of the World and he took the
child in his arms when he said, '*Nunc dimittis.*' And as
soon as the good lady Anna, who was walking through
the temple as she performed her duties, saw the Virgin

holding her child enter the temple, she knew in her spirit that this was the Savior, and so she knelt and adored Him and said in a loud voice that this was He who had come to save the world. You will find many other women prophets in the Jewish religion, if you pay attention, and in the Christian religion you will find almost an endless number, along with numerous holy women. But let us proceed beyond these ladies—because one could say that God favored them with a special boon—and let us speak more about pagan women again.

"Holy Scripture mentions that when the queen of *II.4.2* Sheba, who was endowed with superior understanding, heard about Solomon, whose fame had spread throughout the world, she desired to see him. For this reason she traveled from the regions of the Orient, from the farthest corner of the world, leaving her country and riding through the lands of Ethiopia and Egypt, accompanied by a distinguished entourage of princes, lords, knights, and noble ladies of high estate and carrying many precious treasures, she arrived in the city of Jerusalem in order to see and visit wise King Solomon and to test and verify what was said about him throughout the world. Solomon received her with great honor, as was fitting, and she spent a long time with him, testing his wisdom in many fields. She put many problems and questions to him, as well as several obscure and cryptic riddles, all of which he solved so well as soon as she would propose them that she declared that he possessed such extraordinary wisdom not because of human wit but thanks to a special gift from God. This lady gave him many precious presents, including the saplings of small trees which product sap and yield balm and which the king had planted near a lake called Allefabter, ordering that they be carefully cultivated and tended there. And the king likewise gave her many precious jewels.

"Several writings mention this woman's wisdom and *II.4.3* prophecies. They relate that while she was in Jerusalem and Solomon was leading her to see the noble temple which he had had built, she saw a long board lying over a mud puddle which served as a plank to cross this mire. Thereupon, seeing this board, the lady stopped and worshiped it, saying, 'This board, now held in such great contempt and set under foot, will, when the time comes, be honored above all other pieces of wood in the world and adorned with precious gems from the treasuries of princes. And He who will destroy the law of the Jews will die on the wood of this plank.' The Jews did not take this pronouncement as a joke but removed the board and buried it in a place where they thought it would never be found. But what God wishes to save is well protected, for the Jews did not know how to hide it so well that it was not rediscovered during the time of the Passion of our Lord Jesus Christ. And it is said that from this plank the Cross was fashioned upon which our Savior suffered His death and passion, and thus this lady's prophecy was fulfilled."

5. MORE CONCERNING NICOSTRATA, CASSANDRA, AND QUEEN BASINE.

II.5.1   "This Nicostrata, discussed here earlier, was also a woman prophet: for as soon as she had crossed the river Tiber and had climbed the Palentine Hill with her son Evander, frequently mentioned in histories, she prophesied that a city would be built upon this hill, the most famous city in the world ever, which would rule over all worldly dominions. In order to be the first to lay a stone there, she built a fortified castle on that site where, just as was said earlier, Rome was founded and built.

II.5.2   "Likewise, was not the noble Trojan virgin Cassandra, daughter of Priam, king of Troy, and sister of the brave Hector, a woman prophet in addition to being such a great scholar who knew all the sciences? For since this maiden never desired a man as her ruler, regardless of how great a prince he might be, and since she knew in her mind what would happen to the Trojans, she was sad at all times. When she realized that Troy's great prosperity would wax and flourish in great magnificence before the start of the war which the Trojans would subsequently fight against the Greeks, she wept and lamented and mourned all the more. Viewing the nobility and richness of the city and thinking of her fair brothers who were so famous, especially the noble Hector who had so much merit, she could not remain quiet about the enormous evil which would befall him. And seeing the start of the war, she redoubled her grief and could not cease from lamenting and wailing and trying to incite her father and brothers for the gods' sake to make peace with the Greeks—for otherwise, she knew, they would, without a doubt, be destroyed by this war. But they paid no attention to her words and did not believe her in the least. When, however, she would grieve—and rightly so—over the great loss and destruction, for she simply could not stay quiet, she would be beaten by her father and brothers who claimed she was crazy. But she would nevertheless not be still; she would neither remain silent nor put up with their talk in order to avoid death. For this reason, if they wanted to have any peace, they had to shut her up in a room far away from people in order to get her racket out of their ears. However, it would have been better for them if they had believed her, for everything which she had predicted happened to them, and so finally they regretted not having listened, but it was too late for them.

"Similarly, was not the prognostication equally mar- *II.5.3* velous made by Queen Basine, who was first the wife of the king of Thuringia and who subsequently became the wife of Childeric, the fourth king of France, just as the chronicles relate? For the history states that, on the night of her wedding to King Childeric, she told him that if he kept himself chaste that night, he would see a wonderful vision, and then she told him to get up, go to the chamber door, and note what he saw. The king did so and it seemed to him that he saw huge beasts, commonly called unicorns, leopards, and lions, coming and going in the palace, and so he returned totally frightened and asked the queen what it meant. She replied that she would tell him in the morning and that he should not be afraid but go back again. And he did so, and it seemed to him that he beheld large bears and wolves eager to attack one another. The queen sent him back a third time, and it seemed to him that he saw dogs and small animals tearing each other completely apart. And, as the king was greatly frightened and amazed by these sights, the queen explained to him that the vision of the beasts which he had seen signified different generations of princes who would descend from them and who would reign in France, whose mores and deeds could be inferred from the nature and diversity of the animals which he had seen. Thus, you can see clearly, dear friend, how our Lord has often revealed his secrets to the world through women."

6. CONCERNING ANTONIA, WHO BECAME EMPRESS.

II.6.1   "It was no small secret which God revealed through a woman's vision to Justinian, who subsequently became emperor of Constantinople. This Justinian was a guard of the treasures and coffers of Emperor Justin. One day, when Justinian went out to relax in the fields and brought along a woman named Antonia, whom he loved to keep him company, the noon hour arrived and he was overcome with fatigue. Justinian lay down under a tree to sleep and placed his head in his girl friend's lap. Just as he fell asleep, Antonia saw a large eagle come and fly over their heads, spreading its wings to shield Justinian's face from the heat of the sun. Antonia was wise and understood the significance of this sign. When Justinian awoke, she spoke to him with fair words and said, 'Sweet friend, I have loved and I love you very much. You are the master of my body and my love, and you know it. Since it is right that a beloved lover should refuse his mistress nothing, in exchange for my virginity and my love, I want to ask you for a boon, which, although quite important to me, will seem quite insignificant to you.'

Justinian answered his girlfriend that she should ask boldly and that she would never lack for anything which he could grant. Then Antonia asked, 'The boon which I am asking from you is that, when you are emperor, you will not disdain your poor friend Antonia but will let her be the companion of your honor and your empire through faithful marriage. And so from this moment on, promise me this.' When Justinian heard the maiden speak this way, he began to laugh, thinking that she had said this as a joke. Since he considered it impossible that it could ever happen that he would be emperor, he promised her that he would without fail take her as his wife when he was emperor; he swore it to her by all the gods, and she thanked him for it. As a sign of this promise, she made him give her his ring and she gave him hers. Thereupon she said, 'Justinian, I tell you in all certainty that you will be emperor and that this will happen to you in a short time.' And with that, they left. Shortly afterward, after the emperor Justin had assembled his army to attack the Persians, he caught an illness from which he died. Later, when the barons and princes assembled to elect a new emperor and could not reach a consensus, it happened that out of spite for one another they elected Justinian emperor, who did not waste time dreaming but immediately moved in great strength with a large army against the Persians and won the battle, captured the king of the Persians, and won great honor and booty. After he had returned to the palace, his girlfriend Antonia was not out amusing herself but through great subtleness she had managed to make her way to where he sat on the throne surrounded by princes. And there, kneeling before him, she began her plea, explaining that she was a maiden who had come to him to ask for justice from a young man who was engaged to her and who had given her his ring and taken hers. The emperor, not thinking of her at all, replied that if a young man was engaged to her as she said, the right thing was for him to take her as his wife and that he, the emperor, would gladly see that she receive justice, provided that she could prove her claim. Antonia then took the ring from her finger and handed it to him, saying, 'Noble Emperor, I can prove it with this ring. See whether you recognize it.' At this point the emperor realized that he had been caught by his own words, yet all the same he wished to keep his promise to her and immediately had her led to his chambers and dressed in noble garments, and he took her as his wife."

7. CHRISTINE SPEAKS TO RECTITUDE.

II.7.1 "My lady, because I understand and clearly see that women are overwhelmingly innocent of what they are so frequently accused, now make me better acquainted than ever with their accusers' great guilt. Once more I cannot remain quiet regarding a practice with widespread currency among men—and even among some women—that when women are pregnant and then give birth to daughters, their husbands are upset and grumble because their wives did not give birth to sons. And their silly wives, who should be supremely joyful that God has delivered them to safety and, similarly, should heartily thank Him, are unhappy because they see their husbands upset. Why does it happen, my lady, that they grieve so? Are daughters a greater liability to their parents than sons, or less loving and more indifferent toward their parents than sons are?"

"Dear friend," she replied, "because you ask me the cause from which this springs, I can assure you that it comes from the excessive simplemindedness and ignorance of those who become so upset. Yet the principal reason which moves them is the cost which they fear the marriage of their daughters will force them to pay. Also, some are upset because they are afraid of the danger that, by bad advice, their daughters could be deceived when they are young and naïve. But all of these reasons are nothing when examined with common sense. For, as regards their fear that their daughters might do something foolish, one need only instruct them in wisdom when they are young, making sure that the mother herself sets a good example of integrity and learnedness, for if the mother lives foolishly, she will hardly be an example for the daughter. The daughter should also be protected from bad company and raised in accordance with strict rules which she respects, for the discipline exercised over children and young people prepares them to live upright lives for their whole lifetime. Similarly, as far as cost is concerned, I believe that if the parents looked closely at that incurred on account of their sons—whether in teaching them knowledge or skills, or in simple upkeep, and even in superfluous expenses, whether on a large, middle, or small scale, for silly companions or for a lot of frivolities—they will hardly find a greater financial advantage in having sons rather than daughters. And if you consider the anger and worry which many sons cause their parents—for they often get involved in harsh and bitter riots and brawls or pursue a dissolute life, all to the grief and expense of their parents—I think that this anguish can easily exceed the worries which they have because of their daughters. See how many sons you will find who gently and humbly care for their parents and mothers in their old age, as they are supposed to. I insist that they are few and far between, although there are and have been many who have helped when it was too late. Thus, after a father and mother have made gods out of their sons and the sons are grown and have become rich and affluent—either because of their father's own efforts or because he had them learn some skill or trade or even by some good fortune—and the father has become poor and ruined through misfortune, they despise him and are annoyed and ashamed when they see him. But if the father is rich, they only wish for his death so that they can inherit his wealth. Oh! God knows how many sons of great lords and rich men long for their parents' deaths so that they can inherit their lands and wealth. Petrarch observed the situation accurately when he remarked, 'Oh foolish men, you desire children, but

111   *Christine de Pizan*

you could not have such mortal enemies; for, if you are poor, they will be annoyed with you and will wish for your death, in order to be rid of you; and if you are rich, they will wish for your death no less, in order to have your possessions.' I certainly do not mean that all sons are like this, but there are many who are. And if they are married, God knows their enormous greed to sap their fathers and mothers. It hardly matters to them whether these miserable old people die of hunger, provided, of course, that they inherit everything. Some sustenance indeed! Nor does it matter to them when their mothers are widowed, then—when they ought to comfort them and be the support and aid in their old age—those same mothers, who so cherished and so lovingly and tenderly nourished their children, are well rewarded for all their trouble! For these evil offspring think that everything should be theirs, and if their widowed mothers do not give them everything they want, they do not hesitate to vent their displeasure on them. God knows how much reverence is shown there! Moreover, what is worse, they have no pangs of conscience about bringing lawsuits and court proceedings against their mothers. This is the reward which many parents have after having spent all their lives trying to acquire some wealth or put their children ahead. There are many sons like this, and there may well be daughters like this, too. But if you are very attentive, you will find more sons than daughters who are so corrupt. And let us suppose that all sons were good, nevertheless one usually sees the daughters keep their fathers and mothers company more often than the sons, and the daughters visit them more, comfort them more, and take care of them in sickness and old age more frequently. The reason is that the sons wander through the world in every direction and the daughters are calmer and stay closer to home, just as you can see from your own experiences; for even though your brothers are quite normal, very loving, and virtuous, they went out into the world and you alone remained to give your mother a little company, which is her greatest comfort in old age. For this reason, I tell you in conclusion that those who are troubled and upset when daughters are born to them are exceedingly foolish. And since you have got me onto this topic, let me tell you about several women mentioned among others in various writings who were quite natural and most loving toward their parents."

8. HERE SHE BEGINS TO TALK ABOUT DAUGHTERS WHO LOVED THEIR PARENTS, AND FIRST, ABOUT DRYPETINA.

"Drypetina, queen of Laodacia, was much beloved of *II.8.1* her father. She was the daughter of the great king Mithridates and loved him so much that she followed him in all his battles. She was quite ugly, for she had an extra row of teeth—a monstrosity—but she was so well loved by her father that she never left his side, whether in prosperity or in misfortune. Although she was queen and lady of a great kingdom which would have allowed her to live in ease and leisure in her own country, she shared in all the pains and labors which her father suffered during his many campaigns. After he was conquered by Pompey the Great, she never left his side but attentively and diligently took care of him.

9. HERE SHE SPEAKS OF HYPSIPYLE.

"Hypsipyle placed herself in mortal danger in order to *II.9.1* save her father, who was named Thoas and who was king of Lemnos. When his country rebelled against him and a raging mob stormed the palace to kill him, his daughter Hypsipyle hid him in a chest and then went outside to calm the people down. This did not do her much good at all, and after they had searched for the king everywhere and could not find him, they turned their swords against Hypsipyle and threatened to kill her unless she told them where the king was. They also promised that if she told them, they would crown her queen and obey her. But the good and true daughter, who loved her father's life more than being queen, was not in the least swayed by the fear of death and replied boldly that he had of course fled a long time before. Finally, because they could not find him and because she had assured them with such certainty that he had fled, they believed her and crowned her queen. For a while she reigned peacefully over them. But, after having secretly guarded her father for some time, she became frightened that in the end he could be discovered by some jealous subject and so took him out at night and safely sent him off by sea with a great deal of wealth. However, when this was revealed to the disloyal subjects, they drove out their queen Hypsipyle. And they would have killed her too, but since she was so good, some of them were moved to pity."

10. CONCERNING THE VIRGIN CLAUDINE.

II.10.1   "And what a great sign of love the virgin Claudine showed her father, when, because of his good deeds and the great victories which he had won in many battles, he returned victorious to Rome and received the highest honor called a triumph, which was a particularly high distinction accorded to princes returning as conquerors from a campaign. While Claudine's father, a most valorous prince of Rome, was receiving the triumphal honor, he was violently attacked by another lord of Rome who hated him. But when his daughter Claudine, who had been consecrated to the service of the goddess Vesta (now we would say she was the sister of an abbey) and who was with the ladies of the order who had accompanied the procession going out to meet this prince, as was the custom, heard the scuffle and realized that her father had been attacked by his enemies, then the great love which the daughter had for her father made her completely forget the simple and serene conduct that a virgin was usually wont to follow; she laid aside all fear and fright, jumped out of the wagon in which she had been riding with her companions, went rushing through the crowd and boldly planted herself between the swords and lances which she saw drawn on her father and forcefully grabbed the nearest assailant by the throat and with her own bare strength began to defend her father bravely. The struggle was intense and the mêlée was quickly over. As the Romans were accustomed to venerating anyone who performed an act worthy of admiration, they greatly esteemed this virgin and bestowed great praise upon her for what she had done."

11. CONCERNING A WOMAN WHO BREAST-FED HER MOTHER IN PRISON.

"Similarly, a Roman woman spoken of in the histories *II.11.1* had great love for her mother. Her mother was condemned to die in prison as punishment for a crime, and no one was to give her anything to eat or drink. Her daughter, prompted by great filial love and saddened by this condemnation, requested a special favor from those who guarded the prison, that she be able to visit her mother each day, as long as her mother was alive, so that she could admonish her to be long-suffering. And, put briefly, she wept and begged so much that the prison guards took pity on her and allowed her to visit her mother daily. But before she was brought to her mother, they would search her thoroughly to see whether she was bringing her any food. After these visitations went on for so many days that it seemed impossible to the jailers that their woman prisoner could have lasted so long without dying, and yet she was not dead, and considering that no one visited her besides her daughter, whom they carefully searched before she entered her mother's cell, they wondered a great deal how this could be. In fact, one day they watched the mother and daughter together, and then they saw that the unhappy daughter, who had recently had a child, would give her teat to her mother until the mother had taken all the milk from her breasts. In this way the daughter gave back to her mother in her old age what she had taken from her mother as an infant. This continual diligence and great love of daughter for mother moved the jailers to great pity, and when this deed had been reported to the judges, they, also moved by human compassion, freed the mother and turned her over to her daughter.

II.11.2   "Turning again to the question of a daughter's love for her father, one can mention the most virtuous and wise Griselda, who was the marquise of Saluces, whose great virtue, firmness, and constancy I will presently describe to you. What a great love, enlivened in her by her loyal nature, made her so diligent in serving her poor father Giannucolo, old and sick, in such humility and faithfulness—a love which she so diligently cultivated and maintained in her purity, virginity, and in the flower of her youth! With great care and solicitude she earned a poor living for the two of them, through the labor and skill of her hands. Daughters with such kindness and such great love for their fathers and mothers are born at truly propitious times, for although they do what they are supposed to do, they nevertheless acquire great merit for their souls; indeed, great praise in the world ought to be given them, and also to sons who act likewise.

II.11.3   "What more do you want me to say? I could give you countless examples of similar cases, but let this one be enough for you now."

12. HERE RECTITUDE ANNOUNCES THAT SHE HAS FINISHED BUILDING THE HOUSES OF THE CITY AND THAT IT IS TIME THAT IT BE PEOPLED.

II.12.1   "It seems to me at this point, most dear friend, that our construction is quite well advanced, for the houses of the City of Ladies stand completed all along the wide streets, its royal palaces are well constructed, and its towers and defense turrets have been raised so high and straight that one can see them from far away. It is therefore right that we start to people this noble City now, so that it does not remain vacant or empty, but instead is wholly populated with ladies of great excellence, for we do not want any others here. How happy will be the citizens of our edifice, for they will not need to fear or worry about being evicted by foreign armies, for this work has the special property that its owners cannot be expelled. Now a New Kingdom of Femininity is begun, and it is far better than the earlier kingdom of the Amazons, for the ladies residing here will not need to leave their land in order to conceive or give birth to new heirs to maintain their possessions throughout the different ages, from one generation to another, for those whom we now place here will suffice quite adequately forever more.

"And after we have populated it with noble citizens, *II.12.2* my sister, Lady Justice, will come and lead the Queen, outstanding over all, and accompanied by princesses of the highest dignity who will reside in the uppermost apartments and in the lofty towers. It is fitting that on her arrival the Queen find her City supplied and peopled with noble ladies who will receive her with honors as their sovereign lady, empress of all their sex. But what citizens will we place here? Will they be dissolute or dishonored women? Certainly not, rather they shall all be women of integrity, of great beauty and authority, for there could be no fairer populace nor any greater adornment in the City than women of good character. Now let us go, dear friend, for now I am putting you to work, and I will go ahead so that we can go look for them."

13. CHRISTINE ASKS LADY RECTITUDE WHETHER WHAT THE BOOKS AND MEN SAY IS TRUE, THAT MARRIED LIFE IS SO HARD TO ENDURE BECAUSE OF WOMEN AND THE WRONG THEY CAUSE. RECTITUDE ANSWERS AND BEGINS TO SPEAK OF THE GREAT LOVE SHOWN BY WOMEN FOR THEIR HUSBANDS.

Then, as we were searching for these women by order *II.13.1* of Lady Rectitude, I spoke these words as we went along, "My lady, truly you and Reason have solved and settled all the problems and questions which I could not answer, and I consider myself very well informed about what I asked. I have learned a great deal from you: how all things which are feasible and knowable, whether in the area of physical strength or in the wisdom of the mind and every virtue, are possible and easy for women to accomplish. But could you now please confirm for me whether what men claim, and what so many authors testify, is true—a topic about which I am thinking very deeply—that life within the institution of marriage is filled and occupied with such great unhappiness for men because of women's faults and impetuosity, and because of their rancorous ill-humor, as is written in so many books? Many assert that these women care so little for their husbands and their company that nothing else annoys them as much? For this reason, in order to escape and avoid such inconveniences, many authorities have advised wise men not to marry, affirming that no women —or very few—are loyal to their mates. Valerius wrote to Rufus along similar lines, and Theophrastus remarked in his book that no wise man should take a wife, because there are too many worries with women, too little love, and too much gossip, and that, if a man marries in order to be better taken care of and nursed in sickness, a loyal servant could better and more loyally care for him and serve him and would not cost him nearly as much, and that if the wife becomes sick, the languishing husband does not dare budge from her side. But enough of such things, which would take too long to recite in full, therefore I say to you, dear lady, that if these remarks are true, so evil are these faults that all the other graces and virtues which women could possess are wiped out and canceled by them."

"Certainly, friend," she replied, "just as you yourself once said regarding this question, whoever goes to court without an opponent pleads very much at his ease. I assure you that women have never done what these books say. Indeed, I have not the slightest doubt that whoever cared to investigate the debate on marriage in order to write a new book in accordance with the truth would uncover other data. How many women are there actually, dear friend—and you yourself know—who because of their husbands' harshness spend their weary lives in the bond of marriage in greater suffering than if they were slaves among the Saracens? My God! How many harsh beatings —without cause and without reason—how many injuries, how many cruelties, insults, humiliations, and outrages have so many upright women suffered, none of whom cried out for help? And consider all the women who die of hunger and grief with a home full of children, while their husbands carouse dissolutely or go on binges in every tavern all over town, and still the poor women are beaten by their husbands when they return, and *that* is their supper! What do you say to that? Am I lying? Have you never seen any of your women neighbors so decked out?"

And I said to her, "Certainly, my lady, I have seen many, and I feel very sorry for them."

"I believe you, and to say that these husbands are so unhappy with their wives' illnesses! Please, my friend, where are they? Without my having to say any more to you, you can easily see that such foolishness spoken and written against women was and is an arbitrary fabrication which flies in the face of the truth. For men are masters over their wives, and not the wives mistresses over their husbands, who would never allow their wives to have such authority. But let me hasten to assure you that not all marriages are conducted with such spite, for there are those who live together in great peacefulness, love, and loyalty because the partners are virtuous, considerate, and reasonable. And although there are bad husbands, there are also very good ones, truly valiant and wise, and the women who meet them were born in a lucky hour, as far as the glory of the world is concerned, for what God has bestowed upon them. You know this perfectly well from your own experience, for you had such a good husband that, given a choice, you could not have asked for better, whom no other man in your judgment could surpass in kindness, peacefulness, loyalty, and true love, and for whose sake the remorse over Fate's having taken him from you will never leave your heart. In spite of what I have told you—and it is true that there are many women greatly mistreated by their husbands—realize, however, that there are very different kinds of women, and some unreasonable, for if I claimed that they were all good, I could easily be proven a liar, but that is the least part. I will not meddle with evil women, for such women are like creatures alienated from their own nature.

II.13.2   "But to speak of good women, as for this Theophrastus, whom you have mentioned, and who says that a man can be cared for by his servant as loyally and as carefully as by his wife—ha! How many good women there are who are so conscientious in caring for their husbands, healthy or sick, with a loyal love as though their husbands were gods! I do not think that you will ever find such a servant. And since we have taken up this question, let me give you numerous examples of the great love and loyalty shown by women for their husbands. Now we have come back to our City, thank God, with all the noble company of fair and upright women whom we will lodge there. Here is the noble queen Hypsicratea, long ago the wife of the rich king Mithridates. We will lodge her first of all in the noble residence and palace which has been readied for her because she is from such an ancient time and of such worthiness."

14. HERE SHE SPEAKS OF QUEEN HYPSICRATEA.

II.14.1   "How could any creature show greater love for another than the fair, good, and loyal Hypsicratea showed for her husband? She demonstrated this well. She was the wife of the great king Mithridates, who ruled over a realm consisting of countries of twenty-four different languages. Although this king was supremely powerful, the Romans waged a very harsh war against him. No matter where he went, during his long absences from court or in the thick of battle, his faithful wife never left him. Even though this king had several concubines, as was the barbarian custom, this noble lady was nevertheless surrounded by a perfect love, so that she could not bear him to go off without her, and she often would accompany him in the great battles when he was in danger of losing his kingdom, risking death against the Romans. He could never venture into a strange region or distant country, or cross the sea or perilous desert, or go anywhere without her constant and loyal companionship. For she loved him with such a perfect love that she was sure that no one could serve her lord as purely, as faithfully, or as fully as she did. And in refutation of what Theophrastus said on this subject, consider how this lady resolved to follow her lord always, intending to administer at all times what was fitting and necessary for him, regardless of whatever pain she might suffer, since she knew that kings and princes frequently have faithless servants who serve them deceitfully. Since women's clothes were not suitable for such activity, nor was it proper for a woman to be seen in battle at the side of such a great king and noble warrior, she cut her long golden blond hair—the most beautiful adornment of women—in order to look like a man. Nor did she spare the fair freshness of her face, but wore a helmet, under which her face was often dirty and covered with sweat and dust. And she clothed her fair and soft body with armor and a coat of mail. She took off her precious rings and rich ornaments, and in place of them she carried hard axes in her hands, as well as lances and bows and arrows; she buckled on a sword rather than costly belts. Thanks to the force of her strong and loyal love, this noble lady conducted herself so valiantly that her fair and soft body, so young, delicate, and tenderly nourished, was transformed, as it were, into a powerful and vigorous armed knight. Boccaccio, who tells this story, could only wonder, 'What can love not achieve if such a woman, accustomed to living so delicately and to sleeping in soft beds and to having everything at her ease, can drive herself by sheer force of will, as though she were a tough and strong man, through mountains and valleys, day and night, sleeping in deserts and forests, often on the ground, afraid of enemies, and surrounded on all sides by wild animals and snakes?' But everything was easy for her, simply by being at her husband's side at all times in order to comfort, advise, and serve him in all his affairs. Later, after she had suffered many harsh trials for a long time, her husband was savagely beaten by Pompey, commander of the Roman army, and he was forced to flee. But after he had been abandoned by all his men and was completely alone, his good wife did not leave him but followed him through mountains, valleys, and dark and savage places, accompanying him at all times. Though abandoned and deserted by all his friends, with all hope gone, he was comforted by his good wife, who gently urged him to hope for better fortune. When he and she found themselves in the greatest desolation, she would console him all the more and encourage him with her sweet words so that he could briefly forget his melancholy through the gracious and consoling games which she knew how to devise. With these and with her extreme gentleness, the lady was able to console him so well that, regardless of the suffering in which he found himself, regardless of how much tribulation he suffered, she would make him forget; therefore he frequently remarked that he was not an exile, but that it seemed to him that he were at his leisure in the palace with his loyal spouse."

15. CONCERNING THE EMPRESS TRIARIA.

II.15.1 "The noble empress Triaria, wife of the Roman emperor Lucius Vitellius, strongly resembled Queen Hypsicratea, discussed above, in her fortune and in her loyal love for her husband. She loved him with such devotion that she followed him everywhere; and in every battle, armed like a knight, she stayed bravely at his side and fought vigorously. When Lucius Vitellius was fighting Vespanianus for the dominion of the empire, it happened, as he was moving against a city of the Volscians one night, that he managed to gain entry inside, where he found the people asleep whom he then savagely attacked. But this noble lady Triaria—who had followed her husband all through the night—was nearby and fully armed, girded with her sword. In her eagerness for her husband to win the victory she fought fiercely in the fray next to him, now here, now there, in the darkness of the night. She felt neither fear nor revulsion but conducted herself so bravely that after this battle she enjoyed everyone's respect and was able to accomplish many amazing deeds. Thus she demonstrated well the great love which she had for her husband, as Boccaccio himself noted, approving the marriage bond which others want to attack."

16. MORE CONCERNING QUEEN ARTEMISIA.

"Of all the ladies who have loved their husbands *II.16.1* devotedly and who have demonstrated their love in fact, I would like to add, regarding that noble lady Artemisia, queen of Caria, that, just as was said above, insofar as she had followed King Mausolus into so many battles and was stricken and overcome with as much grief as anyone could bear when he died, she showed no less devotion in the end than she had demonstrated during his lifetime. For she performed all the solemn rites which could be administered to a king, in observance of the customs of that time, and during a dignified funeral in the presence of the princes and barons, she had his body cremated. She herself gathered his ashes together, washing them with her tears before she placed them in a gold vessel. Now it struck her that there was no reason why the ashes of the man whom she had so loved should have any other sepulcher than the heart and body where the root of this great love resided, and so for this reason, little by little, over a period of time, she drank these ashes mixed with wine until she had consumed them all. Nevertheless, she still wished to build a sepulcher to her husband's memory to serve forever as his memorial. Toward this end she spared no expense, but sought out four artisans who knew how to plan and execute wonderful edifices, named Scopa, Briaxes, Thimotheus, and Leocares, all outstanding craftsmen. The queen told them how she wished the sepulcher to be constructed for her lord, King Mausolus, and for it to be the most imposing sepulcher which any king or prince in the world had ever had, for she wished her husband's name to last forever through this marvelous work. And the artisans replied that they would gladly follow her instructions. The queen ordered a large amount of marble along with as much jasper in various colors as they might want. The work was arranged in the same way in which these same artisans had erected a great stone structure of superbly carved marble before the city of Halicarnassus, the chief city of Caria. Its base was a square with each side forty-four feet in length and one hundred forty feet in height. There was an even greater wonder, for this massive edifice rested entirely on thirty large stone columns carved out of marble. Each of the four artisans carved one façade, all the while trying to outmatch the others. Their workmanship was so marvelous that it commemorated not only the man for whom it had been built but also evoked admiration for the subtlety of the artisans. A fifth artisan, named Ytheron, came to complete the work, and he built a spire for this edifice which rose forty steps above what the others had constructed. Afterward came a sixth worker, named Pithis, who carved a chariot out of marble and placed it on top of the entire monument. This work was so marvelous that it was reputed to be one of the seven wonders of the world. Because it had been built for King Mausolus, the edifice took its name from him and was called the 'Mausoleum.' Furthermore, because this sepulcher was the most imposing ever built for a king or prince, every other sepulcher for a king or prince has since been called a mausoleum, according to Boccaccio. Artemisia's loyal love for her faithful spouse thus was clear both in her acts and in this token, a love which lasted as long as she lived."

17. HERE SHE SPEAKS OF ARGIA, DAUGHTER OF KING ADRASTUS.

"Who could dare say a woman had little love for her II.17.1 husband if he considers the great love of Argia, daughter of Adrastus, king of Argos, for Polyneices her husband? This Polyneices, Argia's husband, struggled with his brother for the throne of the kingdom of Thebes which belonged to him in accordance with certain agreements between the two of them. But as Etiocles wished to acquire the entire kingdom for himself, Polyneices, his brother, went to war and his lord Adrastus arrived with all his might to aid him. However fortune turned so badly against Polyneices that he and his brother killed each other in battle, and from the entire army the only survivors were the king Adrastus and three hundred soldiers. Now when Argia learned that her husband had died in battle, she immediately departed, and all the ladies of the city of Argos accompanied her after she left behind her royal throne. Boccaccio tells of what she did as follows, 'The noble lady Argia heard that the corpse of her husband, Polyneices, lay lifeless and unburied among the corpses and rotting carcasses of the common soldiers who had been killed there. Filled with grief, she immediately laid aside her royal dress and adornment as well as the softness and easiness of her life in the sumptuously appointed chambers. Along with this, she overcame and conquered feminine weakness and tenderness through overwhelming force of will and ardor of love. And she traveled for several days until she came to the battlefield, undaunted by the ambushes of enemies lying in wait; nor did the length of the journey or the hot weather tire her. Having arrived at the battlefield, she was not frightened by the savage beasts or large birds hovering around the dead, nor by the evil spirits which some fools believe flutter around men's bodies. What is even more marvelous,' says Boccaccio, 'is that she did not fear the edict and order of King Creon, who had announced his command that under pain of death no one was to visit or bury the bodies, no matter who they were.' But she had not come there to obey this order, indeed, as soon as she arrived there, toward nightfall, and undaunted by the stink given off by the rotting corpses, she began to turn over the bodies, now here, now there, searching everywhere for the man whom she loved. And she did not stop until, by the light of a small torch when she held, she recognized her most beloved husband. And so she found what she had been seeking. 'What marvelous love and most ardent desire and affection in a woman,' notes Boccaccio, for even though her husband's face was half eaten away by the corrosion of his armor and was completely filled with pus, all bloodied, covered with dirt, smeared and stained with filth, sallow, and blackened—already practically unrecognizable—it could never be disguised from that woman, so ardently did she love him. Neither the infection of his body nor the filth covering his face could stop her from kissing him and embracing him tightly. Neither the edict nor the order could prevent her from crying out in a loud voice, 'Alas! Alas! I have found the man I loved!' nor from weeping profusely. For after trying to see whether his body still lodged his soul by kissing him on the mouth, and after washing his already rotting limbs with her tears and calling on him with low cries, tears, and groans, she committed his body to the fire, to the accompaniment of great wailing, thereby fulfilling the final, piteous office for him, and she gathered his ashes into a golden vessel. After having done all this, like some woman wishing to risk death in order to avenge her husband, she struggled and fought so fiercely, aided by a great number of other women, that they pierced the citadel walls, captured the city and put all inside to death."

18. CONCERNING THE NOBLE LADY AGRIPPINA.

II.18.1   "The good and loyal Agrippina, a daughter of Marcus Agrippa and of Julia, daughter of the emperor Octavian, lord of the entire world, must of course be placed among the noble ladies having immense love for their husbands. After this noble lady had been given in marriage to Germanicus, an exceptionally noble, wise, and well-bred prince who cultivated Rome's public welfare, the immoral Emperor Tiberius, who then ruled, became so jealous of the good reports he heard about Germanicus, Agrippina's husband, as well as of the love shown him by everyone, that he had him ambushed and killed. His good wife was so grieved at his death that she wished to be killed in a similar manner. She was, moreover, quite blatant indeed in expressing this intent, for she could not refrain from addressing great insults to Tiberius, for which he had her beaten and cruelly tortured and held in prison. But preferring death to life because she could not forget her grief at her husband's death, she resolved never to drink or eat again. After this decision came to the attention of the tyrant Tiberius, he sought to force her with torture into eating, in order to prolong her torment. Since nothing was of any avail, he decided to have her force-fed. She showed him clearly, however, that while he held the power to put people to death, he did not have the power to keep them alive against their will, and so she ended her days."

19. CHRISTINE SPEAKS, AND THEN RECTITUDE ANSWERS HER, GIVING EXAMPLES, AND SPEAKS OF THE NOBLE LADY JULIA, DAUGHTER OF JULIUS CAESAR AND WIFE OF POMPEY.

After Lady Rectitude had told me all this, I answered *II.19.1* her, "Certainly, my lady, it seems to me an outstanding honor to the feminine sex to hear about so many excellent ladies. Everyone should be extremely pleased that, in addition to their other virtues, such great love could reside in a woman's heart in the bond of marriage. Let Mathéolus and all the other prattlers who have spoken against women with such envy and falsehood go to sleep and stay quiet. But, my lady, I still recall that the philosopher Theophrastus, whom I spoke of above, said that women hate their husbands when they are old and also that women do not love men of learning or scholars, for he claims the duties entailed in the upkeep of women are totally incompatible with the study of books."

She replied, "Oh dear friend, keep still! I can immediately provide you with examples contradicting and disproving such statements.

II.19.2 "The noblest Roman lady in her time was Julia, daughter of Julius Caesar, who was then emperor, and of his wife, Cornelia, both descended from Aeneas and Venus of Troy. This lady was the wife of Pompey, the great conqueror, who, according to Boccaccio, after having conquered kings, deposed them and made others kings in their place, having subjugated nations and crushed pirates, having won the favor of Rome as well as that of the kings of the entire world, having acquired different dominions—on both land and sea, the result of marvelous victories—had attained supreme honor and was already aged and in decline. Nevertheless, the noble lady Julia, his wife, who was still quite young, loved him with such complete, loyal, and profound devotion that she ended her life as a result of a curious twist of fate. One day it happened that Pompey was moved out of piety to praise the gods for the noble victories which he had won, and he wanted to sacrifice according to the customs of that time. When the sacrificial animal was on the altar and Pompey, in his piety, held it from one side, his robe became stained by the blood coming from the beast's wound. For this reason he removed the robe he was wearing and had one of his servants take it back to his residence in order to fetch a clean and fresh one. Unfortunately, the servant carrying this robe met Pompey's wife, Julia, who, upon seeing her lord's robe stained with blood, was overwhelmed—since she knew that prominent Romans were often attacked and killed because of envy—and viewed the robe with a certainty of conviction that some similar misfortune had befallen her husband. For this reason, such excruciating grief overcame her heart that she suddenly seemed moribund. She was great with child and fell in a faint, pale and discolored, her eyes turned into her skull. No remedy could be applied nor could her fear be dissipated to keep her from giving up the ghost. Understandably her death must have been an overwhelming grief for her husband, but it was a terrible loss not only for him and the Romans but also for everyone living then, for if she and her child had lived, the great war between Julius Caesar and Pompey would never have broken out, a ruinous conflict for all lands."

20. CONCERNING THE NOBLE LADY TERTIA AEMILIA.

"Similarly, the fair and virtuous Tertia Aemilia, wife of Scipio Africanus the Elder, did not resent her husband for being old. This lady was exceptionally prudent and upright, and even though her husband was already aged while she was still young and beautiful, he nevertheless slept with a slave of hers who served as her chambermaid, and it happened often enough not to escape this valiant lady's notice. But even though it caused her great pain, she had recourse to her virtue of great learning rather than to the passion of jealousy, for she hid her hurt so cleverly that neither her husband nor any other person heard anything said about it, nor did she wish to tell him because it seemed shameful to her to correct so great a man and even worse to mention it to someone else, for that would be like censuring and belittling the reputation of this wise man and an offense against the honor of his person, for he had conquered many kingdoms and empires. Thus, the good lady never ceased to serve him loyally, to love him, and to honor him. When he died, she freed the slave woman and married her to a free man." *II.20.1*

Then I, Christine, replied, "Indeed, my lady, regarding this, it reminds me that I have seen similar women who, although they knew that their husbands bore them little loyalty, nevertheless did not stop loving them and being *II.20.2* well-disposed toward them. They supported and comforted the women with whom their husbands had children. I have also heard the same about a lady of Brittany, who lived recently, the countess of Coemon, who was in the flower of youth and more beautiful than all other ladies, and thanks to her great constancy and goodness she did the same."

21. RECTITUDE SPEAKS OF XANTHIPPE, WIFE OF THE PHILOSOPHER SOCRATES.

II.21.1   "The noble lady Xanthippe possessed great learning and goodness, and because of these qualities she married Socrates, the greatest philosopher. Although he was already quite old and cared more about searching for knowledge and researching in books than obtaining soft and new things for his wife, the valiant lady nevertheless did not stop loving him but rather thought of the excellence of his learning, his outstanding virtue, and his constancy, which, in her sovereign love and reverence, she considered to be a sign of his excellence. Upon learning that her husband had been condemned to death by the Athenians because he had attacked them for worshiping idols and had said that there was but one God, whom one must worship and serve, this brave lady could not bear it, but completely dishevelled, overcome with grief and weeping, she quickly rushed to the palace where her husband was being held, and she found him among the deceitful judges who were administering to him the poison to end his life. Arriving at the moment when Socrates was about to drink, to put the cup to his mouth to drink the poison, she rushed toward him and angrily tore the cup from his hands and poured it all out on the ground. Socrates reproved her for this and urged her to be patient and comforted her. As she could not prevent his death, she was very grieved and said, 'What a great wrong and what an enormous loss to put such a just man to death wrongfully and sinfully.' Socrates continued to console her, saying that it was better that he died wrongfully than justifiably, and so he died. But the grief in the heart of the woman who loved him did not abate for the rest of her life."

22. CONCERNING POMPEIA PAULINA, WIFE OF SENECA.

"Although Seneca, the wise philosopher, was quite old and dedicated all his effort to study, this did not prevent his young and beautiful wife, Pompeia Paulina, from loving him devotedly. This noble lady's only thought was to serve him and preserve his peace as one who loved him most loyally and dearly. When she learned that the tyrant emperor Nero (whose teacher Seneca had been) had condemned him to bleed to death in his bath, she was beside herself with grief. Like a wife who wished to die with her husband, she went about shouting insults to the tyrant Nero so that he would likewise extend his cruelty to her. But when all this did not work, she so greatly mourned her husband's death that she did not survive for very long afterward."

II.22.1

And I, Christine, then said to the lady, when she finished speaking, "Truly, my honored lady, your words have reminded me and brought back to my recollection many other young and beautiful women who most perfectly loved their husbands even though they were quite ugly and old. Even in my own time, I have often seen a woman love her lord most perfectly and show him loyal love as long as he lived. One noble lady, Jeanne de Laval, daughter of one of the great barons of Brittany, was given in marriage to the most valiant constable of France, my lord Bertrand du Guesclin. Although he had a very ugly body and was old, while she was in the flower of her youth, she paid more attention to the worthiness of his virtues rather than to the manner of his person and loved him with such devotion that she mourned his death for the rest of her life. And I could cite many other similar cases which I will leave out for the sake of brevity."

II.22.2

"I believe you," she replied. "Let me tell you of other ladies who loved their husbands."

23. CONCERNING THE NOBLE SULPITIA.

II.23.1   "Sulpitia was the wife of Lentulus Truscellio, a Roman nobleman, whom she loved with obvious devotion, for when he was condemned by the judges of Rome for certain crimes of which he was accused, to be sent into miserable exile and to spend his life there in poverty, excellent Sulpitia, even though she was quite wealthy in Rome and could have remained in ease and comfort, preferred to follow her husband into poverty and exile rather than remain in the abundance of wealth without him, and so she renounced all her inheritances, her possessions, and her homeland. With great difficulty she managed to escape from her mother and relatives who, for just this reason, were guarding her quite carefully, and in disguise she rejoined her husband."

Then I, Christine said, "Indeed, my lady, this reminds me, because you have spoken of several women, that I have seen a number of women in similar circumstances in my time. For I have known women whose husbands became lepers, and it was necessary for them to be separated from society and placed in leper hospitals. However, their good wives wished never to leave them and preferred accompanying them to serve them in their illness and to uphold the loyal faith promised to them in marriage, rather than remain in comfort in their houses without their husbands. And I even know one such woman today, who is young and good and beautiful, whose husband is very much suspected of having this illness. Yet when her parents repeatedly pressure her and urge her to leave him and to come live with them, she replies that she will not leave him for a single day of her life and that if, after having been tested, he is found to have contracted leprosy (meaning he would have to retire from society), she will of course go with him. For this reason her parents are having him examined.

"Similarly, I know other women—whom I shall not   *II.23.2*
name, since it might displease them—whose husbands
are so perverse and follow such a disordered life that
these women's parents wish that their sons-in-law were
dead, and they take every pain to bring their daughters
back to them and away from their evil husbands, but
these women prefer being beaten and living ill-fed in
extreme poverty and subjugation with their husbands
rather than leaving them, and they tell their friends, 'You
gave him to me; with him I will live and with him I will
die.' And these are things which one sees every day, but
nobody pays them any attention."

24. HERE RECTITUDE TELLS OF SEVERAL LADIES WHO
TOGETHER SAVED THEIR HUSBANDS FROM DEATH.

"I want to tell you about several women who, like   *II.24.1*
the ones mentioned above, together showed great love
for their husbands. After Jason had been in Colchis to
conquer the Golden Fleece, it happened that several
knights whom he had brought along with him who were
from a country in Greece called Orchomenos, in Boetia,
left their own country and city and went to live in
another city of Greece called Lacedaemonia. They were
cordially received and honored there, as much for their
ancient nobility as for their wealth. There they married
the noble daughters of the city. They became so rich and
acquired so many honors that in their pride they conspired against the town rulers in order to transfer power
to themselves. Their plot was discovered, and they were
imprisoned and condemned to death. Their wives were
extremely grieved by this and assembled together as if to
mourn, and they were thereby able to take counsel among
themselves to find some way to deliver their husbands.
In the end their consultation resulted in a plan for them
to dress up at night in old clothes and to cover their
heads with their cloaks in order not to be recognized.
So clothed, they went to the prison and, weeping, they
begged the prison guards to allow them to see their

husbands. Once the ladies were inside, they dressed their husbands in their robes and took for themselves the clothes their husbands were wearing. Then they sent their husbands off, and the guards mistook them for the wives returning home. The next morning when they were supposed to die, the executioners led them out to be tortured, and when it turned out that they were the wives, everyone admired this clever ruse, and they were praised for it. The citizens took pity on their daughters, and no one was executed. In this manner the brave wives delivered their husbands from death."

25. CHRISTINE SPEAKS TO LADY RECTITUDE AGAINST THOSE MEN WHO SAY THAT WOMEN DO NOT KNOW HOW TO CONCEAL ANYTHING. THE RESPONSE MADE BY LADY RECTITUDE DEALS WITH PORTIA, DAUGHTER OF CATO.

II.25.1 "My lady, now I know for certain what I had suspected earlier, that many women have shown, and show, great love and faith toward their husbands. For this reason I am amazed at the opinion which circulates quite commonly among men—even Master Jean de Meung argues strongly (too strongly in fact!) in his *Romance of the Rose*, along with other authors as well—that a man should not tell his wife anything which he wishes to conceal and that women are unable to be silent."

"Dear friend," she replied, "you must know that all women are not wise—nor all men, for that matter—so that if a man possesses such wisdom, he must seriously consider what sense and what goodness his wife has before he tells her anything which he might want to hide, for he may be running a risk. But when a man feels he has a good, wise, and discreet wife, there is nothing in the world more trustworthy, nor is there anyone who could comfort him more.

II.25.2 "The noble Roman Brutus, husband of Portia, never shared the opinion that women are as indiscreet as these men claim and that women love their husbands so little. This noble lady Portia was the daughter of Cato the

Younger, who was the nephew of Cato the Elder. Her husband, who felt that she was quite wise and chaste, told her of the intention which he and Cassius, another Roman nobleman, had to kill Julius Caesar in the senate. Considering the great evil which would arise from this action, the wise lady tried with all her might to dissuade him and advise him against the deed. Because of her worry over this matter, she was so upset that she could not sleep all night long. When morning came, Brutus was leaving his room to carry out his plan, and Portia, who would have gladly turned him away from the deed, took a barber's razor, as if to cut her nails, dropped it, and then as she pretended to pick it up, she deliberately stuck herself in the hand with it, whereupon her women servants, seeing her wounded, cried out so loudly that Brutus returned. When he saw her wounded, he reproached her and remarked that it was not her office to use a razor, but a barber's. She replied that she had not acted as foolishly as he thought, but had done so deliberately to try out a way to kill herself if his plan miscarried. Nevertheless, Brutus did not allow himself to be dissuaded, and departed. Shortly afterward he killed Caesar, who stood between Cassius and himself. All the same, both were exiled; then Brutus was killed, although he had fled Rome. When his good wife Portia learned of his death, her grief was so great that she abjured both joy and life. And since all knives or anything sharp with which she could kill herself had been taken from her, for it was obvious what she wanted to do, she went to the fire, took burning coals, swallowed them, and burned herself to death. In such a strange way—the strangest way in which anyone ever died—the noble Portia ended her life."

26. SHE SPEAKS ON THIS SAME TOPIC REGARDING THE LADY CURIA.

"Let me speak to you once more on this same topic, *II.26.1* in answer to those men who argue that women do not know how to hide anything, and at the same time demonstrate, with more examples, the great love which many women have for their husbands. The Roman noblewoman Curia gave Quintus Lucretius, her husband, wonderful loyalty, constancy, wise counsel, and devotion, for after her husband had been condemned to death with some other men for a particular crime with which they all were charged, they found out that they were being sought for execution and so were lucky to have enough time to flee. However, in their fear of being discovered, they hid themselves in the caves of wild beasts but did not dare to live there. But, because of the sense and sound advice of his wife, Lucretius did not even leave his bedroom. When the men seeking him came there, she held him in her arms in her bed, hiding him so cleverly that they did not notice him at all. She knew how to conceal him so well within the bedroom that none of her servants, nor anyone else, would have known he was there. She also covered up the deed with the clever ruse: she would race like a madwoman through the streets, temples, and monasteries, wearing poor clothes, dishevelled and weeping, beating her palms. And everywhere she would ask whether anyone knew what had become of her husband or where he had fled, for wherever he was, she wanted to go to him to be the companion of his exile and miseries. In this way she managed to pretend so cleverly that no one ever knew the difference, and so she saved her husband and consoled him in his fear. In brief, she was able to save him from exile and death."

27. MORE ON THIS SAME TOPIC.

II.27.1   "Now that we have started citing examples to refute those who claim that women do not know how to conceal anything, I could certainly give you an endless number of them, but be satisfied with the one which I will relate to you. When Nero, the tyrant emperor, ruled in Rome, there were several men who, in view of the atrocities and cruelties committed by Nero, considered that it would be an enormous benefit and advantage to assassinate him. So they conspired against him and deliberated on how to kill him. These men withdrew to the house of a woman in whom they had such great trust that they did not hesitate in the least to discuss their conspiracy in front of her. One evening, as they were dining at her house and planning to put their enterprise into effect the next day, they were not wary enough to keep from speaking. They were overheard by chance by someone who, in order to flatter the emperor and win his favor, went and immediately told him what he had heard. As a result, no sooner had the conspirators left this woman's house than the emperor's sergeants arrived at her door. Failing to find the men, they brought the woman before the emperor, who interrogated her at length on this matter. Yet she proved herself marvelously constant and discreet in that he was totally unable to draw out of her who these men were, nor even an admission that she knew anything, either by offering and promising her wonderful gifts or by force of torture (which he did not spare in the least)."

28. REFUTATIONS OF THE CLAIM THAT A MAN IS DESPICABLE WHO BELIEVES HIS WIFE'S ADVICE OR LENDS IT CREDENCE. CHRISTINE ASKS SOME QUESTIONS TO WHICH RECTITUDE REPLIES.

"My lady, for the reasons which I have heard from you and because I have seen so much sense and well-being in women, I am surprised that several authors claim that men who believe or lend credence to their wives' advice are despicable and foolish." II.28.1

She replied, "I told you before that while all women are not wise, those men who have good and wise wives behave like fools when they fail to believe them. You can see this from what I said to you earlier, for if Brutus had believed Portia, his wife, and not killed Julius Caesar, he himself would not have been killed, nor would the resulting evil have occurred. Because we are on this subject, I will tell you about several other men whom misfortune befell because they did not believe their wives. If Julius Caesar, whom we have discussed, had believed his sagacious and virtuous wife—who, as best she could, because of the many signs which appeared foreboding her husband's death and because of her horrible dream the night before, had tried to prevent him from going to the senate on that day—he would not have gone and would never have been killed.

"However, the same applies to Pompey, who was married to Julia, daughter of Julius Caesar, just as I told you before, and then, after her death, to another very noble lady, named Cornelia. In regard to what was said before, Julia loved Pompey so much that she never wanted to leave him, regardless of what misfortune might happen to him. Even when he was forced to flee by sea after being defeated in battle by Julius Caesar, the good lady remained with him and accompanied him through every danger. And when he arrived in the kingdom of Egypt, Ptolemy, the king there, treacherously pretended to be glad at his arrival and sent his retainers out to meet him, as though he were warmly welcoming Pompey; but this maneuver was designed to kill him. These retainers told Pompey to come into their boat and leave his own people behind so that they could more easily bring him into the harbor in their own lighter vessel. But as he was about to enter their boat, his wise and virtuous wife, Cornelia, tried to dissuade him from going at all and from taking leave of his own people. Seeing that he was not going to believe her (whose heart foretold nothing good coming from this), she tried at all costs to throw herself into the boat with him, but he would not allow it, and it was necessary to restrain her by force. The sorrow of this valiant woman began at this moment and did not decrease for the rest of her life, for he was not very far from her when she (who had trained her look nowhere else but on him and who had followed him the whole way with her eyes) saw him murdered by these traitors in their ship. She would have thrown herself into the sea for grief had she not been forcibly prevented from doing so.

"Moreover, similar misfortune befell the brave Hector II.28.3 of Troy, for on the night before he was killed, his wife Andromache had a marvelous vision that if Hector went into battle the following day, he would surely die. Therefore, the lady, frightened by this vision which was no dream but a true prophecy, begged him first with clasped hands, then by kneeling down before him, and finally by holding their two beautiful children in her arms, to delay his going into battle that day. But he disparaged all her words, considering that it would always be a source of shame for him if he had not gone into battle because of a woman's advice and urgings, nor would he delay for his father's or his mother's sake, whom Andromache invoked. Thus, what she had predicted came true, for Hector was killed by Achilles, and it would have been better if he had believed her.

"I could give you countless examples of men who II.28.4 suffered misfortune in various ways because they did not deign to believe the advice of their good and wise wives. If evil befell these men who disparaged their wives' advice, the wives should not be blamed."

29. RECTITUDE GIVES EXAMPLES OF MEN WHO WERE FAVORED WITH GOOD FORTUNE BECAUSE THEY BELIEVED THEIR WIVES.

"I will tell you about those men favored with good II.29.1 fortune because they followed the advice given by their wives, and let this proof suffice, for I could say so much that it would be an endless process, and what I told you before about many wise and virtuous ladies on this subject applies here, too. The emperor Justinian, whom I mentioned to you before, had a baron as his companion whom he loved as much as himself. This baron was named Belisarius, and he was a very brave knight. Therefore, the emperor made him the master and commander of his cavalry, and had him sit at his table and served with the same dignity, and, in short, he showed Belisarius so many signs of love that his other barons became quite jealous and told the emperor that Belisarius intended to put him to death and assume control of the empire. The emperor believed this report too readily and, intending to put Belisarius to death covertly, commanded him to fight against a people called the Vandals whom he would not be able to defeat because of their overwhelming strength. When Belisarius heard this command, he realized and knew for sure that the emperor would not have charged him with this mission unless he had surely fallen from the emperor's favor and good will. He was grieved that he could do nothing more and he left for home. When his wife, who was named Antonia and who was the empress' sister, saw him lying in bed, pale and pensive, his eyes filled with tears, she took pity on him and repeatedly asked him what the matter was, so that, in great pain, he told her the cause of his sorrow. After having listened to him, the wise lady pretended to be very joyful, and consoled him, saying, 'What! Is that all that is bothering you? You must not be so upset!' As this happened during the time when the faith of Jesus Christ was still quite new, the good lady, who was a Christian, then said, 'Have faith in Jesus Christ, the crucified, and through this faith and with His help, you will surely triumph. If the envious desire to destroy you with their false words, you will show with your good deeds that they are liars and taken in by their own lies. So trust in me and do not disparage my words. Let all your hope be in the Living God, and I promise you that you will conquer. Take care not to give the slightest appearance of being burdened by this matter or of being sad, but instead seem glad, like someone who is quite happy. I will tell you when to assemble your army as hastily as possible. In addition, take care that no one knows where you wish to go. Also arrange to have plenty of ships and then divide your army into two parts, and, as quickly and as secretly as you can, invade Africa with one part of your army and immediately attack your enemies. I will have the other part of your troops with me, and we will arrive by sea from the other side of the port, and, while the enemy will be trying to join battle with you, we will come in from the other flank into the cities and towns and will put everyone to death and everything to the torch and destroy them all.' Belisarius followed this advice and so acted like a wise man and organized the expedition according to what she had said, no more, no less. Everything turned out so well for him that he was able to conquer and subjugate his enemies. He captured the king of the Vandals and won such a noble victory through the good counsel, sense, and valiance of his wife that the emperor loved him more than ever.

"Likewise, a second time it happened that, because of *II.29.2* false gossip spread by envious courtiers, Belisarius again fell from the emperor's grace and was completely stripped of his duties with the cavalry. Nevertheless, his wife comforted him and gave him hope. Then the emperor himself was deposed from his rule over the empire by the same envious courtiers. However, because of his wife's advice, Belisarius managed with all his power intact to return the emperor to his throne, even though the emperor had done him great wrong. Thus the emperor realized the loyalty of his knight and the treason of the others, and this all thanks to the wisdom and sound advice of the shrewd lady.

"Similarly, King Alexander did not disparage the *II.29.3* counsel and worth of the queen, his wife, who was the daughter of Dares, the king of Persia. When Alexander realized that he had been poisoned by his disloyal servants, he wanted to throw himself in the river to end his life more quickly because of the enormous pain he was in. The lady met him while he was on his way and began to comfort him, even though she herself was very grieved. She told him to go back, to lie down in his bed, and to speak to his barons there, and to formulate his ordinances as befitted an emperor of his dignity, for it would have been a great loss of honor if one could say afterward that impatience had completely overcome him. So he believed his wife and thanks to her advice instituted his ordinances."

30. CHRISTINE SPEAKS OF THE GREAT BENEFIT ACCRUED AND ACCRUING EVERY DAY TO THE WORLD BECAUSE OF WOMEN.

II.30.1 "My lady, I see the endless benefits which have accrued to the world through women and nevertheless these men claim that there is no evil which has not come into the world because of them."

"Fair friend," she answered, "you can see from what I have already said to you that the contrary of what they say is true. For there is no man who could sum up the enormous benefits which have come about through women and which come about every day, and I proved this for you with the examples of the noble ladies who gave the sciences and arts to the world. But, if what I have said about the earthly benefits accruing thanks to women is not enough for you, I will tell you about the spiritual ones. Oh, how could any man be so heartless to forget that the door of Paradise was opened to him by a woman? As I told you before, it was opened by the Virgin Mary, and is there anything greater one could ask for than that God was made man? And who can forget the great benefits which mothers bring to their sons and which wives bring to their husbands? I implore them at the very least not to forget the advantages which touch upon spiritual good. Let us consider the Law of the Jews. If you recall the story of Moses, to whom God gave the written Law of the Jews, you will find that this holy prophet, through whom so much good has come about, was saved from death by a woman, just as I will tell you.

II.30.2 "In the time when the Jews were in servitude to the kings of Egypt, it was foretold that a man would be born among the Hebrews who would lead the people of Israel out of servitude to these kings. When Moses, that noble leader, was born, his mother, not daring to nurse him, was forced to place him in a small basket and send him downstream. So it happened—according to the will of God who saves whatsoever pleases Him—that Thermutis, the daughter of Pharaoh, was playing on the riverbank at the very moment when the little basket floated by on the water, and she immediately had the basket brought to her in order to find out what was inside. When she saw that it was such a lovely child that a more beautiful child could not be imagined, she was terribly glad. She had him nursed and claimed him as her own, and, because through a miracle he would not take the breast of a woman of a foreign religion, she had him nursed by a Hebrew woman. When Moses, elected by God, was grown, it was he to whom our Lord gave the Law and who delivered the Jews from the hands of the Egyptians, and he passed through the Red Sea and was the leader and guide of the children of Israel. And this great benefit came to the Jews thanks to the woman who saved him."

31. CONCERNING JUDITH, THE NOBLE LADY AND WIDOW WHO SAVED HER PEOPLE.

"Judith, the noble lady and widow, saved the people *II.31.1* of Israel from perishing when Nebuchadnezzar II sent Holophernes, the leader of his cavalry, to the Jews after he had conquered the land of Egypt. With all his might, Holophernes besieged the Jews in the city and conducted such a savage campaign against them that they were hardly able to resist. He cut off their water pipes, and their food supplies were nearly exhausted. The Jews had no hope of holding out and were practically at the point of being captured by this man who threatened them so much; they were in great distress, so they unceasingly prayed to God to take mercy on His people and to defend them from the hands of their enemies. God heard their prayers and just as He intended to save the human race through a woman, He likewise wished to help and save these Jews through a woman. At this time the noble and upright Judith was in this city and while she was still young and very beautiful, she was above all chaste and virtuous. This woman had great compassion for the people whom she saw in terrible desolation, and so she prayed day and night to our Lord to help them. She began to reflect on a daring strategy, inspired by God in whom she had her trust. One night, after commending herself to our Lord, she left the city, accompanied by a servant woman, and traveled until she came to the army of Holophernes. When the sentries on watch beheld her great beauty in the moonlight, they immediately led her to Holophernes, who was quite happy to receive her because she was so beautiful. He had her sit next to him and greatly valued her knowledge, beauty, and poise, and, looking at her, he became very excited and lusted after her with a great craving. Her thoughts were elsewhere and she continued to pray to God in her heart to help her accomplish her mission. She kept tormenting Holophernes with fair words until her goal was in sight. On the third night following, Holophernes gave a supper for his barons and drank a great deal until he was inflamed with wine and meat and did not want to wait any longer to go to bed with the Hebrew woman, and so he ordered her to come to him. He told her his desire, and she did not refuse him at all but asked that, for the sake of honesty, he have his tent cleared of everyone and that he should go to bed first. She promised without fail to come to him around midnight, after everyone was asleep. He granted her request and the good lady devoted herself to her prayers, beseeching God to give her feminine heart the boldness and force to deliver His people from the evil tyrant. When Judith thought that Holophernes was asleep, she approached very quietly, accompanied by her servant woman, and listened at the door of his tent and heard him sleeping soundly. Then the lady said, 'Let us act boldly, for God is with us.' She entered and fearlessly took the sword which she saw at the head of the bed, withdrew it from its sheath, then raised it with all her strength, and cut off Holophernes' head without being heard by anyone. She placed his head in her lap and, as quickly as she could, proceeded toward the city until she came without hindrance to the gates, where she called out, 'Come, come open, for God is with us.' After she was inside, no one could imagine the joy with which this exploit was celebrated. The next morning they hung the head on a pole from the walls. All the Jews armed themselves and bravely advanced against their enemies, who were still in their beds, for no one was keeping watch. After arriving at their duke's tent, to which they had rushed to awaken and rouse him quickly out of bed, they found him dead. No troops were ever so bewildered, and therefore the Jews captured or killed them all. Then the people of God were delivered from the clutches of Holophernes thanks to Judith, the honest woman, who will forever be praised on this account in the Holy Scriptures."

32. HERE SHE SPEAKS OF QUEEN ESTHER, WHO SAVED HER PEOPLE.

"God also wished to deliver His people from the *II.32.1* servitude of King Ahaseuras through the noble and wise queen Esther. This king Ahaseuras exercised enormous power over all other kings and ruled many kingdoms; he was a pagan and held the Jews in bondage. He summoned from all his kingdoms the noblest, most beautiful, and best educated young women in order to select the one who pleased him most to be his wife. Among the others brought to him was the noble, wise, and good maiden Esther, beloved of God, who was a Hebrew. She pleased him more than all others, and he married her and loved her with such devotion that he would not refuse her anything which she might request. Sometime afterward, a deceitful flatterer named Haman set the king so much against the Jews that he commanded that everywhere they be sought out, rounded up, and put to death. Queen Esther knew nothing of this, for if she had known about it, she would have been terribly upset that her people were being so mistreated. Nevertheless, an uncle of hers named Mordecai, who was head of the Jews, informed her of the situation and asked her to rectify it immediately, for the time remaining before the sentence was to be carried out was quite short. The queen was so upset by this that she dressed and adorned herself as nobly as she could and went into the garden, accompanied by her ladies as though seeking diversion, at a time when she knew the king would be at his window; and as she was returning, she passed the king's chamber, giving the appearance that this was totally unstudied on her part, and upon seeing the king at the window, she immediately fell to her knees and, completely prostrate on her face, she greeted him. The king, greatly pleased with her humility and viewing with enormous pleasure the magnificent beauty which she radiated, called to her and said that should she ask for anything, she would have it. The lady answered that she only wanted him to dine in her chambers and to bring Haman with him; and he willingly granted this to her. When he dined there on the third day following and found the feast as well as the honor, goodness, and beauty of the lady pleasing, he urged her to put any request whatsoever to him. She threw herself at his feet and, weeping, began to beseech him to have mercy on her people and not to dishonor her so much— since he had placed her in such high honor—by having her lineage and compatriots so treacherously destroyed. Aroused and angry, the king replied, 'Who is so bold to dare to do this?' 'Sire, Haman, your provost who is here, has had this done.' To tell you the matter briefly, the king revoked his sentence; Haman, who had arranged all this out of envy, was taken prisoner and hanged for his crimes; and Mordecai, the queen's uncle, was placed in Haman's position; the Jews were freed and were favored and honored more than all the other peoples. Thus, as with Judith, in this instance God wished to save His people through a woman. And do not think that these two ladies are the only ones in the Holy Scriptures through whom God cared to save His people at various times, for there are plenty of others whom I am omitting for the sake of brevity, such as Deborah, whom I spoke of above, who also delivered her people from servitude, and others have acted similarly."

33. CONCERNING THE SABINE LADIES, WHO MADE PEACE AMONG THEIR FRIENDS.

"I can also tell you about many ladies of the ancient   *II.33.1*
pagan religion who were responsible for saving their homelands, cities, and towns. I will acquit myself with two exceptionally noteworthy examples, and nothing more, which will prove the case for them all. After Romulus and Remus had founded the city of Rome and after Romulus had peopled and filled the city with all the knights and men of arms whom he had been able to select and assemble following several victories, Romulus eagerly took pains to find them wives so that they could have children who would take possession of the city and dominion forever. However, he did not know precisely how he could find wives for himself and his companions, for the Sabine kings and princes and countrymen did not want to give them their daughters in marriage because the Romans seemed extremely unstable to the Sabines, who feared having any relationship with the haughty and strange Romans. Therefore, Romulus concocted a ruse whereby he announced throughout the entire land a tournament and joust to which he invited the princes and kings and all people to bring their ladies and daughters to watch the amusement offered by foreign knights. On the day of festivities, the assembled audience was large on both sides, and many ladies and young women had come there to watch the games. Among others, the king of the Sabines brought his beautiful and well-bred daughter, accompanied by all the ladies and girls of the country

who waited on her. The jousts were held outside the city on a plain next to a mountain, and the ladies were all seated according to rank on the mountainside. There the knights competed against one another in performing deeds of valor and prowess, and the sight of the beautiful ladies gave them more strength and daring to perform knightly deeds. To give you a brief account, after the jousting had lasted long enough, when the time seemed right to Romulus to carry out his plan, he took out a great ivory hunting horn and sounded a loud blast. All his men understood well this sound and signal; they left the game and rushed at the ladies. Romulus snatched the king's daughter (with whom he was already quite smitten), and each of the others likewise took a woman for himself. They forcibly lifted them onto their horses and fled to the city, where they securely locked the gates. The outcry and sorrow of the fathers and relatives from outside the city and of the ladies who had been forcibly carried off was enormous, but their weeping was of no avail to them. Romulus married his lady with great ceremony and the others did likewise. A great war broke out because of this incident, for as soon as the king of the Sabines could, he moved against the Romans with a large army. However, it was not easy to defeat them, for they were a valiant people. The war had already lasted five years when, one day, the enemies assembled on a field in all their strength, and it was inevitable that there would be an enormous loss of life and a great slaughter. The Romans had already moved out in great strength when the queen assembled all the ladies of the city in a temple for a discussion. The queen, who was so wise and good and beautiful, began to address them, 'Most honored Sabine ladies, my dear sisters and companions, you are well acquainted with the rape which our husbands committed against us. On this account, our fathers and relatives are waging war against our husbands and our husbands against them. So it is that this deadly war can be neither ended nor continued without our participation.

No matter who is victorious, it will still be disastrous
for us, for if our husbands are conquered, what a terrible
grief and desolation it will be for us, who rightfully
love them and who have already had children by them,
little children who would be left fatherless. If our husbands win and our fathers and relatives are killed, we
will certainly grieve at our misfortune. What is done is
done, and cannot be otherwise. Therefore, it seems to me
that it would be a very good idea if we could find some
other means of re-establishing peace amid all this war. If
you follow my advice and do what I shall do, I am certain
that we will be able to put an end to this.' They all
responded to the lady's words by saying that they would
gladly obey her commands. Then the queen made herself
completely dishevelled and barefoot, and all the ladies
did likewise. Those who had children either carried them
in their arms or brought them along, and so there were
many children as well as pregnant women. The queen
went in the lead, followed by this piteous procession,
and they arrived at the battlefield exactly at the hour
when the armies were poised to fight, positioning themselves between the two armies so that the enemies would
have to fight in the midst of the assembled women. The
queen knelt down and all the other women did the same,
crying out in a loud voice, 'Most dear fathers and kins-
men, our lords and beloved husbands, for God's sake,
make peace! Otherwise we prefer to die under your
horses' hoofs.' Seeing their wives and children weeping
there, the husbands were greatly amazed, and, of course,
greatly pained. Similarly, seeing their daughters touched
and moved the hearts of the fathers. Looking at each
other with pity for these ladies who had so humbly
entreated them, their hostility changed to the loving piety
of sons toward fathers, and both sides were forced to
throw down their arms, embrace one another, and make
peace. Romulus led the Sabine king, his sire, into his
city, and greatly honored him and all his company. Thus,
thanks to the sense and virtue of this queen and these

ladies, the Romans and Sabines were saved from destruction."

34. CONCERNING THE NOBLE LADY VETURIA, WHO PACIFIED HER SON WHEN HE WISHED TO DESTROY ROME.

II.34.1   "Veturia was a noble lady of Rome, mother of a great Roman named Gnaeus Martius, a man of exceptional virtue and wisdom, subtle and quick, brave and bold. This noble knight, son of Veturia, was sent by the Romans with a great army against the Coriolans, whom he conquered and from whom he captured the fortress of the Volscians. Because of this victory over the Coriolans, he was called Coriolanus. He was honored so much for this deed that within a short time he gained control over the entire government of Rome. But it is extremely dangerous for a people to be governed at the will of a single individual, and in the end, the Romans became angered with him, condemned him to exile, and banished him from Rome. However, he knew well how to avenge himself, for he went over to the side of those whom he had previously defeated and led them in rebellion against the Romans. They made him their lord and moved in strength against the city of Rome, wreaking enormous destruction everywhere they went. The Romans greatly feared them, and, because of the danger in which they saw themselves, they sent messengers to Martius to sue for peace, but he would not deign to hear them. They dispatched messengers to him a second time, but nothing was of any use; he continued to ravage them, so they sent their bishops and priests, in all their vestments, to entreat him humbly. However, they could accomplish nothing, until the Romans, with no other recourse, sent the noble ladies of the city to the noble lady Veturia, Martius' mother, to beg her to try to pacify her son Martius toward them. Thereupon the noble lady Veturia left the city, accompanied by all the noble ladies. With this procession she went to her son, who in his goodness and virtue, and upon learning of her arrival, dismounted and went to meet her, receiving her with the proper deference of a son for his mother. After she had begged him for peace, he answered that it was a mother's right to command her son, not to beg from him. And thus this noble lady brought him back to Rome. This time the Romans were preserved from destruction thanks to her, and she alone accomplished what the high dignitaries of Rome could not do."

35. HERE SHE SPEAKS OF CLOTILDA, QUEEN OF FRANCE, WHO CONVERTED HER HUSBAND, KING CLOVIS, TO THE FAITH.

"As for the great benefits brought about by women regarding spiritual matters, just as I told you before, was it not Clotilda, daughter of the king of Burgundy and wife of the strong Clovis, king of France, who first brought and spread the faith of Jesus Christ to the kings and princes of France? What greater good could have been accomplished than what she did? For after she had been enlightened by the Faith, like the good Christian and holy lady she was, she did not cease to prod and beg her lord to receive the holy Faith and be baptized. But he did not wish to assent, and on this account the lady never stopped praying to God in tears, fasts, and devotions to enlighten the king's heart. She prayed so much that our Lord took pity on her affliction and inspired King Clovis, so that once, having gone into battle against the king of the Germans and seeing the battle's fortunes turn against him, he lifted his eyes toward Heaven and in great devotion declared (just as God had wished to inspire him), 'All powerful God, whom my wife, the queen, believes in and worships, please help me in this battle, and I promise that I will accept your holy law.' No sooner had he spoken this vow than the battle turned in his favor and he won a complete victory. So he gave thanks to God and, upon returning, to the great joy and consolation of both himself and the queen, he was baptized, along

II.35.1

with all the barons and then all the people. From that hour on, thanks to the prayers of this good and holy queen Clotilda, God has so generously bestowed His grace that the Faith has never been defeated in France, nor, thank God, has there ever been a heretic king—which has never been the case with other kings or with many emperors—and this fact should be a source of great praise for the French kings who are, for this reason, called 'most Christian.'

II.35.2   "If I wished to tell you all the great benefits which have come about through women, it would require much too long a book. But while we are still on the subject of spiritual good, how many holy martyrs (just as I will tell you later) were comforted, lodged, and fed by young girls, widows, and virtuous honest women? If you read their legends, you will find that it pleased God that all of the martyrs—or the majority—were comforted in their adversity and their martyrdom by women. What did I tell you? The martyrs, indeed the Apostles as well, Saint Paul and the other saints, and even Jesus Christ, were fed and comforted by women.

II.35.3   "Do not the French, who have shown such great devotion—and with good reason—to the body of my lord Saint Denis who first brought the Faith to France, have this blessed body and those of his blessed companions, Saint Rusticus and Saint Eleutherius, thanks to a woman? For the tyrant who had these saints beheaded ordered that their bodies be thrown into the Seine, and the men who were supposed to do this placed them in a sack to carry them there. These men were lodged with a good lady, a widow named Catulla, who got them drunk and then removed the holy bodies and placed dead pigs in the bag, and she buried the blessed martyrs as honorably as she could in her house, placing an inscription over them so that this would be known in the future. Long afterward, likewise, the first chapel in their honor was erected on this spot by a woman—this was my lady Saint Genevieve —which stood there until the good king of France

Dagobert founded the church which still stands there."

36. AGAINST THOSE MEN WHO CLAIM IT IS NOT GOOD FOR WOMEN TO BE EDUCATED.

Following these remarks, I, Christine, spoke, "My lady, I realize that women have accomplished many good things and that even if evil women have done evil, it seems to me, nevertheless, that the benefits accrued and still accruing because of good women—particularly the wise and literary ones and those educated in the natural sciences whom I mentioned above—outweigh the evil. Therefore, I am amazed by the opinion of some men who claim that they do not want their daughters, wives, or kinswomen to be educated because their mores would be ruined as a result." *II.36.1*

She responded, "Here you can clearly see that not all opinions of men are based on reason and that these men are wrong. For it must not be presumed that mores necessarily grow worse from knowing the moral sciences, which teach the virtues, indeed, there is not the slightest doubt that moral education amends and ennobles them. How could anyone think or believe that whoever follows good teaching or doctrine is the worse for it? Such an opinion cannot be expressed or maintained. I do not mean that it would be good for a man or a woman to study the art of divination or those fields of learning which are forbidden—for the holy Church did not remove them from common use without good reason—but it should not be believed that women are the worse for knowing what is good.

"Quintus Hortensius, a great rhetorician and consumately skilled orator in Rome, did not share this opinion. He had a daughter, named Hortensia, whom he greatly loved for the subtlety of her wit. He had her learn letters and study the science of rhetoric, which she mastered so thoroughly that she resembled her father Hortensius not only in wit and lively memory but also in her excellent delivery and order of speech—in fact, he *II.36.2* surpassed her in nothing. As for the subject discussed above, concerning the good which comes about through women, the benefits realized by this woman and her learning were, among others, exceptionally remarkable. That is, during the time when Rome was governed by three men, this Hortensia began to support the cause of women and to undertake what no man dared to undertake. There was a question whether certain taxes should be levied on women and on their jewelry during a needy period in Rome. This woman's eloquence was so compelling that she was listened to, no less readily than her father would have been, and she won her case.

II.36.3   "Similarly, to speak of more recent times, without searching for examples in ancient history, Giovanni Andrea, a solemn law professor in Bologna not quite sixty years ago, was not of the opinion that it was bad for women to be educated. He had a fair and good daughter, named Novella, who was educated in the law to such an advanced degree that when he was occupied by some task and not at leisure to present his lectures to his students, he would send Novella, his daughter, in his place to lecture to the students from his chair. And to prevent her beauty from distracting the concentration of her audience, she had a little curtain drawn in front of her. In this manner she could on occasion supplement and lighten her father's occupation. He loved her so much that, to commemorate her name, he wrote a book of remarkable lectures on the law which he entitled *Novella super Decretalium*, after his daughter's name.

II.36.4   "Thus, not all men (and especially the wisest) share the opinion that it is bad for women to be educated. But it is very true that many foolish men have claimed this because it displeased them that women knew more than they did. Your father, who was a great scientist and philosopher, did not believe that women were worth less by knowing science; rather, as you know, he took great pleasure from seeing your inclination to learning. The feminine opinion of your mother, however, who wished to keep you busy with spinning and silly girlishness, following the common custom of women, was the major obstacle to your being more involved in the sciences. But just as the proverb already mentioned above says, 'No one can take away what Nature has given,' your mother could not hinder in you the feeling for the sciences which you, through natural inclination, had nevertheless gathered together in little droplets. I am sure that, on account of these things, you do not think you are worth less but rather that you consider it a great treasure for yourself; and you doubtless have reason to."

And I, Christine, replied to all of this, "Indeed, my lady, what you say is as true as the Lord's Prayer."

37. HERE CHRISTINE SPEAKS TO RECTITUDE, WHO ARGUES AGAINST THOSE MEN WHO SAY THAT THERE ARE FEW CHASTE WOMEN, AND SHE TELLS OF SUSANNA.

"From what I see, my lady, all good and virtuous *II.37.1* things are found in women. Where does the opinion that there are so few chaste women come from? Were this so, then all their other virtues would be nothing, since chastity is the supreme virtue in women. But from what I have heard you say, the complete opposite of what those men claim seems to be the case."

She replied, "From what I have already actually told you and from what you know about this, the contrary is quite obvious to you, and I could tell you more about this and then some. How many valiant and chaste ladies does Holy Scripture mention who chose death rather than transgress against the chastity and purity of their bodies and thoughts, just like the beautiful and good Susanna, wife of Joachim, a rich man of great authority among the Jews? Once when this valiant lady Susanna was alone relaxing in her garden, two old men, false priests, entered the garden, approached her, and demanded that she sin with them. She refused them totally, where-upon, seeing their request denied, they threatened to denounce her to the authorities and to claim that they had discovered her with a young man. Hearing their threats and knowing that women in such a case were customarily stoned, she said, 'I am completely overwhelmed with anguish, for if I do not do what these men require of me, I risk the death of my body, and if I do it, I will sin before my Creator. However, it is far better for me, in my innocence, to die than to incur the wrath of my God because of sin.' So Susanna cried out, and the servants came out of the house, and, to put the matter briefly, with their disloyal testimony, these false priests managed to have Susanna condemned to death. Yet God who always provides for those dear to Him, opened the mouth of the prophet Daniel, who was a little child in his mother's arms and who, as Susanna was being led to her execution, with a great procession of people in tears following her, cried out that the innocent Susanna had been condemned because of a very grave mistake. So she was led back, and the false priests were thoroughly interrogated and found guilty by their own confessions. The innocent Susanna was freed and these men executed."

38. HERE SHE SPEAKS OF SARAH.

II.38.1   "The Bible, in the twentieth chapter or so of Genesis, speaks of the chastity and goodness of Sarah. This lady was the wife of Abraham, the great patriarch. Many great and good things are said about this lady in the Holy Scripture, which I omit telling you for the sake of brevity. But while we are on the subject of the chastity of beautiful women, which we were discussing before, we might speak of her chastity, for in her great beauty she so surpassed all other women of her time that many princes lusted after her. She was so loyal that she would not lower herself to listen to any of them. Among others who lusted after her was the pharaoh, so much so that he took her away by force from her husband. Yet, her great goodness, which surpassed even her beauty, obtained such grace for her that our Lord, in His tender love for her, protected her from every villainy by tormenting the pharaoh and his household with such terrible diseases of mind and body and with such horrible visions that he never touched her and was forced to give her back."

39. HERE SHE SPEAKS OF REBECCA.

"The extremely good and upright woman, Rebecca, wife of Isaac the patriarch and father of Jacob, was no less good or beautiful than Sarah. She is praised most wonderfully in the Holy Scripture for many things, and the twenty-fourth chapter of Genesis tells about her. She was such an upright, virtuous, and honest woman that she provided an example of perfect chastity for all the women who saw her. Moreover, she conducted herself with amazing humility toward her husband, with so much humility in fact that she no longer seemed to be a lady. For this reason the upright Isaac honored and loved her marvelously. Yet through her chastity and goodness, this lady obtained an even greater boon than the love of her husband, that is, the grace and love of God, which she enjoyed so greatly that, although she was already aged and barren, God gave her two children in one womb. These were Jacob and Esau, from whom the generations of Israel descend." *II.39.1*

40. HERE SHE SPEAKS OF RUTH.

"I could tell you a lot about virtuous and chaste ladies whom the Holy Scripture mentions, but I will omit them in order to be brief. Ruth was another noble lady, from whom David descended. This lady was quite chaste during her marriage as well as during her widowhood and clearly loved her husband greatly since she left her own country and nation after his death to reside and spend her life with the Jews, from whom her husband descended, all because of her devotion to him. She particularly wished to live with his mother. In short, this noble lady was so good and chaste that a book was written about her and her life, in which these matters are described." *II.40.1*

41. CONCERNING PENELOPE, WIFE OF ULYSSES.

II.41.1   "One finds, in various writings, many chaste, good, and honest women among pagan ladies. Penelope, wife of Prince Ulysses, was a most virtuous lady, and among her many fine traits, she was much praised for the virtue of chastity. Many histories mention her at great length, for during the ten years her husband spent at the siege of Troy, this lady conducted herself most wisely, and even though she was propositioned by many kings and princes on account of her outstanding beauty, she did not listen or pay attention to a single one of them. She was wise, prudent, and devoted to the gods and to living virtuously. Even after the destruction of Troy she still had to wait another ten years for her husband. It was thought that he had perished at sea, where he had suffered many misfortunes. On his return, Ulysses found her besieged by a king seeking to marry her because of her great chastity and goodness. Her husband arrived disguised as a pilgrim and inquired after her, and he was very happy with the good reports he heard and took great joy in his son Telemachus whom he had left as a little child and whom he found grown up."

Then I, Christine, said, "My lady, from what I have heard you say, these ladies did not fail to be chaste even though they were beautiful. For many men claim it is considerably difficult to find a beautiful and chaste woman."

She replied, "Those who say this fail to note that there have been, there are, and there always will be many beautiful chaste women."

42. HERE SHE ARGUES AGAINST THOSE MEN WHO MAINTAIN THAT THERE ARE VERY FEW BEAUTIFUL CHASTE WOMEN AND SHE TELLS OF MARIANNES.

II.42.1   "Mariannes was a Hebrew woman, daughter of King Aristobolus. She was such a great beauty that it was thought not only that she exceeded and surpassed all the women of her own time in beauty but also that she was a celestial and divine apparition rather than a mortal woman. A portrait of her, painted on a tablet, was sent to King Anthony of Egypt, who, out of admiration for such beauty, judged her to be a daughter of the god Jupiter, for he did not believe in the least that this lady could have been fathered by a mortal man. In spite of her outstanding beauty and the number of princes and kings who tried to win her, with her great virtue and force of courage, she nevertheless resisted all and yet was all the more praised and radiantly extolled. The fact that she was unhappily married increased the praise for her even more. She was the wife of Herod Antipater, king of the Jews, a man of extraordinary cruelty, who even had her own father put to death. For this reason, as well as because of the many hardships he caused her, she hated him and yet did not fail to be an upright and chaste woman. Moreover, she learned that he had ordered her to be put to death immediately if he died before her, so that no one else could enjoy the possession of such great beauty after him."

43. MORE ON THIS SAME TOPIC; SHE SPEAKS OF ANTONIA, WIFE OF DRUSUS TIBERIUS.

"Even though it is widely held to be as difficult for a beautiful woman in the company of young men and courtiers eager for love to protect herself from being seduced as it is to stand in the midst of flames without being burned, the beautiful and virtuous Antonia, wife of Drusus Tiberius, brother of the emperor Nero, knew how to defend herself quite well. Nero's poisoning Tiberius left her a grieving widow in the flower of youth, resplendent in her sovereign beauty. She resolved never to marry again and to live out her widowhood in chastity, an intention which she so completely realized as she grew older that no other lady among the pagans ever earned greater praise for chastity. What makes her continence all the more praiseworthy, according to Boccaccio, was that she resided in a court with many smart and gracious   *II.43.1* young men, handsome and eager for love, and living in leisure. She spent her life there without stain and without reproach for the slightest lapse. Such deeds, says our author, merit praise, just like the example of a young woman of outstanding beauty who was the daughter of Mark Anthony, who himself led a carnal and lubricious life. Nevertheless, his bad example did not keep her from being safe among the burning flames, filled with chastity, and not for a short time either, for she persevered her entire lifetime until her death in old age.

II.43.2 "I could find many examples for you of such beautiful women living quite chastely in a worldly setting, particularly at court and among young men. Even nowadays, rest assured, there are many of them. There is a great need for me to do this, regardless of what malicious gossips might say, for I do not think that in all times past there were so many evil tongues as there are today, nor so many men inclined to slander women without reason as there are today. And there is no doubt that if these beautiful, virtuous women about whom I have spoken to you, were living now, they would be viciously attacked out of jealousy, instead of winning the praise which the Ancients gave them.

II.43.3 "But to return to our subject of those good and chaste ladies leading an honest life even when they resided among and visited the most worldly people, Valerius discusses the noble Sulpitia who was of great beauty and yet reputed to be the most chaste lady in Rome."

44. REFUTING THOSE MEN WHO CLAIM WOMEN WANT TO BE RAPED, RECTITUDE GIVES SEVERAL EXAMPLES, AND FIRST OF ALL, LUCRETIA.

II.44.1 Then I, Christine, spoke as follows, "My lady, I truly believe what you are saying, and I am certain that there are plenty of beautiful women who are virtuous and chaste and who know how to protect themselves well from the entrapments of deceitful men. I am therefore troubled and grieved when men argue that many women want to be raped and that it does not bother them at all to be raped by men even when they verbally protest. It would be hard to believe that such great villainy is actually pleasant for them."

She answered, "Rest assured, dear friend, chaste ladies who live honestly take absolutely no pleasure in being raped. Indeed, rape is the greatest possible sorrow for them. Many upright women have demonstrated that this is true with their own credible examples, just like Lucretia, the noblest Roman woman, supreme in chastity among Roman women, wife of a nobleman named Tarquin Collatinus. Now, when another man, Tarquin the Proud, son of King Tarquin, was greatly taken with love for this noble Lucretia, he did not dare to tell her because of the great chastity he saw in her, and, despairing of achieving his goal with presents or entreaties, he considered how he could have her through ruse. Claiming to be a close friend of her husband, he managed to gain entrance into her house whenever he wished, and once, knowing her husband was not at home, he went there and the noble lady received him with the honors due to someone whom she thought to be a close friend of her husband. However, Tarquin, who had something altogether different on his mind, succeeded in entering Lucretia's bedroom and frightened her terribly. Put briefly, after trying to coax her for a long time with promises, gifts, and favors, he saw that entreaties were getting him nowhere. He drew his sword and threatened to kill her if she made a sound and did not submit to his will. She answered that he should go ahead and kill her, for she would rather die than consent. Tarquin, realizing that nothing would help him, concocted a great malice, saying that he would publicly declare that he had found her with one of his sergeants. In brief, he so scared her with this threat (for she thought that people would believe him) that finally she suffered his rape. Lucretia, however, could not patiently endure this great pain, so that when daylight came she sent for her husband, her father, and her close relatives who were among the most powerful people in Rome, and, weeping and sobbing, confessed to them what had happened to her. Then, as her husband and relatives, who saw that she was overwhelmed with grief, were comforting her, she drew a knife from under her robe and said, 'This is how I absolve myself of sin and show my innocence. Yet I cannot free myself from the torment nor extricate myself from the pain. From now on no woman will ever live shamed and disgraced by Lucretia's example.' Having said this, she forcibly plunged the knife into her breast and collapsed dead before her husband and friends. They rushed like madmen to attack Tarquin. All Rome was moved to this cause, and they drove out the king and would have killed his son if they had found him. Never again was there a king in Rome. And because of this outrage perpetrated on Lucretia, so some claim, a law was enacted whereby a man would be executed for raping a woman, a law which is fitting, just, and holy."

45. ON THIS SAME SUBJECT SHE SPEAKS OF THE QUEEN OF THE GALATIANS.

II.45.1   "The story of the noble queen of the Galatians, the wife of King Orgiagon, is appropriate to this subject. When the Romans were making their great conquests in foreign lands, they captured this king of the Galatians in battle, and his wife along with him. While they were in the Roman camp, the noble queen, who was quite beautiful, simple, chaste, and virtuous, greatly pleased one of the officers of the Roman army, who was holding the king and queen prisoner. He entreated her and coaxed her with fine presents, but after he saw that pleading would not work, he violently raped her. The lady suffered terrible sorrow over this outrage and could not stop thinking of a way to avenge herself, biding her time until she saw her chance. When the ransom was bought to deliver her husband and herself, the lady said that the money should be turned over in her presence to the officer who was holding them. She told him to weigh the gold to have a better count, so that he would not be deceived. When she saw that he intended to weigh the ransom and that none of his men would be there, the lady, who had a knife, stabbed him in the neck and killed him. She took his head and without difficulty brought it to her husband and told him the entire story and how she had taken vengeance."

46. MORE ON THIS SUBJECT; SHE SPEAKS OF THE SICAMBRIANS AND OF SEVERAL VIRGINS.

"I can give you examples of married women—about whom I could tell you much more—whose anguish at having been raped was unbearable. I will tell you no less about several widows and virgins. Hyppo was a woman from Greece; she was captured and carried off by sailors and sea pirates who were the enemies of the country. This woman, since she was very beautiful, was constantly propositioned by these men. Seeing that she could not escape without being raped and holding this fate in such horror and disgust that she preferred to die, she threw herself into the sea and was drowned. *II.46.1*

"Likewise, on one occasion, the Sicambrians (who are now called the French) attacked the city of Rome with a large army and multitude of people. Hoping to destroy Rome, they brought their wives and children with them. The tide of battle turned against the Sicambrians. When the women saw this, they took counsel among themselves and resolved that it would be better to die defending their chastity than to be dishonored, for they knew well that, following martial custom, they would be raped. Therefore they constructed a fortress around them with their wagons and chariots and armed themselves against the Romans. They defended themselves as best they could, and many of the Romans were killed. But almost all the Sicambrian women were killed; those who remained begged with clasped hands not to be treated so shamefully and to be able to spend the rest of their lives *II.46.2* serving in the temple of virgins dedicated to the goddess Vesta. But when this wish was not granted to them, they preferred to kill themselves rather than be raped.

II.46.3 "Similarly, it is exactly the same case for virgins, such as Virginia, the noble maid of Rome, whom the false judge Claudius thought he could have through ruse and force, after he realized that entreaty would be ineffective. But, even though she was just a young girl, she preferred to be killed rather than raped.

II.46.4 "It was the same when a city in Lombardy was once captured by its enemies who killed the lord. The beautiful daughters of this lord, thinking that their enemies were going to rape them, found a strange remedy, for which they deserve much praise: they took raw chicken meat and placed it on their breasts. This meat quickly rotted because of the heat so that when the enemies approached them and smelled the odor, they immediately left, saying, 'God, how these Lombards stink!' But this stink made them quite fragrant indeed."

47. REFUTATION OF THE INCONSTANCY OF WOMEN. CHRISTINE SPEAKS, AND THEN RECTITUDE ANSWERS HER REGARDING THE INCONSTANCY AND WEAKNESS OF CERTAIN EMPERORS.

II.47.1 "My lady, you have given me a remarkable account of the marvelous constancy, strength, endurance, and virtue of women. What more could one say about the strongest men who have lived? Men, especially writing in books, vociferously and unanimously claim that women in particular are fickle and inconstant, changeable and flighty, weak-hearted, compliant like children, and lacking all stamina. Are the men who accuse women of so much changeableness and inconstancy themselves so unwavering that change for them lies outside the realm of custom or common occurrence? Of course, if they themselves are not that firm, then it is truly despicable for them to accuse others of their own vice or to demand a virtue which they do not themselves know how to practice."

She replied, "Fair sweet friend, have you not heard the saying that the fool can clearly see the mote in his neighbor's eye but pays no attention to the beam hanging out of his own eye? Let me point out to you the contradiction in what these men say concerning the variability and inconstancy of women: since they all generally accuse women of being delicate and frail by nature, you would assume that they think that they are constant, or, at the very least, that women are less constant than they are. Yet they demand more constancy from women than they themselves can muster, for these men who claim to be so strong and of such noble condition are unable to prevent themselves from falling into many, even graver faults and sins, not all of them out of ignorance, but rather out of pure malice, knowing well that they are in the wrong. All the same, they excuse themselves for this by claiming it is human nature to sin. When a few women lapse (and when these men themselves, through their own strivings and their own power, are the cause), then as far as these men are concerned, it is completely a matter of fragility and inconstancy. It seems to me right, nevertheless, to conclude—since they claim women are so fragile—that these men should be somewhat more tolerant of women's weaknesses and not hold something to be a crime for women which they consider only a peccadillo for themselves. For the law does not maintain, nor can any such written opinion be found that permits them and not women to sin, that their vice is more excusable. In fact these men allow themselves liberties which they are unwilling to tolerate in women and thus they—and they are many—perpetrate many insults and outrages in word and deed. Nor do they deign to repute women strong and constant for having endured such men's harsh outrages. In this way men try in every question to have the right on their side—they want to have it both ways! You yourself have quite adequately discussed this problem in your *Epistre au Dieu d'Amour.*

"But as for your question whether men are so strong   *II.47.2* and so constant that they are justified in accusing others of inconstancy, if you consider, starting with wise men in Antiquity up to the present, I can tell you that, from books and from what you have seen in your own time and what you can see every day with your own eyes, not in simple men nor in those of low estate but in the most prominent, indeed, generally in the majority of them, you will be able to observe their perfection, strength, and constancy and to see how many wise, constant, and strong men there are and how great the need for them is.

II.47.3   "And if you want me to give you proof, from the past and present, of why they accuse women so often of this vice, as well as whether inconstancy or fickleness are found in men's hearts, you need only consider whether the behavior of the most powerful princes and greatest men is more shameless than that of emperors which I can tell you about. Let me ask you where there was ever a woman's heart so frail, so fearful, so utterly vulgar, and so inconstant as that of Emperor Claudius? He was so changeable that he would countermand orders which he had given an hour before, nor was he consistent in his pronouncements. He could agree to every bit of advice. In his madness and cruelty he had his wife killed, and that same evening asked why she had not come to bed. And he would summon retainers whom he had had beheaded to come and entertain him. He was so weak-hearted that he constantly shook with fear and he trusted no one. What more can I tell you about him? Every misfortune of mores and emotions were combined in this servile emperor. But why am I telling you about him? Was he the only one filled with such weakness who ever ruled over the empire? Was the emperor Tiberius any better? Were not inconstancy, fickleness, and lust more clearly apparent in him than in any woman what-soever?"

48. HERE SHE SPEAKS OF NERO.

II.48.1   "And who was Nero, after all, since we have come to the acts of the emperors? His enormous weakness and fickleness were obvious. In the beginning he was quite virtuous and strove to please everyone, but later there were no restraints to his lust, rapacity, and cruelty. To excite these vices all the more, at night he would often arm himself and then frequent orgies and brothels, accompanied by his fellow profligates as accomplices, running riot in the streets, committing every vice. In searching for a pretext to commit evil, he would purposely collide with anyone he met and, if they said a word, he would attack and kill them. He would break into taverns and whorehouses and take the women by force, and once he was almost killed by the husband of a woman whom he had raped. He would organize dissolute baths and would gorge himself all night long. He would give one order and then another, depending upon how his madness directed him. He practiced every lechery, outrage, passion, excess, and dissipation. He loved evil men and persecuted good ones. He consented to the killing of his father and later had his mother killed, and after she was dead he had her dissected so that he could see the place where he had been conceived, and he remarked upon seeing her that she had been a beautiful woman. He killed Octavia, his wife, who was a good lady, and he took another woman as his wife whom he loved a great deal to begin with, and then he killed her, too. He put Claudia, the daughter of his predecessor, to death because she refused to marry him. He had his stepson, who was under the age of seven, put to death because he was treated by the servant like the son of the prince when he was taken out to play. He had Seneca, his teacher, the noble philosopher, put to death because he could not help feeling ashamed of his actions in front of Seneca. He poisoned his lieutenant while pretending to take care of his teeth. He poisoned the food and drink of the noble princes and ancient barons of high authority who held great power. He had his aunt killed and confiscated her possessions. He had all the noblest men of Rome executed or exiled, and he killed their children. He had a cruel man from Egypt taught how to eat raw human flesh so that he could have them eaten alive. What more should I tell you? One cannot recount all his wickedness and evil. This depravity came to a head when he had fires started throughout the city of Rome, which raged for six days and nights. Many people died in this disaster. Watching a tower collapse in flames, he rejoiced at the beauty of the fire and began to sing. He had the saints Peter and Paul and many other martyrs executed as his dinner entertainment. After he had ruled for fourteen years, the Romans who had suffered too much from his actions revolted against him. He despaired and took his own life."

49. CONCERNING THE EMPEROR GALBA AND OTHERS.

II.49.1 "Do you think I told you about Nero's depravity and wickedness in order to shock you? I assure you that the emperor who succeeded him, who was named Galba, would hardly have been any better, if he had lived as long. His cruelty was boundless, and in addition to his other vices, he was so capricious that he was always vacillating and never stable, now cruel and lacking self-control, now excessively soft and lacking justice, negligent, envious, and suspicious, with little love for his princes and knights, cowardly and fearful-hearted and greedy for everything. He ruled only six months, for he was murdered in order to put an end to his cruelty.

II.49.2 "And how much more was Otho worth, the emperor who succeeded him? Indeed, for all that they say about women being fastidious, this man had such a pretty and delicate body that nothing else was softer. With his servile heart he sought only his own ease—a voracious thief, an extravagant fool, and an unsurpassed glutton, a weak, self-indulgent, and faithless traitor filled with arrogance and depravity. And the end came to him in suicide—he killed himself after a reign of three months because his enemies had won a victory over him.

"Vitellius, who succeeded Otho, was in no way better, *II.49.3*
but full of perversion. I do not know what more I can
say. Do not think I am lying to you. Read the histories
of the emperors and the accounts of their lives and you
will find that a very small number of the total—as many
as there were—were good, upright, and constant, such as
Julius Caesar, Octavian, Trajan, and Titus. But I assure
you that for every one of these virtuous emperors, you
will find ten very bad ones.

"Let me also tell you about the popes and churchmen, *II.49.4*
who must be more perfect and more elect than other
people. But, whereas in the early Church they were holy,
ever since Constantine endowed the Church with large
revenues and riches, the remaining holiness . . . well, you
only have to read through their histories and chronicles.
If you claimed that these things used to be good and
remain so, you need only consider all sorts and conditions
of men to decide whether the world is improving and
whether the words and deeds of temporal and spiritual
princes show much firmness and constancy. The point is
clear—I will not say more. For this reason I do not know
why men speak of women's capriciousness and fickleness,
and why they are not ashamed to talk about it when they
see that their own actions, *not* those of women, show so
little constancy and steadfastness that their behavior
appears childish. They should also consider how well the
propositions and agreements which they make in council
are upheld!

"And to define exactly inconstancy and changeable- *II.49.5*
ness, they are nothing but acting against the commands
of Reason, for it exhorts every reasonable creature to act
well. When a man or a woman allows regard for Reason
to be conquered by sensuality, this is frailty or inconstancy, and the deeper one falls into error or sin, the
greater the weakness is, the more one is removed from
regard for Reason. Therefore, it turns out, according to
what the histories recount—and I believe experience
does not contradict this—that, regardless of what philos-

ophers and other authors may say about the changeableness of women, you will never find such perversion in women as you encounter in a great number of men. The most evil women whom you will find written about were Athalis and Jezebel, her mother, queens of Jerusalem, who persecuted the people of Israel; Brunhilde, queen of France; and several others. But consider, for my sake, the perversity of Judas Iscariot who cruelly betrayed his good Master whose apostle he was and who had done so many good things for him, or the harshness and cruelty of the Jews and of the people of Israel who killed not only Jesus Christ out of envy but also several holy prophets who lived before him as well: they murdered some, and slaughtered the others with other methods. Take the example of Julian the Apostate, whom some consider to have been one of the Antichrists because of his perversity, or of Denis, the treacherous tyrant of Sicily, who was so detestable that just reading about his life is a dishonest act, and along with these consider all the evil kings in various countries, disloyal emperors, heretical popes, and other unbelieving prelates filled with greed— the Antichrists who must come—and you will find that men should really keep quiet and that women should bless and praise God who placed their precious souls in feminine vessels. I will be quiet about all of that. In order to refute with examples the comments of these men who have called women so weak, I will tell you about several very strong women, whose exemplary stories are wonderful to hear."

50. SHE SPEAKS OF GRISELDA, THE MARQUISE OF SALUCES, A WOMAN STRONG IN VIRTUE.

II.50.1   "It is written that there was a marquis of Saluces named Gualtieri. He was a handsome and honest man, but he behaved in an extraordinarily strange manner. His barons would frequently admonish him to marry in order to have a successor. After refusing for a long time, he finally agreed to marry on the condition that they promise to accept whatever woman he might choose, and his barons agreed and swore to this. The marquis often took pleasure in hunting birds and game. Near his fortress was a small country village where a weak, old, and impoverished peasant named Giannucolo lived among the poor laborers there. He had been a good and upright man all his life. This honest man had an eighteen-year-old daughter, named Griselda, who waited upon him with great diligence and supported him with her spinning. The marquis, who often passed by the village, had carefully noted this maiden's upright conduct and integrity, as well as the beauty of her body and face, and therefore he held her in great favor. It happened that the marquis, after having agreed with his barons to take a wife, told them to assemble on a particular day for his wedding, and he ordered all ladies to be present. He had magnificent preparations made, and on the appointed day, after everyone was assembled before him, he had the entire company mount on horseback to accompany him as he sought his bride. He went straight to Giannucolo's house and met Griselda, who was coming back from the fountain with a jug of water on her head. He asked her where her father was, and Griselda knelt down and told the marquis that her father was at home. 'Go fetch him,' he ordered. When the good man arrived, the marquis told him that he wished to marry his daughter. Giannucolo answered that he should do his will, whereupon the ladies entered the little cottage and dressed and adorned the bride in the noble fashion befitting the position of the marquis—with the robes and jewels which he had had readied. Then he brought her to the palace, where he married her. And to make the story short, this lady conducted herself so well toward everyone that the nobles—both the great and minor nobility—and the people greatly loved her and she handled herself to the satisfaction of all and served and cherished her lord as she should have. That year the marquise bore a daughter whose birth was received with great joy, but when the

171   *Christine de Pizan*

child was old enough to be weaned, the marquis, in order to test Griselda's constancy and patience, made her believe that the barons were unhappy that one of her descendants would reign over them and therefore wished the child killed. To this matter (which would be difficult for any mother) Griselda replied that the daughter was his and that the nobles should do as they pleased, and so she gave the child to one of the marquis' squires, who, all the while pretending to have come to fetch the child to kill her, brought her secretly to Bologna to the countess of Panico (a sister of the marquis) for her to shelter and nourish the child. At the end of the following year, the marquise was pregnant and bore a most beautiful son who was joyfully received. Once again the marquis wished to test his wife and told her that the boy would have to be killed to satisfy his barons and subjects. And the lady replied that if her son's death was not enough, she was ready to die if he wanted. So she gave her son to the squire, just as she had done with her daughter, without showing the slightest trace of sadness, nor did she say anything except to beg the squire to bury the child after killing him so that wild beasts and birds would not eat the infant's tender flesh. Faced with such overwhelming harshness, Griselda showed not the slightest change. The marquis, however, did not stop at this but wanted to test her once more. They had been together twelve years, during which time the good lady had acted so well that it should have been more than enough proof of her virtue, when one day the marquis summoned her to his chamber and told her that he was unpopular with his subjects and his people and in danger of losing his dominion because of her, for they felt too much of an aversion to his keeping Giannucolo's daughter as his lady and mistress. Therefore it was necessary, if he wanted to appease his subjects, for her to return to her father's house and for him to marry another, more noble woman. To this proposal, which must have been extremely harsh and severe for her, Griselda replied, 'I have always known very well and often thought there could never be any comparison between your nobility and magnificence and my poverty, nor have I ever reputed myself worthy enough to be either your wife or your maid. From this moment on, I am ready to return to my father's house, where I will spend my old age. As for the dowry which you commanded me to bring, I know, as you well realize, that when you received me at the door of my father's house, you had me stripped completely naked and dressed in the robes with which I came into your company, nor did I bring any other dowry besides faith, maturity, love, reverence, and poverty. Therefore it is right that I restore your property to you. Here is the dress which I myself will strip off, and let me give you back the ring with which you married me, and I will return to you all the other jewels, rings, vestments, and ornaments with which I was adorned and enriched in your chamber. I left my father's house completely naked and I will return there completely naked, except that it does not appear fitting to me that this womb, wherein lay the children which you fathered, should appear totally naked before the people, and so for this reason, if it pleases you, and for no other, I beg you in compensation for my virginity (which I brought when I came into your palace and which I cannot take back with me when I leave it) that a single slip be granted to me, with which I shall cover the womb of your former wife and marquise.' The marquis could hardly keep himself from weeping out of compassion; yet he overcame his feelings, and leaving his chamber he ordered that a single slip be given to her.

"Then Griselda stripped herself before all the knights   II.50.2
and ladies, removing her shoes and all her jewelry, and she had on nothing except her slip. The rumor had spread everywhere that the marquis intended to divorce his wife, and all his subjects arrived at the palace much grieved at the news. And Griselda, completely naked except for her slip, bare-headed, and barefoot, mounted a horse and rode out, accompanied by the barons, knights, and ladies,

who all wept, cursing the marquis and mourning the lady's goodness. But Griselda herself never shed a tear. She was conveyed to the house of her father, that old man who had always been in doubt about this whole affair, thinking that her lord would one day grow tired of his poor marriage. Hearing the uproar, he went out to meet his daughter and brought her an old torn tunic of hers which he had kept, and he covered her with it, showing not the least sign of grief. So Griselda remained with her father for some time, living in humility and poverty and serving her father as she had done before, without a single trace of sadness or regret; rather, she comforted her father in his grief at seeing his daughter fall from such a great height to such lowly poverty.

II.50.3   "When it seemed to the marquis that he had sufficiently tested his loyal wife, he ordered his sister to come to him in the noble company of lords and ladies and to bring his two children without giving the least hint that they were his. He informed his barons and subjects that he intended to take a new wife, to marry a most noble maiden whom his sister had in tutelage. He had a handsome company of knights and ladies assembled in his palace on the day when his sister was supposed to arrive. He also had a great celebration readied. He gave Griselda the following orders: 'Griselda, the maiden whom I will marry will be here tomorrow, and because I want my sister and her entire noble company to be magnificently received, and since you know my customs and are familiar with the chambers and rooms, I want you to be in charge. All the servants shall obey you so that each member of the company can be received according to his rank, particularly my bride-to-be. Take care that everything is well arranged.' Griselda replied that she would gladly do this. The following day when the company had arrived, the celebration was magnificent. Even in spite of her shabby dress Griselda did not hesitate to go out with a glad face to meet the maiden who, she believed, would be the new bride. Humbly curtseying to her, Griselda said, 'My lady, you are most welcome.' She curtseyed to her son and to all the members of the company and she received each cordially, according to their rank. Even though she was dressed so poorly, it was perfectly clear from her bearing that she was a woman of the highest distinction and prudence so that the strangers wondered how such eloquence and honor could simultaneously be present with such poverty. Griselda had arranged everything so well that nothing was out of place. But she was drawn so strongly to the maiden and to her son that she could not leave and she carefully took note of their beauty which she greatly praised. The marquis himself had arranged everything to look as though he were going to marry the maiden. When the time came to celebrate the Mass, the marquis came forward, and in front of all, called to Griselda and said to her before everyone, 'What do you think, Griselda, of my new bride? Is she not beautiful and upright?' She answered loudly, 'Indeed, my lord, there is no woman more beautiful or more upright. I would however make a single request of you and give you only one bit of advice: that you neither trouble nor needle her with the torments which you inflicted upon your first wife. This woman is younger and has been raised more delicately so that she probably cannot bear as much as your other wife did.' The marquis, hearing Griselda's words, recalled her unsurpassed steadfastness, strength, and constancy and was filled with admiration for her virtue. Pity overwhelmed him because he had made and was making her suffer so much and for so long and so undeservedly. Thereupon, in the presence of all, he began to speak:

"'Griselda, this is a sufficient test of your constancy *II.50.4* and of the faith, loyalty and great love, obedience and proven humility which you feel for me. Rest assured that there is no man under the heavens who has come to know the love of the marriage bond through so many trials as I have with you.' Then the marquis approached her, embraced her warmly, kissed her, and said, 'You alone are my wife, I want no other and will have no other. This young girl, who you thought was to be my wife, is your daughter and mine, and this other child is your son. Let all who are here know that everything which I have done has been to test my loyal wife and not to condemn her. I have had my children raised in Bologna with my sister and I did not have them killed—they are right here.' Hearing the words of her lord, the marquise fainted with joy; when she came to, she took her children in her arms and they were soon wet with her tears. There is not the slightest doubt that her heart was filled with great joy. Everyone who saw this wept for joy and pity. Griselda was restored to greater authority than ever before and she was richly fitted out and bejeweled. The celebration was magnificent and joyful, and during it, all spoke in praise of this lady. They lived together another twenty years in joy and peace. The marquis also summoned to the palace Giannucolo, his wife's father, whom he had ignored in the past, and he held him in high esteem. He married his children in great honor. His son succeeded him following his death with the barons' assent."

51. HERE SHE SPEAKS OF FLORENCE OF ROME.

II.51.1   "Just as is written in the *Miracles de Nostre Dame*, the noble Florence, empress of Rome, endured great adversity with amazing patience and greatly resembled Griselda, marquise of Saluces, in strength and constancy of character. This lady was overwhelmingly beautiful and even more chaste and virtuous. Her husband once had to go off on a very long voyage to a distant war and so left the care of his land and wife to a brother of his who, tempted by the devil after the emperor's departure, foolishly desired his sister-in-law Florence. Put briefly, he imposed severe restrictions on her to compel her to do his will either out of fear or, if his entreaties were of no avail, forcibly. The lady had him imprisoned in a tower, and he remained there until the emperor's return. When the news came of the emperor's return, the lady, never imagining her brother-in-law would slander her, had him released so that the emperor would not learn of his brother's treachery and so that he could go out to meet him. But when he arrived before the emperor, he accused the lady of every possible evil, as though she were the most immoral woman ever, and he claimed she had held him in prison in order to carry out her own evil will rather than to follow the emperor's command. Believing his brother's story and without mentioning any of this, the emperor ordered his servants to kill her before he arrived, for he did not wish to see her nor find her alive. However, while astounded by these reports, she managed to beg the servants who had been commissioned to kill her to let her live incognito. Through a strange twist of fate this noble lady came to be entrusted with watching over the child of a great prince. It happened that the prince's brother was so smitten with love for her that, when she would not consent to his numerous petitions, in his spite and in order to destroy her, he killed the little child next to her while she slept. This noble lady endured with great patience and strong, unfailing courage all of these not inconsiderable adversities. After she had been led to the place where she was to be executed as the child's presumed murderer, the lord and lady were over-whelmed with such pity that, for the sake of her fair life and outstanding virtues which they had noted, they did not have the heart to put her to death and instead sent her into exile. Once, during her exile, in all her poverty, long-suffering, and devotion to God and His gentle mother, she fell asleep in a garden after saying her prayers. There she beheld a vision of the Virgin who told her to pick a certain plant which grew under her head, so that she could earn her living by curing every illness with this plant. After a time, thanks to this very plant, the lady, who had already healed so many illnesses, became famous everywhere. Then it happened that God willed that the prince's brother, who had killed the child, should fall ill with a most horrible sickness, and Florence was summoned to heal him. After coming into his presence, she told him that he should know that God was punishing him with His scourges and that if he publicly acknowledged his sin, then he would be cured, but otherwise she could not heal him. Then, moved by great contrition, he confessed his horrible misdeed and told how he himself had killed the child, although he had blamed the good lady who had cared for the child. The prince was furious and wanted to exact justice from his brother at all costs. The noble lady interceded and calmed the prince and cured his brother. In this way she returned good for evil to him, according to God's commandment. Likewise, not long afterward, it happened that the emperor's brother, on whose account Florence had first been exiled, fell sick with such horrible leprosy that his body was almost completely putrid. But, since the news that there was a woman who could cure every sickness had spread everywhere in the world, Florence was summoned by the emperor without his knowing who she was, for he thought that his wife was long dead. When she appeared before the emperor's brother, she told him he must confess publicly, otherwise she could not cure him. Finally, after refusing for a long time, he confessed the entire evil deed which he had without reason or cause perpetrated against the empress, and it was for this sin, he knew, that God was punishing him. Upon hearing this, the emperor flew into a rage because he thought on this account that he had had his beloved wife put to death. He wanted to kill his brother, but the good lady appeared and pacified the emperor. And so Florence regained her standing and good fortune by virtue of her patience, to the great joy of the emperor and all the people."

52. CONCERNING THE WIFE OF BERNABO THE GENOVAN.

II.52.1 "Moreover, as part of the discussion of constant and wise women, the story related by Boccaccio in his *Decameron* might be mentioned, about how several Lombard and Italian merchants in Paris, dining together, came to speak of their wives. A Genovan among them, named Bernabo, began to praise his wife for her beauty, her wit, her virtue, and above all else, for her chastity. There was a disreputable man in this company named Ambrose, who claimed that it was foolish to praise a wife so much, especially for her chastity, since there was no woman, however strong, whom a man could not eventually seduce if he plied her with enough gifts, promises, and fair words. A great dispute on this topic arose, and it went so far that they wagered a sum of five thousand florins. Bernabo bet that Ambrose would never succeed in sleeping with his wife, in spite of all his influence. Ambrose wagered he would bring back such unimpeachable proof that Bernabo would be convinced. The others took great pains to break up the quarrel, but nothing worked. Ambrose left as quickly as he could and went to Genoa. Upon his arrival he inquired in some detail into the conduct of Bernabo's wife. But, to put the matter briefly, he heard so much about her virtue that he lost all hope of ever getting very far. He found himself dumbfounded and sorry for having been such a fool. Therefore he devised a malicious plot, because it grieved him to lose five thousand florins in such a stupid bet. He did, however, manage to speak with a poor old woman who lived in the lady's household. He paid her so much money, and promised her even more, that he was able to hide himself in a chest in the lady's bedroom. The old woman gave her lady to understand that in this chest entrusted to her care were many beautiful objects which thieves had tried to steal. For this reason she asked her lady to watch over the chest for a short time in her bedroom until the people to whom the objects belonged returned. The lady granted her request gladly. Ambrose, inside the chest, spied on the lady at night until he saw her completely naked. He also took a small purse and a belt which the lady had had richly embroidered with needlework, after which he slipped back into the chest so quietly that the lady, who was asleep, and her small daughter, whom she had with her, heard nothing. Three days later the old woman returned and asked for the chest. Extremely happy at the thought he had acted quite cleverly, Ambrose reported to Bernabo in front of this company that he had indeed—and with ease—slept with Bernabo's wife. First of all he described the layout of the bedroom and the paintings hanging there. Then he showed Bernabo the purse and belt which Bernabo recognized immediately, and he claimed that Bernabo's wife had given them to him. Last of all, after describing her naked body, he recounted how she had a mark like a purplish wart under her left breast. Bernabo firmly believed Ambrose on the basis of this evidence and he was, of course, grieved. Nevertheless, fully satisfied, he paid Ambrose the five thousand florins. He left as quickly as he could for Genoa, but before arriving he expressly ordered one of his retainers, who managed his property and in whom he entrusted all his affairs, to kill his wife, explaining why and how she should be killed. According to this order the retainer was to have Bernabo's wife ride out with him in the belief that the retainer was leading her to meet her husband. The lady, gladly and joyfully believing the retainer, went with him. Arriving in a wood, he told her why he had to kill her in accordance with her husband's order. In brief, this fair and good lady knew how to handle this retainer so well that she succeeded in persuading him to let her go on her promise to leave the country. Having escaped, she made her way into a village where she convinced a good woman to sell her some men's clothing. She cut her hair short and disguised herself as a young man. She succeeded in securing herself a place in the service of a rich man from Catalonia named Señor Ferant, who had just disembarked from his ship in port in order to rest and refresh himself. She waited on him so diligently that he considered himself well served; he claimed that he had never found such a good servant. The lady called herself Sagurat da Finoli.

Returning to his ship with Sagurat, Señor Ferant traveled by sea to Alexandria, and there he bought extraordinarily fine falcons and horses. Then he traveled to the sultan of Babylon, a good friend of his. After he had resided there for some time, the sultan took notice of Sagurat, who so diligently served his master and who seemed to the sultan to be so fair and gracious that the sultan requested Señor Ferant to let him have Sagurat as his own servant, adding that he would be a good master. Although it pained him, Señor Ferant obliged the sultan. In short, Sagurat served the sultan so well that the sultan confided only in him. The sultan was such a powerful ruler that he governed practically everything around him. It happened that a very large fair was to be held in one of the sultan's cities, to which merchants from everywhere were invited. The sultan ordered Sagurat to go to this city in order to observe the fair and to look after his interests. It turned out, just as God willed, that this same false Ambrose, considerably enriched by Bernabo's wealth, came there in the company of other Italians who had brought jewels. Sagurat, in his capacity as the sultan's deputy in the city, was honored by all. Because he was such a great ruler and master, every day the merchants, including Ambrose among others, would bring him exotic jewels to sell. When it happened that Ambrose opened a small case filled with jewels in front of Sagurat for him to inspect, the small purse and belt mentioned above were in the case. Seeing the purse, Sagurat recognized it and took it in hand and examined it closely, wondering how it could have gotten there. Ambrose, not at all thinking of any risk, began to smile. Seeing him smile, Sagurat said, 'Friend, I think you are smiling at my amusement over this little purse—a woman's possession—but it is quite beautiful.' Ambrose replied, 'My lord, it is at your disposal, but I am really smiling because I am reminded of the way in which I got it.' 'God bless you,' said Sagurat, 'tell me how you got it.' 'In good faith,' said Ambrose, 'I got it from a beautiful woman who gave it to me after I slept with her once, and with this purse I won a bet of five thousand florins from the woman's foolish husband, who was named Bernabo and who dared to bet me that I could never get his wife into bed. The unfortunate fellow killed his wife on account of this, though he deserved punishment more than she did, for a man should know that every woman is weak and easily seduced, and therefore he shouldn't be too confident.' The lady immediately realized the cause of her husband's anger, which she had never known. But being as prudent and firm as she was, she hid her reaction until the right time and place. She appeared greatly relieved and told him that he was a very fine fellow, that she wanted to be good friends with him and that she wished him to remain in the country and handle a lot of trading for them both, for which she would entrust to him a great deal of money for them both. Ambrose was quite happy with this. Indeed, Sagurat even had a residence built for him, and in order to deceive him all the better, put much money in his hands and showed him so much affection that he spent every day with Sagurat. She had him recount his prank in front of the sultan, as if to make him laugh. To tell briefly how the matter ended, upon learning that Bernabo had fallen into poverty, as much because of the large sum he had wagered away as because of the troubles he had had, Sagurat had a Genovan residing in this country have Bernabo brought, on the sultan's orders. Arriving before the sultan, Sagurat immediately summoned Ambrose. But she let the sultan know in advance that Ambrose was lying when he boasted of having slept with the lady. Sagurat asked the sultan to punish Ambrose justly, according to the merits of the case, if the truth should ever come to his knowledge, and the sultan agreed.

II.52.2   "While Bernabo and Ambrose stood before the sultan, Sagurat began to speak, 'Ambrose, it pleases our sire, the sultan, that you recount at length the prank and how you won from Bernabo, whom you see here, the five thousand florins which you bet him and how you slept with his wife.' Thereupon Ambrose changed color like someone in whom such fraudulent treachery could hardly overcome the truth, for the matter had arisen too suddenly for him to put up his guard. Nevertheless, he regained his composure somewhat and replied, 'My lord, it could never be important for me to tell all this. Bernabo knows it well enough already. I am ashamed on account of his shame.' Then Bernabo, filled with pain and shame, begged never to hear of the matter again and to be allowed to go. But Sagurat answered, smiling, that Bernabo should not be angered and that it was necessary for the matter to be heard. Seeing that he was going to be forced to speak, Ambrose began to relate the story with a trembling voice, just as he had first given Bernabo to understand it and as he had also told them. At the conclusion of the speech, Sagurat asked Bernabo if what Ambrose had said was true, and he replied that it was so, without a doubt. 'And how,' asked Sagurat, 'could you be so sure that this man slept with your wife? Even if he produced some evidence, are you so stupid not to know that he could have found out how her body looked through deceit, without ever having slept with her? And for this reason you put her to death? You deserve to die for not having sufficient proof!' Bernabo became quite afraid. Sagurat, not wanting to delay beyond what seemed to her the right time to speak, said to Ambrose, 'False and disloyal villain, tell the truth, tell the truth so I won't have to have you tortured to get it out of you. For you must tell the truth now, since it is certain you were lying through your false mouth about what you said. The woman whom you boast about is not dead, but rather is close enough to you to contradict your treacherous lies, for you never touched her, and that is a fact.' The assembly, filled with many of the sultan's barons and a large number of Lombards, heard this exchange with astonishment. And, to put the matter briefly, Ambrose was under so much pressure that he confessed in front of the sultan and all present the entire fraud which he had perpetrated in his greed for the five thousand florins. Hearing this, Bernabo practically went out of his mind because he thought his wife had been killed. But the good lady approached him and asked, 'What would you give, Bernabo, to the person who could bring back your wife alive and chaste?' Bernabo said that he would give all he could pay. Then she said to him, 'Bernabo, brother and friend, don't you recognize me?' And since he was so stunned that he had no idea what he was doing, she unbuttoned her breast-plate and said, 'Look, Bernabo, I am your loyal companion whom you condemned to death without reason.' They joyfully embraced. The sultan and all present were extremely amazed by this event, and they greatly praised this lady's virtue. She received wonderful gifts and all the property belonging to Ambrose, whom the sultan had executed in a most painful way. Afterward Bernabo and his wife returned to their own land."

53. AFTER RECTITUDE LISTS THE CONSTANT WOMEN, CHRISTINE ASKS HER WHY ALL THE VALIANT WOMEN WHO HAVE LIVED HAVE NOT OBJECTED TO THE BOOKS AND MEN WHO SPEAK BADLY ABOUT THEM; AND RECTITUDE ANSWERS.

II.53.1   After this story, Rectitude told me many others which I will omit for the sake of brevity, such as, for instance, the one about Leaena, a Greek woman who, in spite of all the torture used on her, refused to accuse the two men with whom she was associated, but instead bit her own tongue off with her teeth in front of the judge so that he would have no chance of making her talk using torture. Rectitude also told me about many other women who were of such constant heart that they preferred to die by drinking poison rather than turn against righteousness and truth. Thereupon I said to Rectitude, "My lady, you have demonstrated for me women's great constancy of heart and all their other virtues so well that no one could say anything better about any man. For this reason I am surprised that so many valiant ladies, who were both extremely wise and literate and who could compose and dictate their beautiful books in such a fair style, suffered so long without protesting against the horrors charged by different men when they knew that these men were greatly mistaken."

She replied, "My dear friend, this question is quite easy to answer. You can see from what has been said to you before how all the ladies whose outstanding virtues I told you about above occupied their minds in various specialized works and not at all in any one activity. The composition of this work has been reserved for you and not for them, for their works have been written to benefit people of clear understanding and true discernment, without their having written any other work on the subject. As for the length of time that has passed in which these accusations and slanders have gone uncontradicted, let me tell you that in the long run, everything comes to a head at the right time, for how could God have long tolerated in the world heresies against His holy law, which were eradicated with such great difficulty and which would still persist today if they had not been challenged and overcome? It is the same with many other things which were tolerated for a long time, but which were then debated and disproved."

Thereupon I, Christine, once more addressed her. *II.53.2* "My lady, you have spoken quite well but I am certain that many complaints will arise among the detractors of this present work, for they will claim that it may be true that some women have been or are good, but that all women are not good, not even the majority."

She answered, "It is wrong to say that the majority of women are not good. This is well proven from what I have told you before about the experiences evident every day in their prayers and charitable acts and virtues and from the fact that the great horrors and evils perpetrated in the world do not come about because of them. But what a surprise that *all* women are not good! In the entire city of Nineveh, which was so large, not a single good man could be found when Jonah the prophet went there on behalf of our Lord to destroy it unless it turned away from its evil. It was even worse in the city of Sodom, as was obvious when fire from Heaven destroyed it after Lot's departure. Moreover, note that in the company of Jesus Christ, where there were only twelve men, there was still one very bad man among them. And men dare to say that all women must be good and that one should stone those who are not! I would simply ask them to look at themselves and then let him who is without sin cast the first stone! And what are they supposed to be? Indeed, I maintain that when men are perfect, women will follow their example."

54. CHRISTINE ASKS RECTITUDE WHETHER WHAT MANY MEN SAY IS TRUE, THAT SO FEW WOMEN ARE FAITHFUL IN THEIR LOVE LIVES; AND RECTITUDE'S ANSWER.

II.54.1   Proceeding further, I, Christine, again spoke, "My lady, let us now move on to other questions and for a short while go beyond the topics developed up to now, for I would like to ask you several questions, if I were sure that they would not bother you, since the subject I want to discuss goes somewhat beyond the temperament of reason."

She replied to me, "Friend, ask what you like, for the disciple who must ask the master questions in order to learn ought not to suffer reproof for inquiring about everything."

"My lady, a natural behavior of men toward women and of women toward men prevails in the world which is not brought about by human institutions but by the inclination of the flesh, and in which men and women love one another with a very strong love strengthened in turn by foolish pleasure. And they do not know for what reason and to what end such a mutual love is implanted in them. Men usually claim that women, in spite of everything they promise regarding this widespread passion usually called one's 'love life,' are rarely constant, not very loving, and amazingly false and fickle. All of this stems from the frivolousness of their hearts. Among other Latins authors who level this charge is Ovid, who makes serious accusations in his *Ars amatoria*. When he finishes his attack, Ovid (as well as others) says that everything contained in his books regarding women's deceptive manners and malice was for the benefit of the common good, in order to warn men about women's ruses so that they could better avoid them, like the snake hidden in the grass. If you would, dear lady, teach me the truth of this matter."

She replied, "Dear friend, as for the charge that women are deceitful, I really do not know what more I can say to you, for you yourself have adequately handled the subject, answering Ovid and the others in your *Epistre au Dieu d'Amour* and your *Epistres sur le Roman de la Rose*. But, as for the point you mention that these men attack women for the sake of the common good, I can show you that it has never been a question of this. And here is the reason: the common good of a city or land or any community of people is nothing other than the profit or general good in which all members, women as well as men, participate and take part. But whatever is done with the intention of benefiting some and not others is a matter of private and not public welfare. Even less so is an activity in which one takes from some and gives to others, and such an activity is perpetrated for the sake of private gain, and at the same time it constitutes, quite simply, a crime committed for the benefit of one person and to the disadvantage of the other. For they never address women nor warn them against men's traps even though it is certain that men frequently deceive women with their fast tricks and duplicity. There is not the slightest doubt that women belong to the people of God and the human race as much as men, and are not another species or dissimilar race, for which they should be excluded from moral teachings. Therefore, I conclude that if these men had acted in the public good—that is, for both parties—they should also have addressed themselves to women and warned them to beware of men's tricks just as they warned men to be careful about women. But leaving behind these questions and pursuing the others, that is, whether women show so little love where they set their hearts and whether women are more constant than these men claim, it will be enough for me to deduce the point for you from examples of women who persevered in their love until death. First, I will tell you of the noble Dido, queen of Carthage, whose great value I discussed above and which you yourself have spoken of earlier in your works."

55. CONCERNING DIDO, QUEEN OF CARTHAGE, ON THE SUBJECT OF CONSTANT LOVE IN WOMEN.

II.55.1   "Just as was said above, during the time in which Dido, queen of Carthage, was living happily in her city and ruling gloriously in peace, it happened by chance that Aeneas, fugitive from Troy following its destruction, leader and captain of many Trojans, tossed about by many storms, his ships wrecked and provisions exhausted, having lost many of his men, in need of rest, out of money, weary of wandering at sea, and in need of shelter, arrived in the port of Carthage. And when, out of fear of inadvertently landing without permission, he sent to the queen to know whether it would please her that he come into port, the noble lady, full of honor and valiance and well aware that the Trojans enjoyed a better reputation than any other nation of the world at that time and that Aeneas was of the royal house of Troy, not only gave him leave to land but also went out with a most noble company of barons and ladies and maidens to the shore to meet him and there received him and his entire company with the greatest honor. She brought him into her city and honored and feasted him and put him at ease. Why should I give you a long account? Aeneas was able to rest so long there that he hardly recalled the torments he had suffered. Dido and Aeneas spent so much time with one another that Love, who knows how to subjugate all hearts with the greatest of skill, made them become enamored of one another. But as experience showed, Dido's love for Aeneas was far greater than his love for her, for even though he had given her his pledge never to take any other woman and to be hers forever, he left after she had restored and enriched him with property and ease, his ships refreshed, repaired, and placed in order, filled with treasure and wealth, like a woman who had spared no expense where her heart was involved. He departed at night, secretly and treacherously, without farewells and without her knowledge. This was how he repaid his hostess. His departure caused so much grief for the unhappy Dido, who had loved too much, that she wished to renounce all joy and her own life. Indeed, after lamenting a great deal, she threw herself into a large fire which she had lit. Others say she killed herself with Aeneas' own sword. And so the noble queen Dido died in such a pitiful manner, who has been honored so greatly that her fame has surpassed that of all other women of her time."

56. CONCERNING MEDEA IN LOVE.

"Medea, daughter of the king of Colchis, and who possessed such great knowledge, loved Jason with a too great and too constant love. This Jason was a knight of Greece and exceedingly brave at arms. He had heard that on the island of Colchis— which was part of the country over which Medea's father was king— there lived a marvelous golden sheep, protected by different enchantments and that, even though the fleece of this sheep seemed impossible to win, it was nevertheless prophesied that a knight would win it. On hearing this, Jason, eager to increase his fame even more, left Greece with a large company seeking to test himself in such a quest. After arriving in Colchis, the king of the land told him that it was impossible for the Golden Fleece to be won by arms

II.56.1

or by any man's bravery because it was enchanted and that many knights had perished trying; therefore he should not risk losing his life in such a quick way. Jason replied that since he had undertaken the quest he would not abandon it out of fear of death. Medea, the king's daughter, noting Jason's beauty, royal lineage, and fame, and seeing that he would make a good husband for her and that she could not make better use of her love elsewhere, resolved to protect him from death, for too much pity overwhelmed her at the thought that this knight would have to die in such a way, and so she spoke to him for a long time at leisure. Put briefly, she gave him charms and enchantments, and, in her expertise, she taught him how to win the Golden Fleece on the condition that Jason promise to take her as his wife and no other woman and to show her forever loyal faith and love. However, Jason lied about his promise, for after everything went just as he wanted, he left Medea for another woman. For this reason, Medea, who would rather have destroyed herself than do anything of this kind to him, turned despondent, nor did her heart ever again feel goodness or joy.

57. CONCERNING THISBE.

II.57.1 "Just as you know, Ovid tells in his *Metamorphoses* that in the city of Babylon there were two wealthy noblemen who were such close neighbors that the walls of the palaces in which they resided were joined together. They had two children, fair and comely above all others; the one, a son named Pyramus, the other, a daughter named Thisbe. Even at the age of seven these two children were without malice and loved each other so perfectly that one could not live without the other. They were anxious to get up in the morning and take their meals at home so that they could go out and play with the other children and find one another. The two children were always seen together at play. So it remained for a very long time until they were grown, and their love's flame waxed in their hearts at the same rate that their age increased—so much so that suspicions arose, so frequent were their meetings. For this reason, the situation was reported to Thisbe's mother who locked her up in her chambers, saying angrily that she would protect her daughter from Pyramus' obsession. The children were overwhelmingly grieved at this imprisonment, and their cries and complaints were quite pitiful. Their grief at not being able to see one another was too hard for them. This distress lasted for a long time but in no way lessened or diminished their love. Even if they did not see one another, they grew stronger according to the manner of their years until they reached the age of fifteen. One day, as Fortune would have it, it happened that Thisbe, who could think of nothing except Pyramus, sat alone in her room, completely exhausted from weeping, and, looking at the wall between the two palaces, pitifully spoke, 'Oh hard stone wall which separates my love and me, if you had any pity, you would crack open so that I could see him whom I desire so much.' Just as she spoke these words, she saw by chance that the wall had a crack through which filtered light from the other side. She immediately rushed to the crack and, with the clip of her belt buckle—for she had no other tool—she opened up the hole somewhat until she could stick the clip all the way through so that Pyramus might see it—which in fact happened. And after the two lovers had frequently met, thanks to this sign, and spoken together at this crack where they made their piteous complaints, at last, overwhelmed by too much love, they plotted how they would flee from their parents secretly, by night, and meet outside the city near a spring, under a white mulberry tree where they had used to play in their childhood. After Thisbe—who loved the more—had arrived first at the spring, she was frightened away while she waited for her lover by a roaring lion whom she heard come to drink at the spring, and she fled and hid herself in a bush nearby. As she fled, she dropped a white scarf which she had and upon which the lion vomited the entrails of the animals it had devoured. Pyramus arrived before Thisbe could dare to budge from the bush, and seeing in the moonlight Thisbe's scarf covered with entrails, he firmly believed that his love had been devoured. He felt such grief that he killed himself with his sword, and as he was dying Thisbe arrived and found him. Seeing him clutching her scarf to his breast, she knew the cause of this misfortune and felt such grief that she did not wish to live any longer. Seeing her lover's spirit pass away, she mourned piteously and then killed herself with the same sword."

58. HERE SHE SPEAKS OF HERO.

II.58.1   "Hero, the noble maid, loved Leander no less than Thisbe loved Pyramus. In order to protect Hero's honor, Leander preferred to expose himself to great danger rather than go to her gaily in view of all. In order to hide their love, he often resorted to the following manner of seeing his lady: he would quickly leave his bed at night, without anyone noticing, and then, completely alone, he would go to a wide branch of the sea called the Hellespont and, completely nude, he would swim across it to a castle called Abydos which lay on the other shore where Hero lived and where she would wait for him at a window. During the long, dark winter nights she would hold up a lit torch from the window to show him the right direction to come to her. The two lovers spent several years in this way until Fortune grew jealous of their happy life and wished to turn them away from it, for once it happened, during the winter, that the sea turned tempestuous, rough, turbulent, and dangerous from a storm. This storm lasted so long without let-up that the long wait to see one another distressed the two lovers, and they lamented the wind and stormy weather which lasted so long. Finally, one night, seeing the torch which Hero was holding at the window and driven too much by his great desire, Leander thought that Hero was signaling to him and that it would be considered great cowardice on his part if he did not go, regardless of whatever danger he would place himself in. Alas! The unfortunate maid, who was afraid and who would, of course, have forbidden him to come and to put himself in such danger if she could have, held up the torch by chance to give him the right direction in case he risked it. And so the misfortune came to pass that Leander, stripped down, could not struggle against the waves which carried him so far away that he could not help but drown. Poor Hero, whose heart told her what had happened, could not stop weeping. At dawn, unable to rest or sleep, she went back to the window where she had been all night. She saw her lover's dead body floating on top of the waves and, having no desire to live on after him, she threw herself into the sea. She managed to swim out and embrace his body and so perished from having loved too much."

59. CONCERNING GHISMONDA, DAUGHTER OF THE PRINCE OF SALERNO.

"Boccaccio tells in his *Decameron* that there was a prince of Salerno, named Tancredi, who had a most beautiful daughter, well-bred, wise, and courteous, named Ghismonda. This father loved his daughter with such devotion that he could not live unless he saw her, and only with the greatest reluctance and under great pressure did he consent to have her married. Nevertheless, she was given in marriage to the count of Campania, but she did not remain married for long, for this count died shortly afterward, and her father took her back into his household, intending never to let her marry again. The lady, who was the complete joy of her father's old age, was well aware of her own beauty, youth, and fine upbringing, and thought that it was not particularly pleasant to spend her youth without a husband, though she did not dare to contradict her father's will. During the time which she spent in court at her father's side, this lady happened to see a squire among the nobles at court who seemed to her more handsome than all the others—although there were a great many knights and noblemen there—and even better mannered and, in all, quite worthy of being loved. To put the matter briefly, she had studied his behavior so closely that she decided to take her pleasure in this squire in order to pass her youth more joyfully and to satisfy the gaiety of her pretty heart. Every day, even for a long time before she revealed her love, while she sat at the table she watched the behavior and deportment of this young man who was named Guiscardo. The more attention she paid to him, the more he seemed to her from day to day to be perfect in everything. For this reason, after having observed him a great deal, she summoned him one day and said to him: 'Guiscardo, dear friend, my trust in your goodness and loyalty and integrity moves me and urges me to reveal myself to you regarding several extremely secret matters which concern me and which I would not tell any other. But before I tell you, I want your pledge that they will never be revealed or made known by you.' Guiscardo replied, 'My lady, you must not be afraid that I will ever reveal anything you tell me.' Thereupon Ghismonda said to him, 'Guiscardo, I want you to know that my pleasure lies in a noble man whom I love and wish to love. And because I cannot speak to him, nor do I have anyone who could convey my wishes, I want you to be the messenger for our love. You see, Guiscardo, I trust you so much more than any other that I wish to place my honor in your hands.' Then he knelt down and said, 'My lady, I know that you possess so much good sense and valiance that you would never do anything unseemly; therefore I thank you most humbly for having so much confidence in me, more than in anyone else, that you wish to reveal to me your secret thoughts. So, my dear lady, without having the slightest fear, you may command me to carry out all your good pleasures, as you would command someone who had offered body and soul to obey all your commands to the best of his ability. Moreover, I offer myself as the most humble servant to whomever is so lucky to possess the love of a lady so worthy as you, for truly, he has not been without a lofty and most noble love.' When Ghismonda, who had wanted to test Guiscardo, heard him speak so wisely, she took him by the hand and said to him, 'Guiscardo, my love, you are the one whom I have chosen for my only love and in whom I wish to take all my pleasure, for it seems to me that the nobility of your heart and the good manners with which you are filled make you worthy of such a lofty love.' The young man rejoiced at this and humbly thanked her. And, put briefly, their love flourished for a long time, unknown to all. But Fortune, jealous of their happiness, did not want the two lovers to live in joy and so changed their happiness into the most bitter sorrow. By extraordinary chance one summer day it happened that, while Ghismonda was relaxing in the garden with her maids, her father—whose only wealth was in seeing her—went all alone to her bedroom to chat with her and to relax in her company. But finding the windows closed, the bed-curtains drawn, and not a soul there, he thought she was taking a nap. Not wanting to awaken her he lay down on a couch and fell sound asleep. Ghismonda, thinking she had been in the garden long enough, retired to her bedroom, lay down on her bed as if to sleep, and had her maids leave. She shut the door without noticing her sleeping father. When she saw she was alone, she got up and went to look for Guiscardo, who was hiding in one of her closets, and she led him to her bedroom. While they were speaking with one another behind the bed curtains like a couple who believed they were alone, the prince woke up and heard a man speaking with his daughter. He suffered such enormous grief over this that the consideration that he might be dishonoring his daughter barely prevented him from rushing upon the stranger. Nevertheless, he kept himself under control and listened carefully for who it was. Then he managed to slip out of the bedroom without being heard. After the two lovers had been together for a while, Guiscardo left. But the prince, who had prepared an ambush for him, had him captured and imprisoned immediately. He then went to his daughter and, speaking alone to her in her bedroom with a sad face and tear-filled eyes, he said:

II.59.2   "'Ghismonda, I used to think that I had in you a daughter more beautiful, chaste, and wise than all other women, but now I am more convinced of the opposite in my anger than I would be if I had thought the contrary in spite of myself—for if I had not seen it with my own eyes, there would have been nothing that could make me believe that you could be seduced by the love of any man unless he were your husband. What aggravates my anger even more is that I believed you had the noblest heart of any woman ever born. And I see that the contrary is true because you were taken with one of the lowliest members of my household. For, if you wanted to do such a thing, you could have found in my court an overabundance of nobler men, without having to be smitten with Guiscardo, who, I think, will pay dearly for the grief which I have suffered on his account. I want you to know that I will put him to death and I would do the same to you if I could undo the foolish love I have for you in my heart, a far greater love than any other father ever had for his daughter, which keeps me from doing this.'

II.59.3   "No one need wonder whether Ghismonda was grief-stricken when she realized that her father knew about the one thing she had most wanted to hide, and yet, above all, the greatest grief wrung her heart because he threatened to kill the one man whom she loved so much. She wanted to die at that very moment, but with an unwavering heart and composed countenance and without shedding a tear—although she had prepared herself to die—she replied, 'Father, since Fortune has consented that you discover what I had so wished to keep secret,

I do not need to make any request of you, except that, if I intended to beg for your forgiveness and for the life of the man whom you threaten to kill by offering myself in his place, I would beg you to take my life and spare his. And as for my asking pardon from you, in case you do with him what you say, I will not ask for pardon, for I do not wish to live any longer; I assure you that with his death you end my life. And concerning the cause of your anger against us, you have only yourself to blame, for you are a creature of the flesh and did you ever stop to think that you fathered a daughter from the flesh and not from stone or iron? You should remember, even though you have grown old, what terrible ennui afflicts youth living in luxury and ease and what pricks of temptation must be overcome. Since I saw you had decided never to let me marry again, and feeling young and urged on by my own prettiness, I fell in love with this young man, and not without discussion or long deliberation I granted to my heart what it desired. First I observed his behavior—more perfect in every virtue than any other in your court. This you should realize yourself, for you brought him up. And what is nobility except virtue? It never comes from flesh or blood. Therefore you have no right to say that I was taken in by the least noble of your court, and you have no cause for the great anger which you have expressed against us, considering your own fault. But, most of all, if you wish to exact punishment for this deed, it is not right to take it out on his person, for that would be wrong and sinful. Rather, it would be more fitting that I be punished, for I urged him on to this deed which he himself did not think of at all. What was he supposed to do? Indeed, he would have had a base heart to refuse a lady of such high standing. So you must forgive him this misdeed but not me.' The prince immediately took leave of Ghismonda but was not in the least pacified toward Guiscardo because of this, and on the following day had him killed and ordered his heart torn out of his body. The father placed Guiscardo's heart in a gold goblet and had one of his secret messengers take it to his daughter and inform her that he was sending her this present to give her joy in the one thing which she loved most, just as she had made him joyful in the one thing he had held most dear. The messenger came to Ghismonda, presented his gift, and said what he had been charged. She took the goblet, opened it, and immediately realized what had been done. But in spite of the inestimable grief she felt, nothing could shake her lofty heart and she replied without any change of expression, 'My friend, tell the prince that I perceive that he is wise in one matter, that is, he has given such a noble heart a fitting sepulcher, for it ought not to have any but of gold and precious stones.' Then she leaned over the goblet and kissed the heart, saying piteously, 'Oh most sweet heart, vessel of all my pleasure, cursed be the cruelty of him who has shown you to my eyes, you who were always visible to my mind's eye. Now, through a bizarre turn of events, you have passed the course of your noble life. Yet in spite of such misfortune you have received from your own enemy a sepulcher worthy of your merit. Thus it is most fitting, my sweet heart, that for the last rites you be bathed and washed in the tears of her whom you loved so much, for you will never beat again. Besides, your soul will not be bereft of hers, since that would not be right, for she will shortly join you. And yet, in spite of this treacherous Fortune, which has harmed you so much, it has still turned out well for you, insofar as my cruel father sent you to me so that you could be honored all the more and so that I could speak to you before I leave this world and so that my soul could go with yours whose company I desire, for I know that your spirit is asking and longing for mine.' Ghismonda spoke these words and many others as well, so pitiful that no one who heard her could not collapse in tears. She wept so much that it seemed as if she had two fountains in her head which poured without stop into this goblet. She made no uproar or cry, but with a low voice kept kissing the heart. The ladies and maids who stood around her were quite amazed at this, for they knew nothing of what had happened nor the possible cause of her sorrow; they wept out of pity for their mistress and tried to comfort her, but nothing was of any use. Her intimates could only ask in vain about the cause of her sorrow. After Ghismonda, overcome with incredible grief, had wept for a long time, she said, 'Oh most beloved heart, I have carried out my duties on your behalf, nothing remains but to send my soul to keep your soul company.' Having said these words, she stood up, went to open a cupboard, and removed a small flask where she had placed poisonous herbs in water to dissolve to be ready should need ever arise. She poured this water into the goblet containing the heart and, without the slightest fear, drank it all. She lay down on her bed to wait for death, still clutching the goblet tightly in her arms. When her maids saw her body change with the signs of death, in their terrible grief they summoned the father, who had gone out to amuse himself in order to forget his melancholy. The poison had already spread through her veins by this time. Filled with grief for what had happened and remorse for what he had done, he began to speak to her sweetly, mourning greatly, and he thought he was comforting her. His daughter, speaking as best as she could, replied, 'Tancredi, save your tears for something else, for they have no place here, nor do I desire or want them. You are like the serpent which kills a man and then weeps for him. Would it not have been better for your daughter to have lived as she pleased, secretly loving a good man, than to watch such a horrible death—to your own grief but caused by your own cruelty—a death which makes what had been secret public knowledge.' With that she could speak no more; her heart burst as she held the goblet. And the poor man of a father died of grief. So died Ghismonda, daughter of the prince of Salerno."

199   *Christine de Pizan*

60. HERE SHE SPEAKS OF LISABETTA AND OTHER LOVERS.

II.60.1   "Boccaccio also recounts in his *Decameron* that in the city of Messina, in Italy, there lived a young girl named Lisabetta. Her three brothers were anxious in their greed to have her married off. They had a servant and administrator for all their affairs—a very handsome and good-looking young man whom their father had raised from infancy. It happened that Lisabetta and he fell in love because of their frequent visits together, and they nurtured their love most joyfully for some time. But when the brothers finally found out, considering it to be a great shame, and even though they wanted to avoid making a large outcry over it, they decided to kill the young man. In fact, one day they brought this young fellow, who was named Lorenzo, along with them to their estate. After arriving there they murdered him in the garden and buried him between some trees. Upon their return to Messina they led their retainers to believe that they had sent Lorenzo far away on some matter of business. Lisabetta, who loved the youth with deep devotion, was unhappy with her lover's absence, and her heart told her that something was amiss. Finally, as though forced by too great a love, she could not keep herself from asking one of her brothers where they had sent Lorenzo, whereupon the brother haughtily replied, 'What business is it of yours to know where? If you talk about him any more, it will be worse for you.' Lisabetta then realized that her brothers had discovered their affair and she was convinced that they had killed Lorenzo. For this reason she mourned deeply when she was all alone, and at night, without resting at all, she wept so much in mourning for her lover that she became sick. Because of her illness she asked her brothers to allow her to go to recover on their estate outside of the city. After her request had been granted, she found herself alone in the garden where Lorenzo lay buried, and, as she looked around everywhere, she saw that the earth had been recently disturbed where the body lay. Then, using a pick which she had brought along, she removed the earth until she discovered the body. Embracing it in her great sorrow, she mourned beyond measure. But knowing well she could not remain in the garden too long for fear of being discovered, she covered the body over again with earth and took her lover's head, which her brothers had cut off. After covering it with her kisses, she placed it in a beautiful scarf and buried it in one of the large pots for violets, and over it she planted five shoots of the fair and sweet-smelling herb basil, and with this pot she returned to the city. This pot was so dear to her that day and night she would not leave the window where she had placed it, nor would she water it with any water except for her tears. And her behavior did not change after a few days, as men claim who argue that women easily forget, but rather it seemed that her grief grew from day to day. And the basil grew thick and tall, thanks to the richness of the soil. In short, she spent her life so centered around this pot that several neighbors noticed how she wept unceasingly over this pot at the window, and they told her brothers, who spied on her and saw her amazing sorrow. They were dumbfounded as to what this all meant and stole the pot away from her that night, and on the next morning her anguish was all the greater when she failed to find it. She begged for mercy's sake that it be given back to her, promising to turn over her share in the family properties to her brothers if she could have the pot back. She lamented and said pitifully, 'Alas! In what an hour did my mother give birth to me with such cruel brothers who so detest my modest pleasure that they are unwilling to let me keep a poor pot of basil which costs them nothing or even to give it back to me, and I ask nothing more of them for my dowry. Alas! They have given me only immeasurable grief.' Thus the poor woman mourned so unceasingly that she ended up very sick in bed. During this illness, in spite of everything administered to her, she asked for nothing else but her pot to make her happy, and she died in such a miserable state. I do not believe that this story is a lie, for afterward people composed a song about this woman and her pot which they still sing.

II.60.2 "What more can I tell you? I could always relate to you the stories of women overcome by such great love that they loved too much, too deeply, and too constantly. Boccaccio tells of another woman whose husband had her eat the heart of her lover and who therefore, afterward, never ate again. The Dame de Fayel who loved the Castellan de Coucy did the same. The Dame de Vergi died from excessive love, just as Iseut who loved Tristan too much. Deianeira, whom Hercules loved, killed herself when he died. Thus there is no doubt that the love of a constant woman in which she commits herself totally is very great, despite other women who are not constant.

II.60.3 "But these pitiful examples, as well as many others which I could also tell you, should in no way move women's hearts to set themselves adrift in the dangerous and damnable sea of foolish love, for its end is always detrimental and harmful to their bodies, their property, their honor, and—most important of all—to their souls. Women should conduct themselves wisely and with good sense and should know how to avoid this kind of love and not to listen to those who incessantly strive to deceive them in such cases."

61. HERE SHE SPEAKS OF JUNO AND OF SEVERAL CELE-BRATED LADIES.

II.61.1 "Now I have told you about a great many ladies mentioned in historical works. But since I have not undertaken to tell about them all—that would be an endless task—let it suffice for me to bring forth evidence to disprove what various men have claimed which you have repeated to me. I want to conclude by telling you about several women who were extremely famous throughout the world as a result of coincidence rather than their own virtue.

"Juno, daughter of Saturn and Ops, according to the *II.61.2* works of the poets and the errors of the pagans, was more famous than all the other women of her culture more because of her good looks than for some other outstanding quality. She was Jupiter's sister and married to him. Since he was proclaimed as the supreme god and because she lived luxuriating in such incredible wealth and good fortune, she was reputed to be the goddess of riches. The inhabitants of Samos believed her idol (which they possessed after her death) gave them luck, and they attributed to her the privileges and prerogatives of marriage. In prayer, women had recourse to her help, and they established temples to her everywhere, as well as altars, priests, games, and sacrifices. Thus she was honored for a long time by the Greeks and Carthaginians. Moreover, her idol was brought to Rome and placed in the temple of Jupiter in the Capitol next to her husband's, and there she was honored in various ceremonies for a long time by the Romans, who ruled the world.

"Similarly, Europa, daughter of the Phoenician Age- *II.61.3* nor, became quite famous because Jupiter, who loved her, named a third of the world after her. It should be remembered that various lands, cities, and towns have been named after many women, just like England, after a woman named Angela, and many others.

"Likewise, Jocasta was the queen of Thebes, famed *II.61.4* for her terrible fate, for it was her misfortune to marry her own son after he had killed his father, something which neither she nor her son realized, and she saw how he despaired when he realized his fate, and subsequently she saw her two sons by him kill each other.

"Similarly, Medusa (or Gorgon) was celebrated for *II.61.5* her outstanding beauty. She was the daughter of the very wealthy king Phorcys whose large kingdom was surrounded by the sea. This Medusa, according to the ancient stories, was of such striking beauty that not only did she surpass all other women—which was an amazing and supernatural thing—but she also attracted to herself, because of her pleasing appearance—her long and curly blond hair spun like gold, along with her beautiful face and body—every mortal creature upon whom she looked, so that she seemed to make people immovable. For this reason the fable claimed that they had turned to stone.

II.61.6   "Helen, wife of Menelaus, king of Lacedaemonia, daughter of Tyndareos, king of Sparta, and of Leda, his wife, was renowned for her great beauty. And because Troy was destroyed as a result of Paris' rape of Helen, in spite of what had been said concerning the beauty of other women, the histories claim that she was the most beautiful woman ever born. For this reason the poets claimed Jupiter as her father.

II.61.7   "Likewise, Polyxena, the oldest daughter of King Priam, is also mentioned as the most beautiful maiden in any history. Besides being beautiful, she had a very stable and constant heart, just as she demonstrated when she was beheaded on Achilles' tomb, dying without any change of expression, after she said she preferred to die rather than to be led away into slavery. I could tell you much more about other women, which I will omit for the sake of brevity."

62. HERE CHRISTINE SPEAKS, AND RECTITUDE REPLIES IN ANSWER TO THOSE MEN WHO CLAIM WOMEN ATTRACT MEN THROUGH THEIR COQUETTISHNESS.

II.62.1   Then I, Christine, spoke, "Indeed, my lady, to return to the question mentioned earlier, from what I see, the dangerous life of foolish love ought to be avoided by women who possess any learning whatsoever, for it is quite harmful to them. Yet great blame has been placed upon those women who enjoy being pretty in both their clothes and ornaments, and it is said that they do this in order to attract men to their love."

She replied, "My dear friend, it is not fitting for me to excuse women who are too vain and elegant in their dress. This is doubtless a vice, and not a small one, for excessive elegance is not without blame. Nevertheless, and I say this not to excuse the sin but to avoid placing more blame than is required upon such women who are pretty, I can assure you that all these women have not acted this way because of foolish love, but that many people, men and women, take delight in coquettishness or in beautiful and rich clothes and cleanliness and in stately and dignified things. If such a desire occurs to them naturally, it would be difficult for them to avoid it, no matter how great their virtues. Is it not written that the apostle Bartholomew, who was a gentleman, wore clothes of silk with fringe and precious stones his entire life in spite of our Lord's preaching poverty? It occurred to him naturally to be richly dressed, which is normally vain and pompous, and yet he did not sin in this. And some people claim that for this reason our Lord suffered that Bartholomew in his martyrdom give up his skin and be flayed. I tell you these things to show that no one should judge someone else's conscience from dress, for it is God's office alone to judge His creatures. Let me give you several examples of this."

63. CONCERNING CLAUDIA QUINTA, A ROMAN WOMAN.

"Boccaccio tells, and Valerius reports the same thing, *II.63.1* that Claudia Quinta, a noble lady of Rome, took great pleasure in vain and beautiful clothing and in pretty ornaments. Because she was more refined than the other ladies of Rome, some people spoke badly of her and of her chastity, to the detriment of her reputation. In the fifteenth year of the Second Punic War, the Magna Mater of Pessinus, the mother of the gods, according to their beliefs, had to be transported to Rome. All the noble ladies of Rome were assembled to meet her. The image was placed on a boat in the Tiber, but, in spite of all their strength, the sailors could not reach the shore. Thereupon, Claudia, who was well aware that she was wrongly perceived because of her beauty, knelt before the image and loudly prayed, as truly as the goddess knew her chastity was complete and wholly uncorrupted, that the goddess grant her mercy enough to draw the boat to shore. Then, trusting in her purity, she took her belt, tied it to the gunwales of the ship, and drew the ship to shore, as easily as if all the sailors of the world had been there, a feat which amazed everyone.

II.63.2   "I do not mention this example to you because I think this idol, which the foolish unbelievers called a goddess, had the power to fulfill Claudia's prayer, but rather in order to demonstrate that such a pretty woman was also chaste. She showed thereby that she believed the truthfulness of her chastity would help her, and indeed it was her chastity which helped her, not some goddess.

64. RECTITUDE SAYS THAT MANY WOMEN ARE LOVED FOR THEIR VIRTUES MORE THAN OTHER WOMEN FOR THEIR PRETTINESS.

II.64.1   "If we assumed that women who wished to be loved tried, for this reason, to be pretty, conceited, cute, and vain, then I can show you that such action will not make wise and worthwhile men love them more quickly or better and that, in fact, honest, virtuous, and simple women will more readily and more deeply be loved by men who love honor than pretty women, even if we suppose that these honest women are less beautiful. One could answer that, since women attract men with virtue and integrity and since it is bad that men be attracted, it would be better if women were less good. But of course this argument has no validity at all, for one should not neglect the cultivation and advancement of the good in spite of however much fools abuse it, and everyone must do his duty by acting well regardless of what might happen. I will give you an example to prove that women are loved for their virtue and integrity. First I could tell you about the many women who are saints in Paradise who were desired by men because of their honesty.

"Consider Lucretia, whom I spoke to you about before and who was raped: her great integrity was the reason why Tarquin became enamored, much more so than because of her beauty. For once, when her husband was dining with this Tarquin (who afterward raped her) and with many other knights, the subject of their conversation turned to their wives, and each one claimed that his own was the best. In order to discover the truth and to prove which one of their wives was worthy of the highest praise, they got up and rode home, and those women found occupied in the most honest occupation and activity were to be the most celebrated and honored. Lucretia, of all these wives, turned out to be the most honestly occupied, for her husband found her, such a wise and upright woman, clothed in a simple gown, sitting at home among her women servants, working in wool, and discoursing on various subjects. This same Tarquin, the king's son, arrived there with her husband and saw her outstanding honesty, her smile and fair conduct, and her serene manner. He was so captivated by her that he began to plan the folly which he committed later." *II.64.2*

65. HERE SHE SPEAKS OF QUEEN BLANCHE, THE MOTHER OF SAINT LOUIS, AND OF OTHER GOOD AND WISE LADIES LOVED FOR THEIR VIRTUE.

"The most noble Queen Blanche, mother of Saint Louis, was similarly loved for great learning, prudence, virtue, and goodness by Thibault, the count of Champagne. Even though she had already passed the flower of her youth, this noble count—hearing the wise and good queen speak to him so judiciously after he had gone to war against Saint Louis, sensibly reproving him, telling *II.65.1* him he ought not to have acted this way, considering the good deeds her son had done for him—looked at her intently, amazed by her enormous goodness and virtue, and was so overwhelmed by love that he did not know what to do. He did not dare confess his love for fear of death, for he realized that she was so good that she would never consent to his proposition. From that time onward he suffered much grief because of the mad desire which oppressed him. Nevertheless, he told her then not to fear his continuing to wage war against the king and that he wished to be her subject totally, that she should be certain that everything he possessed, body and soul, was entirely subject to her command. So he loved her all his life, from that hour on, and he never stopped loving her in spite of the slight chance he had of ever winning her love. He made his laments to Love in his poems, where he praised his lady most graciously. These beautiful poems of his were put to music in a charming way. He had them inscribed in his bedroom in Provins and also in Troyes, and they appear there to this day. And so I could tell you about many others."

II.65.2 And I, Christine, replied, "Indeed, my lady, I have seen in my own experience several cases similar to the one you mention, for I know of virtuous and wise women who, from what they have confessed to me in lamenting their distress, have been propositioned more frequently after their peak of beauty and youthfulness than when they were in their greatest flower. Concerning this, they have told me, 'Gods! What can this possibly mean? Do these men see in me some foolish behavior which would give them the slightest glimmer of hope that I would agree to commit such foolishness?' But I realize now, from what you say, that their outstanding goodness caused them to be loved. And this is very much against the opinion of many people who claim that an honest woman who intends to be chaste will never be desired or propositioned unless she herself so wishes."

66. CHRISTINE SPEAKS, AND RECTITUDE RESPONDS IN
HER REPLY TO THOSE MEN WHO CLAIM THAT WOMEN
ARE NATURALLY GREEDY.

"I do not know what more to tell you, my dear lady,   *II.66.1*
for all my questions are answered. It seems to me that
you have disproven the slanders put forth by so many men
against women. Likewise, what they so often claim is not
true, that greed is, among feminine vices, a very natural
thing."

She answered, "My dear friend, let me assure you that
greed is no more natural in women than it is in men, and
God only knows whether men are less greedy! You can
see that the latter is in fact the case because considerably
more evil occurs and recurs in the world because of the
rapacity of different men than because of the greed of
women. But, just as I told you before, the fool sees his
neighbor's peccadillo and fails to see his own enormous
crime. Since one commonly sees women taking delight in
collecting cloth and thread and such trifles which go into
a household, women are thought to be greedy. I can,
however, assure you that there are many women who,
were they to possess anything, would not be greedy or
stingy in bestowing honors and giving generously where
what they have could be used well, just as one poor
person would do for an even poorer person in need.
Women are usually kept in such financial straits that they
guard the little that they can have, knowing they can
recover this only with the greatest pain. So some people
consider women greedy because some women have
foolish husbands, great wastrels of property and gluttons,
and the poor women, who know well that their households need what their husbands spend foolishly and that
in the end their poor children will have to pay for it, are
unable to refrain from speaking to their husbands and
from urging them to spend less. Thus, such behavior is
not at all avarice or greed, but is a sign of great prudence.
Of course I am referring to those women who act with

discretion. One sees so much quarreling in these marriages because the husbands do not like such urging and so blame their wives for something which they should praise them for. It is clear from the alms which these women so freely give that the vice of avarice is not to be found in them. God knows how many prisoners, even in the lands of the Saracens, how many destitute and needy noblemen and others have been and are every day, in this world here below, comforted and helped by women and their property."

II.66.2   And I, Christine, then said, "Indeed, my lady, your remarks remind me that I have seen women show themselves honorable in prudent generosity, and today I am acquainted with women who rejoice when they can say, 'See, the money is put to good use there, and no greedy man can hoard it away in some coffer.' For although Alexander the Great was said to be generous, I can tell you that I never saw any examples of it."

Rectitude then began to laugh and said, "Indeed, my friend, the ladies of Rome were not greedy when their city was gravely afflicted with war, when the public treasury was completely spent on warriors. The Romans had terrible trouble finding money to finance a large army which they had to raise. But the ladies, with their liberality—even the widows—collected all their jewels and property together, sparing nothing, and freely gave them to the princes of Rome. The ladies received great praise for this deed, and afterward their jewels were given back to them, and quite rightly so, for they had saved Rome."

67. HERE SHE SPEAKS OF THE RICH AND GENEROUS LADY NAMED BUSA.

II.67.1   "In the *Faits des Romains* the generosity of a rich and upright woman named Busa, or Paulina, is described. She lived in Apuleia during the time when Hannibal was ravaging the Romans with fire and arms, despoiling almost all of Italy of men and goods. Many Romans retreated after the great defeat at the battle of Cannae, where Hannibal won such a noble victory, and they fled the battlefield wounded or injured. But this valiant Lady Busa received as many as she could take in, until she sheltered some ten thousand in her household, for she was extremely wealthy and had them cared for at her expense. All of them, having been helped by her wealth as much as by the aid and comfort she afforded them, were able to return to Rome and put the army back on its feet, for which she was highly praised. So do not doubt, dear friend, that I could tell you more about the endless generosity, bounty, and liberality of women.

"And even without going back to look for historical *II.67.2* examples, how many other examples of the generosity of ladies from your own time could be mentioned! Was not the generosity great which was shown by the Dame de la Rivière, named Marguerite, who is still alive and was formerly the wife of Monsieur Burel de la Rivière, first chamberlain of the wise King Charles? On one occasion among others it happened that this lady, as she was always wise, valiant, and well-bred, was attending a very fine celebration which the duke of Anjou, later king of Sicily, was holding in Paris. At this celebration there were a large number of noble ladies and knights and gentlemen in fine array. This lady, who was young and beautiful, realized while she watched the noble knights assembled there, that a most noteworthy knight of great fame among those then living, named Emerion de Poumiers, was missing from the company of knights. She, of course, allowed that this Sir Emerion was too old to remember her, but his goodness and valiance made the lady remember him, and she felt there could be no more beautiful an ornament for such an assembly than so noteworthy and famous a man, even if he were old, so she inquired where the missing knight was. She was told that he was in prison in the Châtelet in Paris because of a debt of five hundred francs that he had incurred during his frequent travels in arms. 'Ah!' said the noble lady, 'what a shame for this kingdom to suffer a single hour of such a man imprisoned for debt!' Whereupon she removed the gold chaplet which she was wearing on her rich and fair head and replaced it with a chaplet of periwinkle on her blond hair. She gave the gold chaplet to a certain messenger and said, 'Go and give this chaplet as a pledge for what he owes, and let him be freed immediately and come here.' This was done and she was highly praised for it."

68. SHE SPEAKS HERE OF THE PRINCESSES AND LADIES OF FRANCE.

II.68.1 Then I, Christine, spoke again. "My lady, since you have recalled a lady from my own time and since you have come to the history of the ladies of France and of those ladies still living, let me ask you whether you think it is a good idea to lodge some of them in our City. For why should they be forgotten, and foreign women as well?"

She replied, "I can answer you, Christine, that there are certainly a great many virtuous ladies of France, and I would be more than pleased if they were among our citizens. First of all, the noble queen of France, Isabella of Bavaria, will not be refused, reigning now by the grace of God, and in whom there is not a trace of cruelty, extortion, or any other evil vice, but only great love and good will toward her subjects.

II.68.2 "We can equally praise the fair, young, good, and wise duchess of Berry, wife of Duke John, son of the late King John of France and brother of wise King Charles. In the flower of her youth this noble duchess conducted herself so chastely, so sensibly, and so wisely that all the world praised and reputed her for her excellent virtue.

II.68.3 "What could I say about Valentina Visconti, the duchess of Orléans, wife of Duke Louis, son of Charles, the wise king of France, and daughter of the duke of Milan? What more could be said about such a prudent lady? A lady who is strong and constant in heart, filled with devotion to her lord and good teaching for her children, well-informed in government, just toward all, sensible in her conduct, and virtuous in all things—and all this is well known.

"What more could be said concerning the duchess of II.68.4 Burgundy, wife of Duke John, son of Philip, the son of the late King John of France? Is she not extraordinarily virtuous, loyal to her lord, kind in heart and manners, excellent in her morals and lacking a single vice?

"Is not the countess of Clermont, daughter of the duke II.68.5 of Berry mentioned above from his first marriage, and wife of Count John of Clermont, son of the duke of Bourbon and heir to the duchy, is she not everything which every lofty princess must be, devoted to her love, well-bred in everything, beautiful, wise, and good? In short, her virtues shine forth in her good conduct and honorable bearing.

"And what about that one woman among others whom II.68.6 you love singularly as much for the goodness of her virtues as for the favors she has extended to you and to whom you are much beholden, the noble duchess of Holland and countess of Hainault, daughter of the late Duke Philip of Burgundy mentioned above, and sister of the present duke? This lady should be ranked among the most perfect ladies, loyal-hearted, most prudent, wise in government, charitable, supremely devoted to God, and, in short, wholly good.

"Should not the duchess of Bourbon also be recalled II.68.7 among princesses known for their honor and laudability in all things?

"What more shall I tell you? I would need much time II.68.8 to recount all their great virtues.

"The good and beautiful countess of Saint-Pol, noble II.68.9 and upright, daughter of the duke of Bar, second cousin of the king of France, should also be ranked among the good women.

II.68.10   "Similarly the woman whom you love, Anne, daughter of the late count of La Marche and sister of the present duke, married to Ludwig of Bavaria, brother of the queen of France, does not discredit the company of women endowed with grace and praise, for her excellent virtues are well-known to God and the world.

II.68.11   "In spite of the slanderers, there are so many good and beautiful women among the ranks of countesses, baronesses, ladies, maidens, bourgeois women, and all classes that God should be praised who upholds them all. May He correct those women with shortcomings! Do not think otherwise, for I assure you of its truth, even if many jealous and slanderous people say the opposite."

And I, Christine, replied, "My lady, hearing this from you is a supreme joy for me."

She answered, "My dear friend, it seems to me I have now more than adequately executed my office in the City of Ladies. I have built it up with beautiful palaces and many fair inns and mansions. I have populated it for your sake with noble ladies and with such great numbers of women from all classes that it is already completely filled. Now let my sister Justice come to complete the rest, and this should satisfy you."

69. CHRISTINE ADDRESSES HERSELF TO ALL PRINCESSES AND TO ALL WOMEN.

II.69.1   "Most excellent, revered, and honored princesses of France and of all lands, and all ladies and maidens, and, indeed, all women who have loved and do love and will love virtue and morality, as well as all who have died or who are now living or who are to come, rejoice and exult in our new City which, thanks to God, is already formed and almost finished and populated. Give thanks to God who has led me to undertake this great labor and the desirable task of establishing for you honorable lodging within city walls as a perpetual residence for as long as the world endures. I have come this far hoping to reach the conclusion of my work with the aid and comfort of Lady Justice, who, in accordance with her promise, will unfailingly help me until the City is finished and wholly completed. Now, my most honored ladies, pray for me."

HERE ENDS THE SECOND PART OF THE BOOK OF THE CITY OF LADIES.

HERE BEGINS THE THIRD PART OF THE BOOK OF THE CITY OF LADIES, WHICH TELLS HOW THE HIGH ROOFS OF THE TOWERS WERE COMPLETED AND BY WHOM AND WHICH NOBLE LADIES WERE CHOSEN TO RESIDE IN THE GREAT PALACES AND LOFTY MANSIONS.

1. THE FIRST CHAPTER TELLS HOW JUSTICE LED THE QUEEN OF HEAVEN TO LIVE IN THE CITY OF LADIES.

Lady Justice then turned to me in her sublime manner and said, "Christine, to tell the truth, it seems to me that you have worked extraordinarily well at building the City of Ladies, according to your capacities and with the aid of my sisters which you have put to excellent use. Now it is time for me to undertake the rest, just as I promised you. That is, to bring and to lodge here the most excellent Queen, blessed among women, with her noble company, so that she may rule and govern the City, inhabited by the multitude of noble ladies from her court and household, for I see the palaces and tall mansions ready and furnished, the streets paved to receive her most excellent and honorable company and assembly. Let princesses, ladies, and all women now come forward to receive her with the greatest honor and reverence, for she is not only their Queen but also has ministry and dominion over all created powers after the only Son whom she conceived of the Holy Spirit and carried and who is the Son of God the Father. And it is right that the assembly of all women beg this most lofty and excellent sovereign princess to reside here below in her humility with them in their City and congregation without disdain or spite because of their insignificance compared to her highness. Yet, there is no need to fear that her humility, which surpasses all others, and her more than angelic goodness will allow her to refuse to inhabit and reside in the City of Ladies, and above all, in the

III.1.1

217

palace already prepared for her by my sister Rectitude, which is constructed solely of glory and praise. Let all women now accompany me, and let us say to her:

III.1.2   " 'We greet you, Queen of Heaven, with the greeting which the Angel brought you, when he said, *Hail Mary*, which pleased you more than all other greetings. May all the devout sex of women humbly beseech you that it please you well to reside among them with grace and mercy, as their defender, protector, and guard against all assaults of enemies and of the world, that they may drink from the fountain of virtues which flows from you and be so satisfied that every sin and vice be abominable to them. Now come to us, Heavenly Queen, Temple of God, Cell and Cloister of the Holy Spirit, Vessel of the Trinity, Joy of the Angels, Star and Guide to those who have gone astray, Hope of the True Creation. My Lady, what man is so brazen to dare think or say that the feminine sex is vile in beholding your dignity? For if all other women were bad, the light of your goodness so surpasses and transcends them that any remaining evil would vanish. Since God chose His spouse from among women, most excellent Lady, because of your honor, not only should men refrain from reproaching women but should also hold them in great reverence.' "

III.1.3   The Virgin replied as follows: "O Justice, greatly beloved by my Son, I will live and abide most happily among my sisters and friends, for Reason, Rectitude, and you, as well as Nature, urge me to do so. They serve, praise, and honor me unceasingly, for I am and will always be the head of the feminine sex. This arrangement was present in the mind of God the Father from the start, revealed and ordained previously in the council of the Trinity."

Here Justice answered, while all the women knelt with their heads bowed, "My Lady, may honor and praise be given to you forever. Save us, our Lady, and pray for us to your Son who refuses you nothing."

2. CONCERNING THE SISTERS OF OUR LADY AND MARY MAGDALENE.

"Now the incomparable Empress resides with us, *III.2.1* regardless of whether it pleases the malicious slanderers. Her blessed sisters and Mary Magdalene must also dwell with her, for they stayed steadfastly with her, next to the Cross, during the entire Passion of her Son. What strong faith and deep love those women possess who did not forsake the Son of God who had been abandoned and deserted by all His Apostles. God has never reproached the love of women as weakness, as some men contend, for He placed the spark of fervent love in the hearts of the blessed Magdalene and of other ladies, indeed His approval of this love is clearly to be seen."

3. CONCERNING SAINT CATHERINE OF ALEXANDRIA.

"We must lodge holy women with the Blessed Virgin *III.3.1* — the holy Queen of Heaven, Empress and Princess of the City of Ladies— to keep her company and to demonstrate God's approval of the feminine sex with examples of His giving young and tender women (just as He has done with men) the constancy and strength to suffer horrible martyrdom for His holy law, women who are crowned in glory and whose fair lives serve as excellent examples for every woman above all other wisdom. For this reason these women are the most outstanding of our City.

"First let me tell of the blessed Catherine, the daughter *III.3.2* of King Costus of Alexandria. This holy maiden found herself at the age of eighteen the heiress of her father and governed herself and her inheritance nobly. She was a Christian woman, totally dedicated to God, and refused to marry. It happened that the emperor Maxentius came to Alexandria on a solemn feast day when the city was busy with splendid preparations for the imposing sacrifices to the gods. Catherine was in the palace and so heard the bellowing of the sacrificial animals and the din of the musical instruments. After inquiring about what was going on, she learned that the emperor had already gone to the temple to sacrifice, and she hurried there and began to reprimand the emperor with learned arguments. As a well-lettered woman, versed in the various branches of knowledge, she proceeded to prove on the basis of philosophical arguments that there is but one God, Creator of all things, and He alone should be worshiped and no other. When the emperor heard this beautiful, noble, and authoritative maiden speak, he was completely amazed and utterly speechless; nevertheless, he stared at her intently. He summoned from everywhere the wisest philosophers known in the land of Egypt, then quite famous for philosophy, and some fifty philosophers were assembled who were quite unhappy to learn why they had been sent for, and said that a trifle had moved the emperor to assemble them from such distant lands in order to debate with a maiden. In short, when the day of the debate arrived, the blessed Catherine so successfully overwhelmed them with her arguments that they were confounded and unable to answer her questions. On this account the emperor was beside himself with anger, which had no effect at all, for they all converted, thanks to the divine grace in the holy words of the virgin, and confessed the name of Jesus Christ. The emperor had them burnt alive for this disrespect, and the holy virgin comforted them in their martyrdom, assuring them that they would be received in eternal glory, and she prayed to God to uphold them in true faith. Thus, because of her, they were ranked among the blessed martyrs. And through them, God demonstrated a great miracle, for the fire destroyed neither their bodies nor their clothes and, after the fire went out, they remained entirely whole, not missing so much as a single hair, and their faces looked as if they were still alive. The tyrant Maxentius, in his great lust for the blessed Catherine, tried through flattery to bend her to his will.

Seeing that this was of no use to him, he turned to threats and then to tortures. After having her roughly beaten and then imprisoned for twelve days without visitors, he tried to weaken her with hunger. The angels of the Lord, however, were with her and comforted her. And when she was brought before the emperor after the twelve days, he saw that she was healthier and fresher than before and, convinced she had received visitors, ordered the prison guards tortured. But Catherine, taking pity on them, claimed that she had received no comfort except from Heaven. The emperor did not know what harsher tortures he could use to compel her, and so, following his prefect's advice, he had wheels built and fitted out with razors which turned against one another so that whatever was between them would be sliced in two. Then he had Catherine placed naked between these wheels. During the entire time, with her hands clasped in prayer, she worshiped God, whereupon the angels descended and with great force broke the wheels apart so that the torturers themselves were killed. Upon seeing the miracles which God had performed for Catherine, the emperor's wife was converted and attacked the emperor for what he was doing. She went to visit the holy virgin in prison and asked her to pray to God on her behalf, and because of this the emperor had his wife tortured and her breasts torn off. And the virgin told her, 'Do not be afraid of the tortures, most noble queen, for today you will be received into endless joy.' The emperor had his wife beheaded, along with a large number of other converts. The emperor then asked Catherine to be his wife, but, after he realized that she was rejecting all of his requests, he finally issued the sentence that she be beheaded. And she prayed, asking intercession for all who remembered her passion and for all who invoked her name in their suffering, and a voice came from Heaven declaring that her prayer had been granted. So she finished her martyrdom, and milk poured from her body rather than blood. And the angels took her holy body and carried it to Mount Sinai, located some twenty days' journey away from there, and buried it. At her tomb God has performed many miracles, which I will omit in order to be brief, except to say that an oil flows from this tomb which heals many illnesses. And God punished the emperor Maxentius horribly."

4. CONCERNING SAINT MARGARET.

III.4.1   "Let us also not forget the blessed virgin Saint Margaret, whose legend is quite well known. Born in Antioch of noble parents, she was introduced to the Faith as a young girl by her nurse, whose goats she humbly tended every day. It happened that Olybrius, who lusted after her, had her summoned. In short, because she would not give in to his will and declared herself a Christian, he had her severely beaten and imprisoned. In prison, feeling herself tempted, she asked God to be able to see what was causing her so much evil, whereupon a horrible dragon appeared who frightened her terribly and tried to devour her. With the Sign of the Cross, however, she slew the dragon. Afterward she saw in a corner of her prison cell a figure as black as an Ethiopian. Margaret bravely went after him and pinned him down; she placed her foot on his throat and he cried aloud for mercy. The prison was immediately filled with light and she was comforted by the angels. Once again Margaret was brought before the judge, who, seeing that his admonitions were useless, had her tortured again, more than the first time. But God's angel appeared and wrecked the torture machines so that the virgin escaped completely whole, and many people were converted. Seeing this, the malicious tyrant ordered her beheaded. But first she prayed and interceded for all those who would remember her passion and invoke her name in their tribulation and for pregnant women and women in childbirth. And God's angel appeared and told her that her prayer had been granted and that she would receive her victory palm in God's name. Thereupon she stretched out her neck and was beheaded, and the angels carried away her soul. This false Olybrius had the holy virgin Regina, a young girl of fifteen, similarly tortured and beheaded because she had refused to give herself to him and had converted many people with her preaching."

5. HERE SHE SPEAKS OF SAINT LUCY.

"In our litany we must not forget the blessed Saint   *III.5.1*
Lucy, virgin, who was born in Rome. This virgin was kidnapped and taken away by the barbarian king Aucejas. When he had returned to his own country and tried to rape her, she began to preach so that he was completely distracted from his evil intent, thanks to divine virtue. He was greatly impressed by her wisdom and said she was a goddess and held her in great esteem and reverence in his palace, and most honorably established a residence for her and her household and ordered no one enter there to bother her. She spent her time unceasingly in fasting and prayer and led a holy life, praying to God on her host's behalf that He might enlighten him. Aucejas consulted with her on all his affairs and gladly received any advice she gave him. When he went to war, he asked her to intercede to God for him. She blessed him and he returned victorious; therefore he wanted to worship her as a goddess and erect temples to her. She answered that he should refrain from this, that there was but one God who ought to be worshiped and that she herself was a simple sinner. She had spent twenty years steadfastly practicing this holy life when our Lord revealed to her that she should return to Rome where she would finish the term of her life with martyrdom. She informed Aucejas, who was quite grieved at this and said, 'Alas! If you leave me, my enemies will assault me, and I will lose my good fortune when I no longer have you.' She

replied, 'Your Majesty, come with me and leave behind your earthly kingdom, for God has elected you to possess a nobler kingdom which shall have no end.' Thereupon he forsook everything and departed with the holy virgin, not as lord but as servant. She was revealed as a Christian after their arrival in Rome and was arrested and led away to martyrdom. This king Aucejas was grief-stricken and ran after her and would have gladly killed her torturers, but she forbade him and told him to control himself. He wept softly and cried out that these torturers were evil to harm this virgin of God. When the time for her beheading came, the king went and placed his head next to hers, crying, 'I am a Christian and offer my head to the Living Christ whom Lucy worships.' Thus were both beheaded together and crowned in glory, and twelve others with them, all converted by the blessed Lucy, so that the feast of their martyrdom is celebrated on the seventh day after the Kalends of July."

6. HERE SHE SPEAKS OF THE BLESSED MARTINA, VIRGIN.

III.6.1 "We must not forget the blessed Martina, virgin. This blessed woman was born in Rome of noble parents and was extraordinarily beautiful. The emperor wanted to force her to become his wife and she refused, saying, 'I am a Christian woman offered to the Living God who delights in a chaste body and pure body and to Him I sacrifice and commend myself.' Out of spite for her answer, the emperor ordered her brought to a temple and forced to worship the idols. She knelt down there, her eyes raised to Heaven and her hands clasped together, and made her prayer to God. Immediately the idols started to sway and fall down, and the temple was wrecked, and the priests serving these idols were killed. The devil residing in the largest idol cried out and proclaimed that Martina was God's servant. The tyrannical emperor delivered Martina to a cruel martyrdom, in order to avenge his gods, and God appeared to her and comforted her. She prayed for her torturers who were thereupon converted through her merits, and a great many spectators along with them. The emperor grew more obstinate than before because of this and had her tortured all the more with various cruel torments, whereupon her torturers cried out that they saw God and His saints standing before her, and they begged for mercy and were converted. As Martina interceded to God on their behalf, a light shone around them and a voice was heard from Heaven proclaiming, 'Out of love for my beloved Martina, I will spare you.' The prefect there shouted at them because they had been converted, 'Fools, this enchantress Martina has deceived you!' Without the slightest fear they replied, 'But the devil in you has deceived you, for you do not recognize your Creator.' In a rage, the emperor ordered them to be hanged and their bodies broken, and they received their martyrdom joyfully praising God. Thereupon the emperor had Martina stripped nude, and her lily-white body dazzled the spectators because of its singular beauty. After the emperor who lusted after her had argued with her for a long time and realized she would not comply, he ordered her body slashed all over, and instead of blood, milk poured from her wounds, and she gave off a sweet scent. Raving all the more at her, the emperor ordered her body to be drawn and staked down and broken, but those who were martyring her became exhausted because God prevented her from dying too quickly so that the torturers and spectators would be moved to convert. They began to cry out, 'Your Majesty, we can do no more, for the angels are beating us with chains.' And fresh executioners arrived to torment her, but they died on the spot, and the confused emperor did not know what to do. He had her stretched out and set on fire with burning oil. She continued to praise God and a strong sweet odor issued from her mouth. When the tyrants were exhausted from torturing her, they threw her into a dark dungeon. The emperor's cousin, Elagabalus, went to keep watch in the prison and saw Martina surrounded by angels, sitting on an ornamental throne, in great radiance, and in the midst of melodious songs. She held a golden tablet upon which she had written, 'Sire, sweet Jesus Christ, your works find great praise among your blessed saints.' Elagabalus, amazed by this, reported everything to the emperor, who replied that his cousin had been deceived by her enchantments. The following day the tyrant had her brought out, and all were astonished to find her completely healed, whereupon many were converted. He had her taken to the temple once more, in order to force her to sacrifice to the false gods. The devil in the idol began to moan, 'Alas! I am vanquished!' And the virgin commanded him to appear and show his ugliness. Immediately there was a loud thunderclap with lightning which fell from Heaven and overturned the idol and burnt up the priests. The emperor raged all the more and ordered her stretched out and her flesh to be ripped off with iron hooks. She continued to worship God. When the emperor saw she was not dying, he ordered her thrown to the wild beasts. A large lion who had not eaten for three days approached her, bowed down, and lay down next to her as though he were a pet dog, and licked her wounds. And she blessed our Lord, saying, 'God, may you be praised, who tame the cruelty of wild beasts with your virtue.' The tyrant, angered by this, ordered the lion taken back to its pit, whereupon the lion arose in a rage, bounded up and killed Egalabalus, the emperor's cousin, which grieved the emperor greatly. He commanded her to be thrown into a large fire; as she stood joyfully in the flames, God sent a strong wind which extinguished the flames around her but burnt her torturers. Thereupon the emperor ordered her long and beautiful hair to be shaved off, for he claimed the power of her spells lay in her hair. And the virgin told him, 'If you cut off the hair which, as the Apostle has said, is the ornament of women, God will take away your kingdom from you and will persecute you. You will wait for death in enormous pain.' Then he commanded her to be shut up in a temple dedicated to his gods, and he himself sealed and nailed the door shut and affixed the door with his seal. He returned after three days and found the idols of his gods overturned and the virgin playing with the angels, healthy and whole. The emperor asked her what she had done with his gods and she replied, 'The virtue of Jesus Christ has confounded them.' Then he ordered her throat cut, whereupon a voice was heard from Heaven saying, 'Martina, virgin, because you fought in My name, enter into My Kingdom with the saints and rejoice in eternity with Me.' And in this way the blessed Martina died. The bishop of Rome, accompanied by all the clergy, then came and buried her body honorably in a church. That same day, the emperor, who was named Alexander, was stricken with such a grievous affliction that he ate his own flesh."

7. HERE SHE SPEAKS OF ANOTHER SAINT LUCY, VIRGIN, AND OF OTHER MARTYRED VIRGIN SAINTS.

"There was another Saint Lucy, who came from the city of Syracuse. Once, while praying for her sick mother at the tomb of Saint Agatha, she beheld Saint Agatha in a vision, surrounded by angels and adorned with jewels, who said to her, 'Lucy, my sister, virgin devoted to God, why do you ask me for something which you yourself can give to your mother? I tell you that, just as the city of Catania is protected by me, so too will the city of Syracuse receive your aid, for in your purity you have gathered together choice jewels for Jesus Christ.' Lucy arose and after her mother's healing, she gave away all she owned for God and ended her life in martyrdom. Among her other tribulations, a judge threatened to have her imprisoned in an asylum for crazy women and there, in spite of her husband, she would be raped. She replied, 'The soul will never be sullied without

III.7.1

the mind's consent. For if you rape me, my chastity will be doubled, as well as my victory.' Just as they tried to take her there, she became so heavy that in spite of the oxen and other animals to which they hitched her, she could not be moved. They placed ropes around her feet to drag her away, but she remained as firm as a mountain. At her death she prophesied the future of the empire.

III.7.2 "The glorious virgin Saint Benedicta, born in Rome, is similarly worthy of great reverence. She was accompanied by twelve virgins who had been converted by her preaching. She longed to increase the Christian religion through preaching, and departing with these blessed virgins, she traveled fearlessly through many lands, for God was with them. Through our Lord's will, they were separated from one another and scattered in different countries so that each one could profit. After converting many countries to the faith of Jesus Christ, the virgin Saint Benedicta ended her life with the palm of martyrdom, and her holy companions likewise.

III.7.3 "Saint Fausta, a virgin of fourteen, was no less perfect. The emperor Maximianus had her sawed in two with an iron saw because she refused to sacrifice to the idols. Her executioners started to saw at the third hour of the day and continued until the ninth and could not even scratch her and so asked, 'How have you kept us here so long through your enchantments without our having accomplished anything?' And Fausta began to preach about Jesus Christ and His Law and so converted them. The emperor was angered by this and ordered her to be tortured with various torments, such as having a thousand nails hammered into her head as though it were a knight's helmet. Yet she prayed for her persecutors. The prefect was converted when he saw the heavens open up and God sitting among His angels. When Fausta was placed in a cauldron of boiling water, the prefect cried out, 'Holy servant of God, do not depart without me!'

and dived into the cauldron. Two others whom she had converted saw this and also dived into the cauldron where the water was at a rolling boil, and Fausta touched them, and they felt no pain. Thereupon she said, 'I am in the middle, just like the vine bearing fruit, recalling what our Lord said, that when two or three gathered in His name, He would be in their midst.' A voice was then heard, which exclaimed, 'Come, blessed souls, the Father calls you.' Upon hearing this, they joyfully gave up their spirits."

8. HERE SHE SPEAKS OF SAINT JUSTINE AND OF OTHER VIRGINS.

"Justine, a holy virgin born in Antioch, very young   *III.8.1* and extraordinarily beautiful, overcame the Devil, who boasted during the invocation of a necromancer that he would succeed in making her do the will of a man who was completely taken with her love and who would not leave her in peace, for he thought the Devil could help where entreaties and promises were useless. But nothing helped, for the glorious Justine repeatedly chased away the Devil, who presented himself in various forms to tempt her, but she vanquished and conquered him, and with her preaching she converted the foolish man who lusted after her. The necromancer himself was also converted, a man named Cyprian, who had led an evil life and whom she changed into a good man. And many others were converted by the signs which our Lord showed forth in her. She departed this world in the end as a martyr.

"Similarly, the blessed virgin Eulalia, born in Spain,   *III.8.2* stole away at the age of twelve from her parents who held her shut in because she would not stop talking about Jesus Christ. She fled by night and went to a temple where she threw down the idols to the ground, and she cried out to the judges who persecuted the martyrs that they were deceived and that she wished to die in the

Faith. So she was ranked among the soldiers of Jesus Christ and suffered many tortures. Many were converted by the signs which our Lord manifested through her.

III.8.3   "Another virgin saint, named Macra, was also harshly tortured because of her faith in God. Among the torments she suffered was having her breasts ripped off. Afterward, as she lay in prison, God sent His angel to her, who restored her health, so that the prefect was completely stunned the following day. All the same he did not cease having her tortured with various torments. At last she gave up her spirit to God. Her body lies buried near the city of Reims.

III.8.4   "In like manner, the glorious virgin Saint Fida suffered martyrdom in her childhood and endured much torture. And our Lord finally crowned her in the view of the world when He sent His angel to bring her a crown of precious stones. God manifested many signs in her, through which many were converted.

III.8.5   "Similarly, the blessed virgin Marcianna saw a false idol being worshiped, whereupon she threw the idol to the ground and smashed it. For this deed she was brutally beaten and left for dead and then imprisoned where a treacherous priest thought he could rape her after night-fall. However, through divine grace, a high wall appeared between him and her so that he could not reach her. The following day all the people saw this wall and many were converted. She suffered horrible tortures but continued to preach in the name of Jesus Christ and finally she prayed that He take her soul to Himself to end her torment.

III.8.6   "Saint Eufemia likewise suffered many tortures for the name of Jesus. She was of very noble birth and had a singularly beautiful body. The prefect Priscus urged her to worship the idols and to renounce Jesus Christ. In answering, she put such a difficult question to him that he was unable to reply, and angered at having been beaten by a woman, he ordered her tortured with a variety of harsh torments. Even though her body was painfully broken, her mind constantly grew stronger and her answers were filled with the Holy Spirit. During her torture, God's angel descended and smashed the torture machine and tormented her persecutors. She came away from this completely whole and with a joyful countenance. The treacherous prefect ordered a fire lit in an oven, whose flame reached eleven cubits high, and he had her thrown in. She sang such melodious praises to God so loudly from within that all nearby could hear her. And when the fire had gone out, she came out safe and sound. The judge, angered all the more, had red-hot pincers brought in, to tear off her limbs, but her tormentors were too frightened to dare even to touch her, so that the tortures were interrupted, whereupon the false tyrant had four lions and two other ferocious wild beasts led in, but they approached her and bowed. And then the blessed virgin, longing to go to her God, prayed to Him to take her, so that she died without a single beast having touched her."

9. HERE SHE SPEAKS OF THE VIRGIN THEODOSINA, OF SAINT BARBARA, AND OF SAINT DOROTHY.

"For our purposes it is good to remember the stead- *III.9.1* fastness shown by the blessed Theodosina in her martyrdom. This noble and beautiful eighteen-year-old virgin argued with amazing skill against the judge Urban, who threatened her with martyrdom unless she renounce Jesus Christ. After she had answered with divine reasoning, he had her hanged by her hair and severely beaten. And she said to him, 'Certainly that man is servile who seeks to rule others but does not know how to rule himself. Woe to him who is overly concerned with having his stomach full of delicacies and takes no care for the famished; woe to him who wishes to be warm but fails to warm or clothe those dying of cold; woe to him who wants to rest and makes others work; woe to him who claims everything is his which he has received from God; woe to him who desires that everyone do him good and who does evil to all.' The virgin repeatedly spoke these words as she was being tortured. But because in her heart she suffered from the shame of having all her limbs appear naked to the people, God sent a white cloud which covered her completely. And Urban threatened her more and more, to whom she said, 'You can take away none of the dishes in the feast which is prepared for me.' The tyrant threatened to corrupt her virginity, whereupon she replied, 'Your threat to corrupt is useless, for God resides in honest hearts.' The prefect, all the more enraged, had her thrown into the sea with a heavy stone around her neck, but she was upheld by the angels and led back to land, singing, and in her arms the virgin carried the stone, which outweighed her. The despot then set two leopards loose on her, but instead they bounded around her to give her a show. Finally the tyrant, not knowing what to do, had her beheaded, and her soul visibly departed from her body in the shape of a resplendent white dove. And that same night she appeared to her parents with a radiance brighter than the sun, wearing a precious crown, accompanied by virgins, holding a cross of gold, and she said to them, 'Behold the glory which you sought to take away from me,' whereupon they were converted.

III.9.2   "Similarly in the time of the emperor Maximianus, the blessed virgin Barbara flourished in virtue. Because of her beauty, her father had her shut up in a tower. She was inspired by faith in God, and because no one else could baptize her, she herself took water and baptized herself in the name of the Father, the Son, and the Holy Spirit. Her father sought a noble marriage for her, but she refused all offers for a long time. Finally she declared herself a Christian and dedicated her virginity to God. For this reason her father tried to kill her, but she was able to escape and flee. And when her father pursued her to put her to death, he finally found her through information provided by a shepherd, who immediately was turned to stone, both he and his animals.

The father brought her before the prefect, who ordered her to be executed with excruciating tortures because she had disobeyed all his commands. And she said to him, 'Coward, are you unable to see that tortures will not harm me?' Whereupon, flying into a rage, he commanded that her breasts be torn off, and in this state he had her led throughout the city. During the entire time she praised God, and because of her shame at having her virgin body seen naked, our Lord sent His angel who healed all of her wounds and covered her body with a white robe. After she had been led around enough, she was taken back to the prefect, who was beside himself with rage when he saw her completely healed and her face radiant like a star. He had her tortured again until her torturers were exhausted with tormenting her. She prayed to God to help all those who would entreat Him in her memory and who remembered her passion. And when she finished her prayer, a voice was heard, saying, 'Come, beloved daughter, rest in your Father's kingdom and receive your crown, and all that you have asked for will be granted you.' After she had climbed the mountain where she was to be beheaded, her criminal father cut off her head himself, and as he was coming down from the mountain, fire from heaven struck him down and reduced him to ashes.

"The blessed virgin Dorothy likewise suffered martyrdom in Cappadocia. Because she did not want to take any man as her husband but spoke constantly of her husband Jesus Christ, the schoolmaster, named Theophilus, said to her mockingly as she was being led to be beheaded that when she was with her husband she could at least send him roses and apples from her husband's orchard. She said she would, and it happened that immediately following her martyrdom, a very beautiful child, around four years old, came to Theophilus and brought him a small basket filled with exquisitely beautiful roses and apples which had a marvelous aroma, and said that the virgin Dorothy had sent them to him. He was astonished,

III.9.3

for this took place during the winter, in the month of February, whereupon he converted and subsequently suffered martyrdom for the name of Jesus Christ.

III.9.4   "If you want me to tell you about all the holy virgins who are in Heaven because of their constancy during martyrdom, it would require a long history, including Saint Cecilia, Saint Agnes, Saint Agatha, and countless others. If you want more examples, you need only look at the *Speculum historiale* of Vincent de Beauvais, and there you will find a great many. However, I will tell you about Saint Christine, both because she is your patron and because she is a virgin of great dignity. Let me tell you at greater length about her beautiful and pious life."

10. HERE SHE SPEAKS OF SAINT CHRISTINE, VIRGIN.

III.10.1   "The blessed Saint Christine, virgin, was from the city of Tyre and was the daughter of Urban, master of the knights. Her father shut her up in a tower because of her great beauty, and she had twelve maids with her. Her father also had a very beautiful chapel with idols built near Christine's chamber so that she could worship them. She, however, even as a twelve-year-old child, had already been inspired by the faith of Jesus Christ and did not pay any attention to the idols, so that her maids were astonished and repeatedly urged her to sacrifice. Yet when she took the incense, as if to sacrifice to the idols, she knelt at a window facing east, looked up to Heaven, and offered her incense to the immortal God. She spent the greater part of the night at this window, watching the stars, and sighing, piously praying to God to help her against her enemies. The maids, clearly aware her heart was in Jesus Christ, would often kneel before her, their hands clasped together, begging her not to place her trust in a strange God but to worship her parents' gods, for if she were discovered they would all be killed. Christine would answer that the Devil was deceiving them by urging them to worship so many gods and that there was but one God. When her father at last realized that his daughter refused to worship his idols, he was terribly grieved and upbraided her a great deal. She replied that she would gladly worship the God of Heaven. He thought she meant Jupiter and he was overjoyed and wanted to kiss her, but she cried out, 'Do not touch my mouth, for I wish to offer a pure offering to the celestial God.' The father was even happy with this. She returned to her chamber and nailed the door shut, then she knelt down and offered a holy prayer to God, weeping all the while. And the angel of the Lord descended and comforted her and brought her white bread and meat which she ate, for she had not tasted food for three days. Once, afterward, when Christine saw from her window several poor Christians begging at the foot of her tower, seeing that she had nothing to give them, she searched for her father's idols which were made of gold and silver, and she smashed them all and gave the fragments to the poor. When her father learned of this, he beat her cruelly. She openly declared he was deceived to worship these false images and that there was but a single God in the Trinity and that her father should worship Him whom she confessed, and she refused to worship any other in order to escape death. Thereupon her enraged father had her tied up with chains and led from square to square to be beaten and then thrown into prison. He himself wanted to be the judge of this dispute, so on the following day he had her brought before him and threatened her with every conceivable torture if she would not worship his idols. After he realized that he could not convince her with entreaties or threats, he had her sprawled completely nude and beaten so much that twelve men wearied at the task. And the father kept asking her what she thought and he said to her, 'Daughter, natural affection wrings my heart terribly to torment you who are my own flesh, but the reverence I have for my gods forces me to do this because you scorn them.' And the holy virgin replied, 'Tyrant who should not be called my father but rather enemy of my happiness, you boldly torture the flesh which you engendered, for you can easily do this, but as for my soul created by my Father in Heaven, you have no power to touch it with the slightest temptation, for it is protected by my Savior, Jesus Christ.' The cruel father, all the more enraged, had a wheel brought in, which he had ordered built, and ordered her tied to it and a fire built below it, and then he had rivers of boiling oil poured over her body. The wheel turned and completely crushed her. But God, the Father of all mercies, took pity on His servant and dispatched His angel to wreck the torture machines and to extinguish the fire, delivering the virgin, healthy and whole, and killing more than a thousand treacherous spectators who had been watching her without pity and who blasphemed the name of God. And her father asked her, 'Tell me who taught you these evil practices!' She replied, 'Pitiless despot, have I not told you that my Father, Jesus Christ, taught me this long-suffering as well as every right thing in the faith of the Living God? Because of this, I scorn your tortures and will repel all the Devil's assaults with God's strength!' Beaten and confounded, he ordered her thrown into a horrible, dark prison. While she was there, contemplating the extraordinary mysteries of God, three angels came to her in great radiance and brought her food and comforted her. Urban did not know what to do with her but could not stop devising new tortures for her. Finally, fed up completely and wishing to be free of her, he had a great stone tied around her neck and had her thrown into the sea. But as she was being thrown in, the angels took her, and she walked on the water with them. Then, raising her eyes to heaven, Christine prayed to Jesus Christ, that it please Him for her to receive in this water the holy sacrament of baptism which she greatly desired to have; whereupon Jesus Christ descended in His own person with a large company of angels and baptized her and named her Christine, from His own name, and He crowned her and placed a shining star on her forehead and set her on dry land. That night Urban was tortured by the Devil and died. The blessed Christine, whom God wanted to receive through martyrdom (which she also desired), was led back to prison by these criminals. The new judge, named Dyon, knowing what had been done to her, summoned her to appear before him, and he lusted after her because of her beauty. When he saw that his alluring words were of no use, he had her tortured again. He ordered that a large cauldron be filled with oil and that a roaring fire be built beneath it; he had her thrown in, upside down, and four men used iron hooks to rotate her. And the holy virgin sang melodiously to God, mocking her torturers and threatening them with the pains of Hell. When this enraged criminal of a judge realized that nothing was of any avail, he ordered her to be hanged by her long golden hair in the square, in front of all. The women rushed up to her, and, wailing out of pity that such a young girl be so cruelly tortured, they cried out to the judge, saying, 'Cruel felon, crueler than a savage beast, how could a man's heart conceive such monstrous cruelty against such a beautiful and tender maiden?' And all the women tried to mob him. Then the judge, who was afraid, said to her, 'Christine, friend, do not let yourself be tortured anymore, but come with me and we will go worship the supreme God who has upheld you.' He meant Jupiter, who was considered the supreme god, but she understood him in a completely different way and so she replied, 'You have spoken well, so I consent.' He had her taken down and brought up to the temple, and a large crowd followed them. Then he led her before the idols, thinking she would worship them, and she knelt down, looked up at Heaven, and prayed to God. Thereupon she stood up and, turning toward the idol, said, 'I command you in the name of Jesus Christ, oh evil spirit residing in this idol, to come out.' Whereupon the Devil immediately came out and made a loud and frightening din which scared all the spectators, who fell to the ground in fear. When the judge stood up again, he said, 'Christine, you have moved our omnipotent god, and, out of pity for you, he came out to see his creature.' This remark angered her, and she reproached him harshly for being too blind to recognize divine virtue, so she prayed to God to overturn the idol and reduce it to dust, which was done. And more than three thousand men were converted through the words and signs of this virgin. The terrified judge exclaimed, 'If the king finds out what this Christine has done against our god, he will utterly destroy me.' Thereupon, full of anguish, he went out of his mind and died. A third judge, named Julian, appeared, and he ordered Christine seized, boasting that he would make her worship the idols. In spite of all the force he could apply, he was unable physically to move her from the spot where she was standing, so he ordered a large fire built around her. She remained in the fire for three days, and from inside the flames were heard sweet melodies. Her tormentors were terrified by the amazing signs they saw. When the fire had burned out, she emerged fully healthy. The judge commanded that snakes be brought to him and had two asps (with their deadly poisonous bite) and two adders released upon her. But these snakes dropped down at her feet, their heads bowed, and did not harm her at all. Two horrible vipers were let loose, and they hung from her breasts and licked her. And Christine looked to Heaven and said, 'I give You thanks, Lord God, Jesus Christ, who have deigned to grant through Your holy virtues that these horrible serpents would come to know in me Your dignity.' The obstinate Julian, seeing these wonders, yelled at the snake-tender, 'Have you too been enchanted by Christine, so that you have no power to rouse the snakes against her?' Fearing the judge, he then tried to provoke the snakes into biting her, but they rushed at him and killed him. Since everyone was afraid of these serpents and no one dared approach, Christine commanded them in God's name to return to their cages without harming anyone, and they did so. She revived the dead man, who immediately threw himself at her feet and was converted. The judge, blinded by the Devil so that he was unable to perceive the divine mystery, said to Christine, 'You have sufficiently demonstrated your magic arts.' Infuriated, she replied, 'If your eyes would see the virtues of God, you would believe in them.' Then in his rage he ordered her breasts ripped off, whereupon milk rather than blood flowed out. And because she unceasingly pronounced the name of Jesus Christ, he had her tongue cut out, but then she spoke even better and more clearly than before of divine things and of the one blessed God, thanking Him for the bounties which He had given to her. She prayed that it please Him to receive her in His company and that the crown of her martyrdom be finally granted to her. Then a voice was heard from Heaven, saying, 'Christine, pure and radiant, the heavens are opened to you and the eternal kingdom waits, prepared for you, and the entire company of saints blesses God for your sake, for you have upheld the name of Your Christ from childhood on.' And she glorified God, turning her eyes to Heaven. The voice was heard saying, 'Come, Christine, my most beloved and elect daughter, receive the palm and everlasting crown and the reward for your life spent suffering to confess My name.' The treacherous Julian, who heard this voice, castigated the executioners and said they had not cut Christine's tongue short enough and ordered them to cut it so short that she could not speak to her Christ, whereupon they ripped out her tongue and cut it off at the root. She spat this cut-off piece of her tongue into the tyrant's face, putting out one of his eyes. She then said to him, speaking as clearly as ever, 'Tyrant, what does it profit you to have my tongue cut out so that it cannot bless God, when my soul will bless Him forever while yours languishes forever in eternal damnation? And because you did not heed my words, my tongue has blinded you, with good reason.' She ended her martyrdom then, having already seen Jesus Christ sitting on the right hand of His Father, when two arrows were shot at her, one in her side and the other in her heart. One of her relatives whom she had converted buried her body and wrote out her glorious legend."

O blessed Christine, worthy virgin favored of God, most elect and glorious martyr, in the holiness with which God has made you worthy, pray for me, a sinner, named with your name, and be my kind and merciful guardian. Behold my joy at being able to make use of your holy legend and to include it in my writings, which I have recorded here at such length out of reverence for you. May this be ever pleasing to you! Pray for all women, for whom your holy life may serve as an example for ending their lives well. Amen.

III.10.2   "What else should I tell you, dear friend, in order to fill our City with such a company? May Saint Ursula come with her multitude of eleven thousand virgins, blessed martyrs for the name of Jesus Christ, all of them beheaded after they had been sent off to be married. They arrived in the land of unbelievers who tried to force them to renounce their faith in God: they chose to die rather than to renounce Jesus Christ their Savior."

11. CONCERNING SEVERAL HOLY WOMEN WHO SAW THEIR CHILDREN MARTYRED BEFORE THEIR VERY EYES.

III.11.1   "What in the world is dearer to a mother than her child, and what greater grief than that which her heart suffers seeing her child in pain? Yet, because of the many valiant women who in their love for Jesus Christ have seen their children given over to torture, like the blessed Felicia, who saw her seven sons (who were beautiful youths) martyred in front of her, I maintain that faith is a much greater feeling. The excellent mother comforted them and exhorted them to be long-suffering and firm in the Faith. Thereby this good lady forgot her mother's heart as far as physical comfort was concerned for the sake of the love of God. Subsequently, after she had offered them all to the sacrifice, she wished to be sacrificed herself and went to be martyred.

"Likewise, the blessed Julitta, who had a son named *III.11.2* Cyricus. As she gave him bodily nourishment, at the same time she also gave him spiritual sustenance, for she drilled him continuously in the Faith so that, as a young child, he could not be overcome by those who sought to martyr him nor be forced to deny the name of Jesus Christ because of tortures. Thus, when he was tortured he cried out as best he could with his small, clear voice, 'I am a Christian and give thanks to our Lord God.' He spoke as distinctly as a forty-year-old. His good mother, who was also being harshly tortured, comforted him. She unceasingly praised God and consoled the other martyrs and spoke of the celestial joy awaiting them so that they should not be afraid.

"What could we say similarly about the wonderful *III.11.3* constancy and strength shown by the blessed Blandina? She saw her dearly beloved fifteen-year-old daughter tortured and martyred in front of her, and she comforted her joyfully. And afterward, as happily as a woman going to meet her husband, she submitted herself to torture. She was tormented with so many kinds of torture that her torturers became weary. She was placed on a grill and roasted, sliced with iron hooks, and all the while she glorified God, persevering to the end."

12. HERE SHE SPEAKS OF SAINT MARINA, VIRGIN.

"Much could be recounted concerning virgin martyrs, *III.12.1* as well as concerning other women who led a religious and holy life in various forms. Let me especially tell you about two of them, whose legends are quite beautiful and at the same time support the contention that women are constant. A layman had an only daughter who was quite young, named Marina, whom he placed in the care of a relative and then entered a monastery, where he led a most holy life. Yet Nature drew him to his daughter, and the pain of separation greatly disturbed him. He became so pensive that the abbot asked him the cause of his grief, and he finally confessed that he was preoccupied with a small son whom he had left behind in the world and whom he could not forget. The abbot told him to summon his son and to bring him into the religious life with him. Thus this virgin came to be with her father, dressed like a little monk, cleverly disguised and well disciplined. When she reached the age of eighteen, after having persevered better and better, her father, who had raised her so religiously, passed away. She remained alone in her father's cell, following the monastic life, so that the abbot and all the other monks acclaimed her way of living, thinking all the while that she was a man. This abbey lay three miles away from a town with a market-place, and from time to time the monks had to go to the market to buy necessities. Sometimes in the winter, night would fall before they had concluded their business, so they stayed the night in the town. And Marina, who was called Brother Marinus, would on occasion, when it was her turn, stay in town in a particular inn where everyone lodged together. It happened that the daughter of the innkeeper turned out to be pregnant and when her parents forced her to identify the father, she laid the blame on Brother Marinus. The parents thereupon went and complained to the abbot who had 'him' called, and the abbot was very sad about this matter. Nevertheless, this holy virgin preferred to accept the blame rather than reveal that she was a woman in order to excuse herself, and she knelt down and said, weeping, 'Father, I have sinned, pray for me and I will do penance.' The enraged abbot had her beaten harshly and thrown out of the abbey and forbidden entrance. She threw herself down on the ground in front of the door, lying there in penance, begging a single morsel of bread from the brothers. The innkeeper's daughter bore a son, whom her mother brought to Marina lying before the abbey and left there. The virgin took the child and, with the morsels of bread which monastery visitors gave her, fed him as though he were her own. Later, moved by pity, the brothers begged the abbot to take Brother Marinus back, for mercy's sake, and they barely succeeded in convincing him, and this was after Marina had already spent five years doing penance. When Marina re-entered the abbey, the abbot ordered her to perform all the filthy and servile duties inside, to fetch water for the latrines and to wait on everyone. The holy virgin did all this humbly and gladly. Shortly afterward she fell asleep in our Lord. Upon being informed by the brothers, the abbot said, 'Even though his sin does not deserve pardon, wash him anyway and bury him next to the abbey.' And when they undressed the corpse and discovered that Brother Marinus was a woman, they began to beat themselves and to cry out, grieved and perplexed by the harm they had done without cause to such a holy creature, and they were overwhelmed with wonder at her way of life. When all this was reported to the abbot, he rushed there and dropped to the ground sobbing at the feet of the holy corpse, beating his breast on account of sin, crying out for mercy, and begging for pardon. He ordered her buried in a chapel inside of the abbey. All the monks went there, including one brother with sight in only one eye who knelt over the body, kissing it with deep devotion, and immediately his sight was restored. On this same day the woman who had bore the child went out of her mind and cried out her sin, whereupon she was led to the holy corpse and recovered her health. And Marina worked and still continues to work many miracles in this place."

13. HERE SHE SPEAKS OF THE BLESSED EUPHROSYNA, VIRGIN.

"Likewise, there lived in Alexandria a virgin named *III.13.1* Euphrosyna, whom God had given to Paphnutius, her father, a man of great wealth, thanks to the prayers of a holy abbot and his monks from a nearby monastery.

When this daughter had grown up, her father wanted to marry her off, but she, in her total dedication to God, was determined to remain a virgin and so she fled, dressed like a man. She asked to be received into the monastery and gave the abbot to believe that she was a young man from the emperor's court who was eager to be admitted. Impressed with her devotion, the abbot gladly received her. Failing to find his beloved daughter, Paphnutius was terribly grieved and went to tell the abbot his grief and to find some consolation, and he begged the abbot to have the monks pray to God that he might hear some news. The abbot consoled him and told him that he could not believe that a daughter given by God in answer to prayer could have perished. The abbot and monks prayed to God for a long time on this score. And as the good man received no news and continued to return to the abbot for comfort in his tribulation, one day the abbot said to him, 'Truly, I do not believe anything has happened to your daughter, for if that were so, I am sure that God would have revealed it to us. Here in the monastery we have a son of prayer who came here from the emperor's court and to whom God has given so much grace that all who speak with him find themselves comforted. You may speak with him if you like.' Paphnutius asked to speak to him for God's sake. Thereupon the abbot had the father brought to his own daughter, whom he did not recognize, but the daughter easily recognized her father. Her eyes immediately filled with tears and she turned away, as though to finish a prayer. The beauty and freshness of her face had withered away because of the harshness of her self-denial. After speaking to her father and consoling him, she assured him that his daughter was in a good place serving God and that he would see her before his death and that he would yet have great joy because of her. The father, thinking she knew all this thanks to divine virtue, left relieved and reported to the abbot that he had not felt so much peace in his heart since he had lost his daughter. 'And I am,' he added, 'as happy as though I had found my daughter.' Then, commending himself to the abbot's and the monks' prayers, he departed. But he did not hesitate at all from coming back frequently to visit the holy brother, and he felt well only while speaking with him. And so the situation remained for a very long time, until this girl, who had herself called Brother Smaragdus, had spent some thirty-eight years in her cell. Then God chose to call her to Himself, and she was taken ill. The good Paphnutius, grieved by this, went there, and when he saw that Smaragdus was dying, he cried out, 'Alas! What happened to your sweet words and the promises which you made to me that I would see my daughter?' Then Smaragdus passed away in God, but the father was not there when he died. The dead monk held something written in his hand which no one could remove. The abbot and all the monks tried, but they could do nothing. Thereupon the father approached in tears, sobbing for his good friend whom he saw dead and in whom had been all his consolation. As soon as he approached the body to kiss it, its hands opened in front of everyone and gave him the writing. He took it and read within how she was his daughter and that no one should touch her body to bury her except for him. This astounded him, the abbot, and all the monks, who greatly praised her holy constancy and virtue. The father's grief was twice as great as before, out of pity for her holy life and for the consolation it afforded, whereupon he sold all he owned and went into the monastery where he ended his life.

"Now that I have told you about several virgins, I *III.13.2* will tell you about other ladies who were martyrs."

14. CONCERNING THE BLESSED LADY ANASTASIA.

"During the great persecutions in Rome under the *III.14.1* emperor Diocletian, there lived in the city a most noble lady of great wealth and wide influence named Anastasia. This lady felt amazing compassion for the blessed Christian martyrs whom she saw daily afflicted with tortures. In order to comfort and visit them every day, she would dress up as poor woman and go with a maid into the prisons where they were held and would comfort them with expensive wines and meats and whatever she could afford. She would wash and clean their wounds and anoint them with precious salves. She kept this up for so long that she was denounced by Publius, a Roman nobleman who wanted her as his wife and who was so angered that he placed guards on her to prevent her from leaving her house. At that time Saint Chrysogonus was in prison with the other martyrs, a man of outstanding excellence who had already suffered many grievous tortures, and he was sustained by the gifts and by the visits of this holy lady Anastasia, to whom this saint secretly sent many letters in care of a Christian lady, exhorting her to be patient, and she likewise sent him letters through this same good lady. Finally, as God willed, this man who had held her in such tight rein died, and she sold all she owned and used it all in visiting and sustaining the martyrs. This noble lady had a large following of Christian ladies and maidens. And among the others there were three virgins, sisters of noble lineage, who were her intimates. The first of the sisters was named Agape, the second, Chionia, the third, Irene. It came to the emperor's knowledge that these three ladies were Christians. He summoned them and promised them enormous gifts and noble marriages if they renounced Jesus Christ. When they paid no attention to any of this, the emperor had them beaten and thrown into a harsh prison where their holy friend Anastasia visited them and did not leave them night or day. And she prayed to God to let her live as long as her wealth lasted so that she could use it all in this holy work. The emperor commanded Dulcitius, his sergeant, that all imprisoned Christians be forced, through torture, to worship the idols, whereupon this sergeant had them all brought before him, including the three blessed sisters. When the evil sergeant saw them, he lusted after them because of their beauty and secretly urged them with alluring words and promises to consent so that he could free them. But when they rejected all of this, he turned them over to one of his aides to guard them and bring them to his house, where he thought he could enjoy their favors whether they were willing or not. When nightfall came, he went alone and without light to the house where he had them brought. And as he went to where he heard the virgins' voices, who all night long repeated praises to God, he passed by where all the kitchen pots were stored. And then, filled with the Devil and his mind blinded by lust—just as God willed—he began to hug and embrace one and then another of these pots, thinking he was with the maidens. He kept doing this until he was quite tired. And when daylight came, he went out to his retainers waiting outside, who thought, upon seeing him, that he was the very image of the Devil: he was filthy, greasy, and covered with soot, his cloak torn and trailing in tatters, and they fled, terrified. Seeing them flee, he realized that they despised him and he was totally baffled at what the reason could be. As he proceeded down the street, everyone who met him mocked him, so he decided to go straight to the emperor to complain about every passerby's making fun of him. When he entered the palace, where several morning attendants were waiting, a great uproar over him broke out in which one attendant beat him with rods, another shoved him back, saying, 'Get out you miserable wretch, you stink all over.' Another spit in his face and the others made fun of him. He was so completely puzzled by what all this could mean that he nearly went crazy, and the Devil had so blinded him that he was unable to see himself, so he returned home, furious.

"Another judge was put in his place, and he had the *III.14.2* three blessed virgins brought before him and tried to make them worship the idols. Because they refused, he ordered them stripped and beaten. Yet for all their power, the judge's henchmen could not strip the virgins, for their robes clung so tightly that no one could remove them; therefore the judge had them thrown into a raging fire, but nothing could injure them. But they prayed to God to end their lives, if it please Him, so they passed away gloriously, and, in order to demonstrate that they had died of their own will, the fire consumed not one hair or piece of clothing they were wearing. And when the fire had gone out, their bodies were found with their heads joined together in prayer, completely whole, with their faces as fresh as though they were only sleeping. The blessed Anastasia, who had cared for them, buried their bodies."

15. CONCERNING THE BLESSED THEODATA.

III.15.1   "Anastasia had another noble companion, named Theodata, who had three small sons. Because she refused to marry the count Leucadius and to sacrifice to the idols, she was cruelly tortured. In order to pressure her more strongly by appealing to her maternal pity, one of her sons was tortured in front of her. But she comforted him with the virtue of faith which transcends nature, saying, 'Son, do not fear these tortures, for through them you will come to glory.' When this lady herself was imprisoned, a son of the Devil tried to violate her chastity, whereupon this incontinent man began to bleed profusely from his nose and therefore cried out that a young boy who was with her had struck his nose with his fist. She was tortured again and finally killed, and also her three sons, who gave up their blessed souls to God, glorifying Him all the while, and the blessed Anastasia buried them.

III.15.2   "This blessed lady so frequently visited the martyrs that she was detained in prison and could no longer visit the saints of God. And she had nothing to eat or drink. But God did not desire that she suffer from want, for she had so diligently comforted and fed His blessed martyrs, and so He sent to her in great radiance the spirit of her blessed companion Theodata, who set a table for her and brought her delectable meals and, in this manner, kept her company for thirty days, during which nothing was brought to her to eat. Her executioners thought she would have already died from starvation, but she was found alive and led before the prefect who was very troubled by this. And because many people converted because of this miracle, he had her placed in a ship with many condemned criminals. Once they were on the high seas, the sailors, carrying out their orders, scuttled the ship and left it for another vessel. Thereupon the blessed Theodata appeared to them and guided them at sea for a night and a day as surely as though it were level ground until they reached the island of Palmaria, where many bishops and holy men had been sent into exile, and there they were welcomed with joyful praises to God. And those who had escaped with Anastasia were baptized and believed in God. When this matter came to the emperor's knowledge, he had them all sent for, more than three hundred men, women, and children, whom he then had tortured to death. And the blessed Anastasia, after delivering several speeches to the emperor and after having been tortured, was crowned with martyrdom."

16. CONCERNING THE NOBLE AND HOLY NATALIA.

"Natalia, who was the noble wife of Adrian, commander of Emperor Maximianus' cavalry, and who was secretly a Christian during the time when so many Christians were being martyred, heard that her husband, Adrian, for whose sake she had prayed to God unceasingly, had suddenly been converted while watching the martyrs being tortured and had confessed the name of Jesus Christ, for which the emperor, in his rage, had ordered him placed in a harsh prison. The blessed lady, overjoyed at her husband's conversion, immediately rushed to the prison to comfort him, praying that he would persevere in what he had started. And she kissed the chains with which he was bound, weeping with pity and joy. She exhorted him to have no regrets for earthly joys which are transient but to hold fast before his

III.16.1

eyes the great glory which was prepared for him. This holy lady stayed there a long time, comforting him and all the other martyrs, praying to God that she could soon join their company. She entreated them to comfort her husband who, she feared, might waver in the firmness of his faith as a result of torture. She visited him every day, constantly preaching to him to remain steadfast, and she spoke many beautiful words to him. But because she and many other women were visiting the holy martyrs, the emperor forbade any women to enter the prison, whereupon Natalia dressed up like a man. When the day of his martyrdom finally came, she was present, and she cleaned his wounds and kissed his blood, weeping in devotion and begging him to pray to God for her. And so the blessed Adrian passed away and Natalia piously buried him. She kept one of his hands which had been cut off and wrapped it up as a holy relic. Following her husband's death, this noble lady was pressured to marry again because she was of noble lineage, beautiful and wealthy. She was constantly in prayer, beseeching God to deliver her from the hands of those who sought to force her, and her husband appeared to her while she slept and comforted her and told her that she would go to Constantinople to bury the bodies of many martyrs there, and this she did gladly. After she had been in God's service for a while, visiting the holy martyrs in prison, her husband again appeared to her and said, 'Sister and friend, chambermaid of Jesus Christ, come to eternal glory, for our Lord calls you.' And she awoke and immediately passed away."

17. CONCERNING SAINT AFRA, A FOOLISH, IMMORAL WOMAN WHO WAS CONVERTED.

III.17.1   "Afra was a prostitute who converted to the faith of Jesus Christ. She was accused by a judge who said to her, 'As though your body's immorality were not enough, you offend the law by your crime of worshiping a foreign god! Sacrifice to our gods so that they will pardon you.' And Afra replied, 'I will sacrifice to my God, who came down from Heaven for sinners, for His Gospel says that a sinful woman washed His feet with her tears and received pardon. And He did not scorn immoral women nor the sinful publicans, rather He let them eat with Him.' The judge said to her, 'If you do not sacrifice, you will not be loved by your clients, nor will you receive gifts from them.' She answered, 'I will never accept another forbidden gift and I have begged the poor to take those gifts which I unlawfully received and to pray for me.' The judge sentenced Afra to be burned to death for refusing to sacrifice. When she was delivered to the torture she prayed, saying, 'Lord God, omnipotent Jesus Christ, who called sinners to repent, receive favorably my martyrdom in the hour of my passion and deliver me from eternal fire with this earthly fire which is akin to my body.' And when she was completely surrounded by flames, she prayed, 'Lord Jesus Christ, deign to receive me, a poor sinful woman, sacrificed for the sake of Your holy name, You who are offered as the one sacrifice for the whole world and who were placed on the Cross without sin for the sake of sinners, wholly good for the benefit of evil men, filled with blessing for the cursed, sweetness for the bitter, clean and innocent of sin on behalf of all sinners. I offer the sacrifice of my body to You who live and reign with the Father and the Holy Spirit for ever and ever.' And so died the blessed Afra, for whose sake our Lord subsequently manifested many miracles."

18. JUSTICE SPEAKS OF MANY NOBLE WOMEN WHO WAITED ON AND LODGED THE APOSTLES AND OTHER SAINTS.

"What more do you want me to tell you, my fair friend, Christine? I could recall other similar examples to you without stop. But because I see that you are surprised—for you said earlier, that every classical author attacked women—I tell you that, in spite of what

III.18.1

you may have found in the writings of pagan authors on the subject of criticizing women, you will find little said against them in the holy legends of Jesus Christ and His Apostles; instead, even in the histories of all the saints, just as you can see yourself, you will find through God's grace many cases of extraordinary firmness and strength in women. Oh, the beautiful service, the outstanding charity which they have performed with great care and solicitude, unflinchingly, for the servants of God! Should not such hospitality and favors be considered? And even if some foolish men deem them frivolous, no one can deny that such works in accordance with our Faith are the ladders leading to Heaven. So it is written regarding Drusiana, an honest widow who received Saint John the Evangelist in her home and waited on him and served him meals. It happened when this same Saint John returned from exile that the city dwellers held a large feast for him just as Drusiana was being led to burial, for she had died from grief over his long absence. And the neighbors said, 'John, here is Drusiana, your good hostess, who died from sorrow at your absence. She will never wait on you again.' Whereupon Saint John addressed her, 'Drusiana, get up and go home and prepare my meal for me.' And she came back to life.

III.18.2   "Likewise, a valiant and noble lady from the city of Limoges, named Susanna, was the first to give lodging to Saint Martial, who had been sent there by Saint Peter in order to convert the country. And this lady did many good things for him.

III.18.3   "Similarly, the good lady Maximilla removed Saint Andrew from the cross and buried him and in so doing risked death.

III.18.4   "The holy virgin Ephigenia in like manner followed Saint Matthew the Evangelist with great devotion and waited upon him. And after his death she had a church built in his honor.

III.18.5   "Similarly, another good lady was so taken with holy

love for Saint Paul that she followed him everywhere
and served him diligently.

"Likewise, during the time of the Apostles, a noble *III.18.6*
queen named Helen (not the mother of Constantine but
the queen of Adiabene, in Assyria) went to Jerusalem,
where there was a terrible shortage of foodstuffs because
of the famine there. And when she learned that the saints
of our Lord, who were in the city to preach to the
people and to convert them, were dying of hunger, she
had enough food purchased to provide them food as long
as the famine lasted.

"Similarly, when Saint Paul was led to be beheaded *III.18.7*
at Nero's command, a good lady named Plautilla, who
had customarily waited on him, walked ahead of him,
weeping profoundly. And Saint Paul asked her for the
scarf which she had on her head. And she gave it to
him, whereupon the evil men who were there taunted
her, saying that it was a fine thing for her to forfeit such
a beautiful scarf. Saint Paul himself tied it around his
eyes, and when he was dead, the angels gave it back to
the woman, and it was completely smeared with blood,
for which she cherished it dearly. And Saint Paul appeared to her and told her that because she had served
him on Earth, he would serve her in Heaven by praying
for her. I will tell you many more similar cases.

"Basilissa was a noble lady by virtue of her chastity. *III.18.8*
She was married to Saint Julian, and both of them took a
vow of virginity on their wedding night. No one could
conceive of the holy way of life of this virgin, nor the
multitude of women and maidens who were saved and
drawn to a holy life through her sacred preaching. And,
in short, she was so deserving of grace because of her
great chastity that our Lord spoke to her as she was dying.

"I do not know what more I could tell you, Christine, *III.18.9*
my friend. I could tell of countless ladies of different
social backgrounds, maidens, married women, and
widows, in whom God manifested His virtues with

amazing force and constancy. But let this suffice for you, for it seems to me that I have acquitted myself well of my office in completing the high roofs of your City and in populating it for you with outstanding ladies, just as I promised. These last examples will serve as the doorways and gates into our City. And even though I have not named all the holy ladies who have lived, who are living, and who will live—for I could name only a handful!—they can all be included in this City of Ladies. Of it may be said, '*Gloriosa dicta sunt de te, civitas Dei.*' So I turn it over to you, finished perfectly and well enclosed, just as I promised. Farewell and may the peace of the Lord be always with you."

19. THE END OF THE BOOK: CHRISTINE ADDRESSES THE LADIES.

III.19.1   My most honored ladies, may God be praised, for now our City is entirely finished and completed, where all of you who love glory, virtue, and praise may be lodged in great honor, ladies from the past as well as from the present and future, for it has been built and established for every honorable lady. And my most dear ladies, it is natural for the human heart to rejoice when it finds itself victorious in any enterprise and its enemies confounded. Therefore you are right, my ladies, to rejoice greatly in God and in honest mores upon seeing this new City completed, which can be not only the refuge for you all, that is, for virtuous women, but also the defense and guard against your enemies and assailants, if you guard it well. For you can see that the substance with which it is made is entirely of virtue, so resplendent that you may see yourselves mirrored in it, especially in the roofs built in the last part as well as in the other parts which concern you. And my dear ladies, do not misuse this new inheritance like the arrogant who turn proud when their prosperity grows and their wealth multiplies, but rather follow the example of your Queen, the sovereign Virgin, who, after the extraordinary honor of being chosen Mother of the Son of God was announced to her, humbled herself all the more by calling herself the hand-maiden of God. Thus, my ladies, just as it is true that a creature's humility and kindness wax with the increase of its virtues, may this City be an occasion for you to conduct yourselves honestly and with integrity and to be all the more virtuous and humble.

And you ladies who are married, do not scorn being *III.19.2* subject to your husbands, for sometimes it is not the best thing for a creature to be independent. This is attested by what the angel said to Ezra: Those, he said, who take advantage of their free will can fall into sin and despise our Lord and deceive the just, and for this they perish. Those women with peaceful, good, and dis-crete husbands who are devoted to them, praise God for this boon, which is not inconsiderable, for a greater boon in the world could not be given them. And may they be diligent in serving, loving, and cherishing their hus-bands in the loyalty of their heart, as they should, keeping their peace and praying to God to uphold and save them. And those women who have husbands neither completely good nor completely bad should still praise God for not having the worst and should strive to mod-erate their vices and pacify them, according to their conditions. And those women who have husbands who are cruel, mean, and savage should strive to endure them while trying to overcome their vices and lead them back, if they can, to a reasonable and seemly life. And if they are so obstinate that their wives are unable to do any-thing, at least they will acquire great merit for their souls through the virtue of patience. And everyone will bless them and support them.

So, my ladies, be humble and patient, and God's grace *III.19.3* will grow in you, and praise will be given to you as well as the Kingdom of Heaven. For Saint Gregory has said that patience is the entrance to Paradise and the way of Jesus Christ. And may none of you be forced into holding frivolous opinions nor be hardened in them, lacking all basis in reason, nor be jealous or disturbed in mind, nor haughty in speech, nor outrageous in your acts, for these things disturb the mind and lead to madness. Such behavior is unbecoming and unfitting for women.

III.19.4 And you, virgin maidens, be pure, simple, and serene, without vagueness, for the snares of evil men are set for you. Keep your eyes lowered, with few words in your mouths, and act respectfully. Be armed with the strength of virtue against the tricks of the deceptive and avoid their company.

III.19.5 And widows, may there be integrity in your dress, conduct, and speech; piety in your deeds and way of life; prudence in your bearing; patience (so necessary!), strength, and resistance in tribulations and difficult affairs; humility in your heart, countenance, and speech; and charity in your works.

III.19.6 In brief, all women—whether noble, bourgeois, or lower-class—be well-informed in all things and cautious in defending your honor and chastity against your enemies! My ladies, see how these men accuse you of so many vices in everything. Make liars of them all by showing forth your virtue, and prove their attacks false by acting well, so that you can say with the Psalmist, "the vices of the evil will fall on their heads." Repel the deceptive flatterers who, using different charms, seek with various tricks to steal that which you must consummately guard, that is, your honor and the beauty of your praise. Oh my ladies, flee, flee the foolish love they urge on you! Flee it, for God's sake, flee! For no good can come to you from it. Rather, rest assured that however deceptive their lures, their end is always to your detriment. And do not believe the contrary, for it cannot be otherwise. Remember, dear ladies, how these men call you frail, unserious, and easily influenced but yet try hard, using all kinds of strange and deceptive tricks, to catch you, just as one lays traps for wild animals. Flee, flee, my ladies, and avoid their company—under these smiles are hidden deadly and painful poisons. And so may it please you, my most respected ladies, to cultivate virtue, to flee vice, to increase and multiply our City, and to rejoice and act well. And may I, your servant, commend myself to you, praying to God who by His grace has granted me to live in this world and to persevere in His holy service. May He in the end have mercy on my great sins and grant to me the joy which lasts forever, which I may, by His grace, afford to you. Amen.

HERE ENDS THE THIRD AND LAST PART OF THE BOOK OF THE CITY OF LADIES.

NOTES ON THE TEXT

These notes may help explain selected, important passages of *The Book of the City of Ladies,* but are in no sense exhaustive. They are intended as a partial interpretation. Curnow gives far more extensive information regarding Christine's sources, and the interested reader is referred to her edition.

I.1.1: The opening stresses Christine's natural affinity for and devotion to study. The small book written by Mathéolus which she comes upon was, in all likelihood, the Old French translation of the Latin *Liber Lamentationum Matheoluli (The Book of the Lamentations of Mathéolus),* a verse work of 5,614 lines, composed around 1300, which Jean le Fèvre de Ressons translated in the last third of the fourteenth century and to which he added his reply, *Le Livre de Leësce.* Mathéolus' tirade against women—couched in Ovidian diction—follows almost standard misogynist conventions and has been summarized (in French) by A. G. van Hamel in his critical edition of *Les Lamentations de Mathéolus et le Livre de Leësce de Jehann le Fèvre de Ressons,* (Paris, 1892-1905), II.lxviii-cvii. Mathéolus has Christine to thank that his work is known, for as van Hamel notes (clvii), its success and fame were not great.

—"my character and conduct as a natural woman": If one chooses to view *The Book of the City of Ladies* as Christine's ongoing commentary on the Quarrel of *The Romance of the Rose,* this phrase takes on a special significance: in the *Rose,* Nature, replying to Reason, presents extended attacks on the chastity of women. Christine turns the tables in *The Book of the City of Ladies.* First, she presents a counterversion of Nature's portrayal of the "natural" behavior of women, and second, she makes Reason—who came off so poorly in the *Rose*—her first guide and helper in constructing the City of Ladies.

I.2.1: The setting for the appearance of the three Virtues makes it clear that Christine is *truly* experiencing their visit, that she is *not* dreaming like Amant, the protagonist of the *Rose,* and consequently that her experiences are more truthful than Amant's. The appearance of Reason, Rectitude, and Justice recalls the appearance of Lady Philosophy to Boethius at the opening of the *Consolation of Philosophy*, as though Christine's work were a kind of "consolation" for ladies. At the same time, Reason's appearance is also reminiscent of that of Vergil to Dante at the opening of the *Commedia*, a work which Christine claimed to have introduced to France.

—"in a fictional way" ("en maniere de fable"): Though Christine has yet to mention the *Rose*, this dismissal of the testimony of poets can be seen as a direct attack on the *Rose* whose opening, "maintes genz dient qu'en songes/n'a se fables non et mensonges" ("many people say that there are only fables and lies in dreams"), anticipates the *Rose's* valorization of the higher truth of poetry.

I.3.2: This section of *The Book of the City of Ladies* recalls the opening of the *Commedia* once again. Reason, Rectitude, and Justice are as concerned for Christine's salvation as the "three blessed ladies" (*tre donne benedette* of *Inferno* 2.124) are for Dante's, just as Christine's straying from the right path recalls Dante's *smarrimento*.

I.4.2: Christine's comparing her building the City of Ladies with the founding of Troy is an interesting variation of the topos of *translatio imperii et studii:* medieval French literature in particular (as, for example, Chrétien de Troyes in *Cligès*) often refers to the shift of political and cultural activity from Greece (or Troy) to Rome and then to France. Political and cultural dignity went hand in hand with political and cultural continuity. By associating the City of Ladies with Troy, Christine bestows a kind of political and cultural legitimacy on her new city. Christine refers to this topos with reference to Charles V in her *Fais et bonnes meurs*.

I.8.3: "these attacks on all women... have never originated with me, Reason": Reason's remarks here and in the remaining sections of the first part of *The Book of the City of Ladies* aim at rehabilitating Reason, whom Christine, writing to Jean Gerson in the course of the Quarrel of the *Rose*, found badly misrepresented by Jean de Meung in his part of the *Rose*.

I.9.2: Cecco d'Ascoli was the *nom de plume* of Francesco Stabili, a professor of astrology in Pisa who died in 1327 and author of the *Acerba*, whose fourth book contains a lengthy misogynist tirade.

I.9.3: *Secreta mulierum (The Secrets of Women)* was a gynecological treatise spuriously attributed to Albert Magnus. As Curnow notes, here Christine is citing the Latin text from memory. — Although the actual sources for Christine's remarks are not Cicero and Cato as she claims, her rhetorical intent is clear. Christine wishes to demonstrate her mastery—albeit sometimes faulty—of the classical canon of rhetorical authorities.

I.13.3-7: Christine demonstrates her fluent control of women's history by skillfully interweaving references to misogynist attacks leveled by classical writers, counter-examples taken from early Christian history, and to noble ladies of the recent past. This management of detail serves to enhance Christine's credibility in rewriting the history of women.

I.15: Semiramis. Liliane Dulac (in "Un mythe didactique chez Christine de Pizan: Sémiramis ou la Veuve héroïque, [Du *De mulieribus claris* de Boccace à la *Cité des Dames*]," *Mélanges de Philologie romane offerts a Charles Camproux*, [Montpellier, 1978], pp. 315-343) has examined in detail the distinctions between Boccaccio's presentation of Semiramis and that of Christine, and demonstrates how carefully Christine reshapes her source, shifting emphasis and changing tone, to fit the political and pedagogical economy of her narrative. Prior to Dulac, scholars tended to view Christine's relationship to her sources (chiefly Boccaccio) in vastly oversimplified terms.

I.19.1: This description of Hector's tomb may have recalled for Christine's readers the depiction of other sumptuous tombs in Old French literature, such as that of Camilla in the *Roman d'Eneas* (vv. 7531 ff.). This is of course a very minor point, but may show that Christine was more familiar with twelfth-century Old French literature than has hitherto been suspected (see below the note to II.60.2).

I.24.1: While Boccaccio is Christine's immediate source for the portrayal of Camilla, one wonders whether Christine might have also known Vergil's description of Camilla (*Aeneid*, XI.532 ff.) or the significant reworking of this Vergilian passage in the Old French *Roman d'Eneas* (whose significance is discussed by Erich Auerbach in his *Literary Language and Its Public in Late Latin Antiquity and in the Middle Ages,* [Princeton, 1965]).

I.28.1: Christine's selection and treatment of earlier women poets such as Cornificia, Proba, and Sappho, is helpful in understanding Christine's perception of herself as a poet. Christine focuses in all of her examples on the erudition of the woman poet. For the mature Christine in *The Book of the City of Ladies,* poetry and erudition are inseparable, an attitude which differs from her position in her early lyric poetry.

I.29.1: By simultaneously rewriting and Christianizing Vergil, Proba showed herself to be the better poet. Christine never says this explicitly. At the same time, Proba's treatment of Vergil exemplifies in part Christine's relationship to Boccaccio, whom she rewrites and Christianizes.

I.31.1: While Boccaccio is Christine's direct source, Manto's importance for both Boccaccio and Christine goes back to Dante's treatment of Manto in *Inferno* 20. Christine adds the detail which is not found in Boccaccio that Mantua was Vergil's birthplace (though this fact was surely common knowledge among an educated public).

I.32.1: By turning to Medea and Manto immediately following her discussion of the three great women poets of Antiquity, Christine seems to be pointing to the affinity of poetry and sorcery, a familiar literary topos.

I.41.4: This enticing remark about Anastasia, in spite of its brevity, is important in showing how closely Christine worked together with the illuminators of her works, a rare if not unique example of a medieval vernacular writer coordinating the physical production of her own work. One should also refer to Millard Meiss' remarks in his *French Painting in the Time of Jean de Berry,* (London, 1967), v. 1, p. 3 and p. 362, n. 3.

I.46.1: Christine prefers to use the name Elissa instead of Dido, certainly an unusual feature of this passage. Perhaps Christine used the "original" name of one of the most vilified women of world literature in order to rehabilitate her. Vergil is conspicuously absent in Christine's account (see below the note to II.3.1).

I.46.3: The word *virago* for Christine does not possess the negative connotations of the word in English (otherwise the word would be completely out of context here). *Virago* functions for Christine as a learned lexical borrowing conveying a certain dignity. One might also think of Gerson's positive description of Christine as *femina ista virilis*, "this manly woman."

II.1.3: Christine's claim that the sibyls were better than Old Testament prophets is a little daring. Christine was probably motivated to make such a comparison because it implicitly pits *feminine* (albeit pagan) augury against masculine (and Church-sanctioned) prophecy. In a sense Christine is lending more weight to the erudition of Antiquity than to the revealed truths of the Old Testament.

—"a subject which Homer wrote about with so many lies": Homer's credibility is also attacked by the earlier Old French poet Benoît de Ste.-Maure in the prologue to his *Roman de Troie*.

II.2.3: One might suspect at first that Christine's repeating Boccaccio's opinion that the sibyl Erythrea was honored among the saints of Paradise is merely another example of medieval syncretism. Since Christine does not often agree with Boccaccio on many subjects, surely a more profound ideological purpose stands behind Christine's reference to Boccaccio here. The legend of the sibyl Erythrea formed the basis for the last episode of the *Epistre d'Othea*.

II.3.1: "several fictions claim that she led Aeneas to Hell and back": In this seemingly off-hand remark, Christine relegates Vergil to the literary scrap-heap without even bothering to name him. Since Christine was well-acquainted with Dante's *Commedia*, perhaps Christine is trying to puncture Vergil's authority for Dante.

II.17.1: When one reads how Argia recognizes her husband's decomposing body thanks to her love, one cannot help thinking of the medieval tradition according to which lovers always recognized each other regardless of all obstacles to recognition or disguises, as in the legend of Tristan and Iseut. For Christine this case of a woman overcoming her "feminine" weakness is *exemplary* whereas for Boccaccio Argia's behavior is praiseworthy because it is unusual.

II.20-24, 30-33, 37-40: The accounts of the various women in these chapters alternate between pagan and sacred (or contemporary) sources and therefore point to the absolute historical continuity of the feminine character for Christine and at the same time refute Boccaccio's positing of a discontinuity between ancient and contemporary women. For Christine, the universal innate goodness of women cuts across all historical and religious barriers. In her striving to write a universal history of women, Christine may have been inspired by Dante's notions of universal history (see Robert Hollander, *Allegory in Dante's Commedia,* [Princeton, 1969], chapter two, "The Roots of Universal History," pp. 57-103).

II.20.1-2: Christine's conjoining the story of Tertia Aemilia given by Boccaccio with that of the countess of Coemon is a good example of how Christine uses her source for her own purposes: the remarkable women whom Boccaccio treated need to be seen as the predecessors of contemporary women of equal or greater stature, and not as historical aberrations or anomalies in the female character. Curnow suggests in her note on the countess of Coemon that Christine was making a veiled reference to Valentina Visconti who, like the countess of Coemon, raised the illegitimate son of her husband.

II.21-22: In both these chapters the "natural" behavior of women is shown to be in complete accord with the conduct followed by the greatest philosophers of Antiquity.

II.22.2: Christine incorporates contemporary examples of old men with young wives into Boccaccio's narrative and once more implicitly refutes Boccaccio's claim that pagan women must be treated separately from Jewish and Christian women. Christine might be implying, as in the case of the sibyl Erythrea, that the conduct of pagan women prefigures (in accordance with medieval notions of universal history) the behavior of women (and men) who consciously participated in "sacred history."

II.25.1: Christine expands her earlier attack on *The Romance of the Rose* here to an attack on all those authors who espouse the kinds of opinions championed in the *Rose.* By disproving misogynistic arguments in general, Christine refutes the *Rose* in particular. This task is all the more difficult because Christine must establish her erudition and credibility by demonstrating her fluency with the very same classical canon whose consistent misogyny she attacks. By being able to "correct" her predecessors, Christine demonstrates her superiority over them and consequently her greater authority and credibility.

II.36.3: Giovanni Andrea (1275-1347) was renowned for his legal scholarship. His erudition even served the Italian humanist Poggio, writing in his *Facetiae* between 1438 and 1452, as the occasion for an elaborate and obscene joke. Christine's source for the scholarly qualitites of Andrea's daughter may have been Jean le Fèvre in his *Livre de Leësce* (11. 1140-1154), as Curnow claims in her note on the passage, or Christine's own personal acquaintance with the story.

II.37: Christine's account of Susanna, argues Curnow, may be a veiled defense of Valentina Visconti (see above the note on II.20.1-2) in that both women were falsely accused. Valentina Visconti is only once explicitly mentioned by Christine in II.68.3.

II.44-45: Christine's remarks on rape, combining ancient and contemporary examples, are perhaps the first of their kind to have been made by a woman. They have lost nothing of their original eloquence and urgency in the intervening centuries.

II.47-49: Christine's comments on the inconstancy and weakness of Nero and other Roman emperors represent a slight departure from Christine's normal line of argument: in general she demonstrates the virtues of women without reference to the vices of men. By giving these examples, Christine provides a basis of comparison for appreciating women's virtues which was lacking in Boccaccio's *De mulieribus claris*, all the while taking the majority of examples for men's vices from Boccaccio's own *De casibus virorum illustrium*. That is, Christine is skillfully able to manipulate Boccaccio for her own argumentative purposes. By extending her account of men's vices to the present, Christine is following her consistent practice of bringing a universal historical perspective to bear on the re-evaluation of women's role in human history.

II.50: While the tale of Griselda owes its greatest fame to Boccaccio, who tells the story at the very end of the *Decameron*, Christine preferred the version of the story given by Petrarch in his *De oboedentia ac fide uxoria mythologia (A Fable on Wifely Obedience and Faithfulness)*, written in 1373, which Philippe de Mézières translated into French and included in his *Livre de la vertu du sacrement du mariage* (1384-89). As Curnow has demonstrated on the basis of verbal parallels, Christine had Philippe de Mézières' translation in front of her as she wrote this part of *The Book of the City of Ladies*. This does not mean that Christine did not know Petrarch's version, in fact Christine might have read Petrarch's story in Latin with the help of Philippe de Mézières' translation. Apart from the question of Christine's immediate source, one needs to consider why Christine explicitly avoided Boccaccio's version here when only two chapters later in II.52 she used Boccaccio's story of the wife of Bernabo. Petrarch had justified his reworking of Boccaccio's story for a specific moral purpose. "It was appropriate to reclothe this story in a different style not because ladies of our time should imitate the suffering of this wife, which seems to me hardly possible to imitate, but because I wanted to inspire my readers at least to imitate this woman's constancy," wrote Petrarch in his introductory letter to Boccaccio (*Hanc historiam stilo nunc alio retexere visum fuit, non tam ideo, ut matronas nostri temporis ad imitandum huius uxoris patientiam, quae mihi vix imitabilis videtur, quam ut legentes ad imitandam saltem foeminae constantiam excitarem*, p. 209 in *Francisci Petrarchae Opuscula historica et philologica*, [Bern, 1604], pp. 182-214). This represents an important shift of emphasis away from that given by Boccaccio. Petrarch's profound correction of Boccaccio could conceivably have influenced Christine to use Petrarch's version. Moreover, utilizing Petrarch's reworking of the story conforms to Christine's desire to undercut Boccaccio's authority in his *De mulieribus claris*, the most characteristic aspect of her reception of Boccaccio. For additional details on the story of Griselda, one should consult: Käte Laserstein, *Der Griseldis-Stoff in der Weltliteratur*, (Weimar, 1926); Elie Golenistcheff-Koutouszoff, *L'Histoire de Griselda en France au XIVe et au XVe siècle*, (Paris, 1933), and Elisabeth Frenzel, "Griseldis," in her *Stoffe der Weltliteratur*, (Stuttgart, 1976₄), pp. 257-261.

II.51: By connecting the story of Florence of Rome to that of Griselda, Christine places the story of the former in a new thematic context. Christine indicates that her source is Gautier de Coinci writing in his *Miracles de Nostre Dame par personnages*, (edited by V. Frédéric Koenig, [Geneva, 1955-1970], 4 vols.).

II.52: Christine, just as she indicates, borrows the story of the wife of Bernabo from Boccaccio's *Decameron* (Second Day, Ninth Tale). In order to utilize this story for her own argumentative purposes, which contrast with Boccaccio's intentions in *De mulieribus claris* (that is, the wife of Bernabo is used by Christine as a contemporary example of feminine excellence), Christine places considerably more emphasis than Boccaccio on the moral aspects of the tale. In medieval rhetorical terms, Christine simultaneously *abbreviates* and *moralizes* her source. A late medieval reader often enjoyed precisely this kind of manipulation and reworking of sources —the new "twist" on a familiar story—much as a modern reader of Joyce's *Ulysses* takes particular pleasure in Joyce's reworking of Homer. At the same time it would be inaccurate to assume that· all of Christine's readers enjoyed the same level of literary culture as Christine herself, so that they could have read and appreciated Christine on a far less complicated—less literate—level, just as the modern reader of Joyce's *Ulysses* who is innocent of Homer can still enjoy that modern classic. Charity Canon Willard indicated in a conversation with this writer that the copying of manuscripts of *The Book of the City of Ladies* ceased abruptly with the appearance in the middle of the fifteenth century of a complete translation of Boccaccio's *De mulieribus claris* in French. In other words, most of Christine's readers probably failed to grasp her reworking of Boccaccio and read her work as the next best thing to a French translation of *De mulieribus claris,* which *The Book of the City of Ladies* clearly does not purport to be.

II.54: Christine explicitly connects her observations on the fidelity of women in love to her earlier remarks in the Quarrel of *The Romance of the Rose,* one additional piece of evidence that Christine viewed *The Book of the City of Ladies* as a continuation of the Quarrel.

II.55-56: In these two chapters Christine returns to Dido and Medea whom she treats in I.46 and I.32, respectively. This repetition presupposes a careful distinction on Christine's part between Dido's and Medea's political accomplishments and their emotional lives. Both Dido and Medea were *primarily* renowned for their disappointments in love rather than for political expertise (Dido) or magical skills (Medea).

Christine emphasizes both women's respective successes before turning to their unhappiness in love, an approach which casts their emotional lives in a more favorable light.

II.57: Christine gives Ovid as her source for the story of Pyramus and Thisbe, though she more likely had the French *Ovide moralisé* at hand rather than the Latin text, as Curnow has shown. Christine notes that of the two lovers the woman, Thisbe, loved the more and suffered the more.

II.59-60: In these two chapters Christine retells three stories from Boccaccio's *Decameron,* all taken from the Fourth Day (Ghismonda, First Tale; Lisabetta, Fifth Tale; the wife of Guillaume de Roussillon, Ninth Tale). The general organizing theme of the Fourth Day is love with an unhappy ending, (*si ragiona di coloro li cui amori ebbero infelice fine*), and by selecting stories specifically from the Fourth Day and specifically those three stories in which women's love is thwarted by the treachery of men, Christine's rehandling of these stories seems to be an effort at "rehabilitating" Ghismonda, Lisabetta, and the wife of Guillaume de Roussillon, and at the same time, an attempt to discredit Boccaccio.

II.60.2: Christine follows up the story of Lisabetta with those of "another woman whose husband had her eat the heart of her lover" (the wife of Guillaume de Roussillon), the Dame de Fayel, the Dame de Vergi, Iseut, and Deianeira. Besides these references to the Dame de Fayel, the Dame de Vergi, and Iseut, we possess very little direct evidence from Christine herself to demonstrate her familiarity with Old French literature apart from *The Romance of the Rose.* One reason for this paucity of remarks on vernacular literature may be that Christine wanted to demonstrate her erudition on the basis of her familiarity with classical authors and consciously avoided referring to Old French works.

II.61: Here Christine addresses herself to a number of famous women whose fame rested on coincidence rather than on their own virtue. This brief excursus serves to buttress Christine's argumentation: in *The Book of the City of Ladies* Christine does not present those women who hitherto necessarily enjoyed the greatest fame. A detractor of the work might claim that Christine presents primarily trivial examples and so does not make a convincing case for a new universal history of women. To forestall such an objection,

Christine distinguishes between women who were famous by chance (that is, those women whom most earlier writers mention) and those women who *deserve* to be famous on the basis of their own achievements. Christine rewrites women's history and forces her potential detractors to argue on her terms rather than from the perspective of an historiographic tradition plagued by misogyny. This excursus serves as a springboard for the remaining chapters in part two, in which Christine discusses individual women who were in fact appreciated for their virtue: Lucretia, Queen Blanche (mother of Saint Louis), Busa, Marguerite, the Dame de la Rivière, and the princesses and ladies of France.

II.68: Christine refers to Valentina Visconti here, not directly by name but only as the duchess of Orléans.

III.1: Part three of *The Book of the City of Ladies* is perhaps the most foreign to contemporary sensibility, since it would hardly occur to a current advocate of feminism to see the Virgin Mary as the culmination of the New Kingdom of Femininity. One might recall that the veneration of the Virgin Mary, as Charles Henry Adams long ago noted in his essay on "The Virgin and the Dynamo," unleashed enormous creative energy in the late Middle Ages. A higher authority for the City of Ladies than the Virgin Mary was inconceivable for the late Middle Ages. We might fail to grasp the absolute indispensability of the Virgin Mary as a guarantee for the validity of this new universal history of women because we have no modern secular equivalent.

—The majority of the saints' lives which Christine recounts are taken from Vincent de Beauvais' *Speculum historiale* which was available to her in French translation. For the purposes of the translation I have used the original Latin names in those cases where the characters in question are not commonly known. I have referred to the 1624 edition of the *Speculum historiale* published in Douai (reprinted, Graz, 1965).

III.1.2: The crescendo of praise for the Virgin—particularly in the enumeration of her various attributes ("Heavenly Queen, Temple of God, Cell and Cloister of the Holy Spirit," etc.), a rhetorical device reminiscent of the topos of the *nomina Christi*, serves to heighten the authority of Christine's work. The women saints whom Christine discusses in the remainder of part three incorporate even more profoundly than their pagan counterparts the essence of femininity. Contemporary secular categories of perception do not reproduce this additional heightening or intensification of femininity which the religious dimension here facilitates.

III.3: Christine uses the example of Saint Catherine to demonstrate the felicitous combination of erudition and saintliness in a woman. Her Christian learnedness overcomes pagan philosophy, or expressed in allegorical terms, the authority of ancient philosophy is subordinate to the confluence of femininity, Christianity, and erudition. It is no thematic coincidence that in the majority of saints' lives recounted here a holy woman resists the sexual overtures of her torturer(s). Part three would suffer from thematic repetition if it were much longer. The significant feature of Christine's use of Vincent de Beauvais' *Speculum historiale* is her concentration of so many stories in such a short space (an example of *abbreviatio*). She uses Vincent de Beauvais to refute Boccaccio's claim that illustrious women were possible only in Antiquity and thereby at the same time connects her new universal history of women to the tradition of universal history represented in the late Middle Ages by Vincent de Beauvais.

III.8-11: In the first of these chapters (8-10) Christine presents a number of virgin martyrs, many of whom, particularly Saint Barbara and Saint Christine, had differences with their (earthly) fathers regarding their Heavenly Father. This theme contrasts with that of III.11, holy women who saw their children martyred before their very eyes. Christine explores the experiences of martyred women both as daughters and as mothers and elucidates the profound connections between the two situations. Charity Cannon Willard pointed out to this writer that medieval opinion held that "Virginity brought women closer to men in both physical and mental powers." See the recent article by Christine Reno, "Virginity as an Ideal in Christine de Pizan's *Cité des Dames*," *Ideals for Women in the Works of Christine de Pizan*, ed. Diane Bornstein, published by the Michigan Consortium for Medieval and Early Modern Studies, 1981, pp. 69-90.

III.12-13: Both these chapters present interesting variations on the theme of filial piety. Saint Marina, in her devotion to her father and to God, is forced to renounce all outward signs of her femininity, and yet she becomes, Christine seems to be saying, an even more perfect example of womanhood understood at an extremely abstract level. The irony of her alleged paternity accentuates her exemplary conduct. Euphrosyne's story resembles that of Marina, but here the disguised virgin comforts her own father who remains unaware of the true identity of his comforter. In this case the father–daughter connection transcends everyday notions of this relationship and becomes a very pure form of friendship and love.

III.19.2: "And you ladies who are married, do not scorn being subject to your husbands, for sometimes it is not the best thing for a creature to be independent." This statement will probably surprise the contemporary reader, since it appears at first glance to be a sell-out. One should recall the political context in which Christine viewed marriage. The wife is the subject of her husband just as the inhabitants of a country are the subjects of their king. This hierarchy implies, in medieval political terms, a system of mutual responsibilities and not a regimen of exploitation. Nevertheless there are good, bad, and mediocre husbands just as there are good, bad, and mediocre kings. On the basis of the wealth of examples given in *The Book of the City of Ladies,* one can see how Christine viewed the responsibilities between men and women in marriage in a wide variety of historical and social settings. In none of them does Christine equate the husband–wife relationship with the *subjugation* of the wife by the husband. The contemporary reader should not overlook this important distinction.

INDEX OF PROPER NAMES

The numbers following the names listed here refer to the sections of the text as these sections are given in the Harley manuscript of *The Book of the City of Ladies*. Several principles have guided the use of proper names in this translation. For the sake of consistency (and in the hope that this translation will encourage comparisons between Christine and her sources to show how intelligently Christine manipulated her sources), the names of characters which Christine borrowed from Boccaccio's *De mulieribus claris* correspond generally to their Latin forms in the 1967 edition prepared by Vittorio Zaccaria, which in turn are largely based on Forcellini's *Onomasticon totius latinitatis*. Similarly, the names of saints and martyrs which Christine borrowed from Vincent de Beauvais' *Speculum historiale* have been given here in their original Latin forms. The few exceptions to this rule are Latin names which are usually cited in an Anglicized form, such as Dorothy, Mark Anthony, Octavian, Tarquin, and Trajan. Italian names, particularly those of characters borrowed from Boccaccio's *Decameron*, are given in their original form, following normal English usage. The general English practice for citing French names, however, is inconsistent. Moreover, since the Middle French forms used by Christine often differ from their modern French counterparts, there is no particular reason to prefer the modern French forms to the English ones for use in this translation. Consequently, following the usage of the Encyclopedia Britannica, French names are generally given in their English forms, (*e.g.*, John, Duke of Berry, rather than Jean, duc de Berri, Isabella of Bavaria rather than Isabeau de Bavière, but Jean de Meung). Titles of works written in foreign languages have been kept in their original form, except for the *Decameron* and *The Romance of the Rose*. I have not corrected Christine's mistakes, (*e.g.*, where she tells in I.30.1 that Plato was inspired by Sappho rather than by Sophron, or in I.48.1 where she calls the son of Aeneas "Julius Silvius" rather than "Aeneas Silvius"). Christine mentions a number of nobles only by their titles; the "Duke of Milan," for example, is listed here under "Milan, Duke of." Christine refers to Valentina Visconti only as the "Duchess of Milan"

(II.68.3). Given her importance for Christine, in this single case, I have supplied her name before her title. All other names and titles are translated exactly as they are given in the original.

Abraham, II.38.1
Absalom, I.14.2
Acerbas Sychaeon, *see* Sychaeus
Achilles, I.19.1, I.19.2, II.28.3, II.61.7
Adam, I.9.3
Adelphus, I.29.1
Adrastus, II.17.1
Adrian, III.16.1
Aeneas, I.24.1, I.48.1, II.3.1, II.19.2, II.55.1
Aeneid, I.29.1
Aetes, I.32.1
Afra, III.17.1
Agape, III.14.1
Agatha, Saint, III.7.1, III.9.4
Agenor, I.46.1, II.61.3
Agnes, Saint, III.9.4
Agrippina, II.18.1
Ahaseuras, II.32.1
Albunia, *see* Tiburtina
Alexander the Great, I.14.2, I.19.3, II.29.3, II.66.2
Alexander (Marcus Aurelius Alexander Severus), III.6.1
Almathea, II.3.1
Amazons, I.16.1, I.17.1, I.18.2, I.18.3, I.18.6, I.19.1, II.12.1
Ambrose (companion of Bernabo), II.52.1, II.52.2
Ambrose, Saint, I.10.4
Anastasia, I.41.4
Anastasia, Saint, III.14.1, III.14.2, III.15.1, III.15.2
Andrea, Giovanni, II.36.3
Andrew, Saint, III.18.3
Andromache, II.28.3
Angela, II.61.3
Anjou, I.13.6, II.67.2
Anna (prophetess), II.4.1
Anne, Countess of Bourbon, II.68.10

Anthony, King of Egypt, II.42.1
Antiope, I.18.3
Antonia (daughter of Mark Anthony and Octavia, wife of Drusus Tiberius), II.43.1
Antonia (sister of Theodora), II.29.1, II.29.2
Antonia (Theodora, wife of Justinian), II.6.1
Apis, I.36.2
Apollo I.4.2, I.30.1, I.31.1, II.1.3, II.3.1
Apostles, I.10.2, I.10.5, I.29.1, I.35.2, II.53.2, III.2.1, III.18.1, III.18.6
Arabians, I.20.1
Arachne, I.39.1, I.39.2
Archelaos, I.41.1
Argia, II.17.1
Ariaractus, I.25.1
Aristobolus, II.42.1
Aristotle, I.2.2, I.9.2, I.9.3, I.11.1, I.14.1, I.30.1, I.38.5, I.43.1
Armenians, I.20.1
Ars amatoria, I.9.2, II.54.1
Artemisia, I.21.1, I.21.2, II.16.1
Ascanius, I.48.1
d'Ascoli, Cecco, I.9.3
Athalis, II.49.5
Athenians, I.34.3, I.34.4, II.21.1
Aucejas, III.5.1
Augustine, Saint, I.2.2, I.10.4
Avernus, II.3.1

Bar, Duke of, II.68.8
Barbara, Saint, III.9.2
Bartholomew, Saint, II.62.1
Basilissa, III.18.8
Basine, II.5.3
Belisarius, II.29.1, II.29.2

Belus, I.46.1
Benedicta, Saint, III.7.2
Berenice, I.25.1
Bernabo, II.52.1, II.52.2
Bible (Scriptures, Holy Scriptures, Gospel), I.10.2, I.10.4, I.12.1, I.29.1, II.4.2, II.31.1, II.32.1, II.37.1, II.38.1, II.39.1, II.40.1
Blanche of France (of Castille), I.13.2, II.65.1
Blanche of Navarre, I.13.5
Blandina, Saint, III.11.3
Boccaccio, I.28.1, I.29.1, I.30.1, I.30.2, I.37.1, I.39.3, I.41.1, II.2.3, II.14.1, II.15.1, II.16.1, II.17.1, II.19.2, II.43.1, II.52.1, II.59.1, II.60.1, II.60.2, II.63.1
Bourbon, Duchess of (Anne), II.68.7
Bourbon, Duchess of (Margaret), II.68.4
Bourbon, Duke of (Louis II), II.68.5
Briaxes, II.16.1
Brunhilde, II.49.5
Brutus (Marcus Junius Brutus), II.25.2, II.28.1
Burgundy, King of (Chilperic), II.35.1
Busa, II.67.1
Byrsa, I.46.2

Cadmus, I.4.2
Camilla, I.24.1
Carmentalis, I.33.2
Carmentis, I.33.2, I.37.1, I.38.4, II.5.1
Carthaginians, I.46.3, II.61.2
Cassandra, II.5.2
Cassius, II.25.2
Castalia, I.30.1
Categoriae, I.11.1
Catherine, Saint, III.3.2
Cato the Elder, II.25.2
Cato Uticensis, I.9.3, I.10.1, II.25.2
Catulla, II.35.3
Cecilia, Saint, III.9.4

Cento, I.29.1
Ceres, I.35.1, I.38.1, I.38.5, I.39.3
Chaldaeans, I.31.1
Charles of Blois, I.13.6
Charles IV, I.13.3
Charles V, I.13.6, II.67.2, II.68.2, II.68.3
(Charles VI), II.68.9
Châtelet, II.67.2
Childeric, II.5.3
Chilperic, King of the Franks, I.13.1, I.23.1
Chionia, III.14.1
Christine, Saint, II.10.1, III.9.4
Chrysogonus, Saint, III.14.1
Cicero, I.9.3
Circe, I.32.2
City of Ladies, The, I.4.1, I.4.2, I.4.3, I.5.1, I.6.1, I.8.1, I.14.4, I.15.2, I.26.3, I.43.2, I.48.1, II.1.1, II.12.1, II.12.2, II.13.2, II.68.11, III.1.1, III.3.1, III.18.9, III.19.1, III.19.6
Claudia, II.48.1
Claudia Quinta, II.63.1, II.63.2
Claudine, II.10.1
Claudius (Claudius Appius), II.46.3
Claudius (Marcus Aurelius Claudius), I.20.1
Claudius (Tiberius Claudius Drusus), II.47.3
Clermont, Countess of (Mary), II.68.5
Cloelia, I.26.1, I.26.2
Clotaire, I.13.1, I.23.1
Clotilda, Saint, II.35.1
Clovis, II.35.1
Coemon, Countess of, II.20.2
Constantine, II.49.4, III.18.6
Coriolans, II.34.1
Coriolanus, II.34.1
Cornelia (wife of Julius Caesar), II.19.2
Cornelia (wife of Pompey), II.28.2
Cornificia, I.28.1
Cornificius, I.28.1
Costus, III.3.2

Gualtieri, Marquis de Saluces, II.50.1

Guesclin, Bertrand du, II.22.2

Guiscardo, II.35.3, II.59.1, II.59.2, II.59.3

Haman, II.32.1

Hannibal, II.67.1

Hebrews, *see* Jews

Hector, I.19.1, I.19.2, II.5.2, II.28.3

Hecuba, I.19.1

Helen of Troy, II.61.6

Helen, Queen of Adiabene, III.18.6

Hellespontina, II.1.3

Hercules, I.18.2, I.18.3, I.18.4, I.18.5, I.18.6, I.41.1, I.46.1, II.60.2

Hero, II.58.1

Herod Antipater, II.42.1

Herod (son of Odenatus), I.20.1

Hippolyta, I.18.3, I.18.4, I.18.5, I.18.6

Hippolytus, I.18.6

Holophernes, II.31.1

Homer, I.29.1, II.1.3

Horace, I.30.1

Hortensia, II.36.2

Hortensius, *see* Quintus Hortensius

Hyppo, II.46.1

Hypsicratea, II.13.2, II.14.1, II.15.1

Hypsipyle, II.9.1

Idmonius of Colophon, I.39.1

Inachos, I.36.1

Indians, I.15.1

Irene (martyr), III.14.1

Irene (painter), I.41.2

Isaac, II.39.1

Isabella of Bavaria, II.68.1

Iseut, II.60.2

Isis, I.36.1, I.38.2, I.38.5

Italians, I.33.2, II.52.1

Jacob, II.39.1

Jason, I.32.1, II.24.1, II.56.1

Jean de Meung, II.25.1

Jeanne (d'Evreux), I.13.3

Jeanne de Laval, II.22.2

Jesus, *passim*

Jews, II.1.3, II.4.3, II.30.1, II.30.2 II.31.1, II.32.1, II.37.1, II.40.1, II.42.1, II.49.5

Jezebel, II.49.5

Joachim II.37.1

Jocasta, II.61.4

John, Saint, III.18.1

John, Count of Clermont, II.68.5

John, Duke of Berry, II.68.2, II.68.5

John the Fearless, Duke of Burgundy, II.68.4, II.68.5

John (error for Philip VI, King of France), I.13.5

Jonah, II.53.2

Judas Iscariot, II.49.5

Judith, II.31.1, II.32.1

Julia (daughter of Julius Caesar), II.19.2, II.28.2

Julia (daughter of Octavian), II.18.1

Julian, III.10.1

Julian the Apostate, II.49.5

Julian, Saint, III.18.8

Julitta, Saint, III.11.2

Julius Caesar, II.19.2, II.25.2, II.28.1, II.28.2, II.49.3

Julius Silvius (Aeneas Silvius), I.48.1

Juno, II.61.2

Jupiter, I.15.1, I.36.1, I.36.2, I.41.1, I.41.4, I.46.1, I.47.1, II.42.1, II.61.2, II.61.3, II.61.6, III.10.1

Justice, part III *passim*

Justin, II.6.1

Justine, III.8.1

Justinian, II.6.1, II.29.1

La Marche, Count of (John), II.68.10

La Marche, Countess of, I.13.7

Lampheto, I.16.1

Octavia, II.48.1
Octavian (Caesar Augustus)
    II.18.1, II.49.3
Odenatus, I.20.1
Odoacre, I.22.1
Oedipus, I.31.1
Olybrius, III.4.1
Olympiad, I.41.1
Ops (Opis), I.47.1, II.61.2
Orchomenos, II.24.1
Orgiagon, II.45.1
Orleans, Duke of, I.13.4
Otho, II.49.2, II.49.3
Ovid, I.9.2, II.1.3, II.54.1, II.57.1

Pallas, I.33.2
Pallas Minerva, *see* Minerva
Palmyrenes, I.20.1
Panico, Countess of, II.50.1
Paphnutius, III.13.1
Paris (of Troy), II.61.6
Paul, Saint, II.35.2, II.48.1, III.18.5,
    III.18.7
Paulina, *see* Busa
Penelope, II.41.1
Penthesilea, I.18.3, I.19.1, I.19.2
Persa (Perseis), I.32.1
Persia (sibyl), II.1.3
Persians, I.20.1, II.6.1
Pessinus, II.63.1
Peter, Saint, I.10.5, II.48.1, III.18.2
Petrarch, II.7.1
Philip the Bold, Duke of Bur-
    gundy, II.68.4, II.68.6
Philip (Philip VI, King of France),
    I.13.4
Phoebus, *see* Apollo
Phoenicians, I.46.1, II.61.3
Phorcys, II.61.5
Phoroneus, I.36.1, I.36.2
Phrygica, II.1.3
Pithis, II.16.1
Plato, I.2.2, I.30.1
Plautilla, III.18.7
Pluto, I.35.1, I.47.1
Polyneices, II.17.1
Polyxena, II.61.7

Pompeia Paulina, II.22.1
Pompey, II.8.1, II.14.1, II.19.2,
    II.28.2
Portia, II.25.2, II.28.1
Poumiers, Emerion de, II.67.2
Priam, I.19.1, II.5.2, II.61.7
Priscus, III.8.6
Proba, I.29.1, I.30.1
Problemata, I.11.1
Proverbs (or Epistle of Solomon),
    I.43.2, I.44.1, I.45.1
Ptolemies, I.20.1
Ptolemy, II.28.2
Publius, III.14.1
Pygmalion, I.46.1
Pyramus, II.57.1, II.58.1
Pyrrhus, I.19.2

Quintus Hortensius, II.36.2
Quintus Lucretius (Quintus Lu-
    cretius Vespillo), II.26.1

Ravenna, I.22.1
Reason, part I, *passim*
Rebecca, II.39.1
Rectitude, part II, *passim*
Regina, III.4.1
Remedia amoris, I.9.2
Remus, I.48.1, II.33.1
Rhodians, I.21.1
Rivière, Burel de la, II.67.2
Rivière, Marguerite de la, II.67.2
Romance of the Rose, The, I.2.2,
    II.25.1
Romans, I.22.1, I.26.1, I.26.2,
    I.33.2, I.34.4, I.36.1, I.41.3,
    I.45.1, II.2.1, II.3.1, II.10.1,
    II.14.1, II.15.1, II.19.2, II.26.1,
    II.33.1, II.34.1, II.45.1, II.46.2,
    II.46.3, II.63.1, II.66.2 II.67.1
Romulus, I.48.1, II.33.1
Rufus (Pomponius Rutillius
    Rufus), II.13.1
Rusticus, Saint, II.35.3
Ruth, II.40.1
Rutulians, I.48.1

Valerianus, I.20.1
Valerius (Valerius Maximus),
    II.13.1, II.43.3, II.63.1
Vandals, II.29.1
Vendôme, Countess of, I.37.1
Venus, II.19.2
Vergi, Dame de, II.60.2
Vergil, I.9.2, I.29.1, I.31.1, II.3.3
Vespasianus, II.15.1
Vesta, I.47.1, II.10.1, II.46.2
Veturia, II.34.1
Vincent de Beauvais, III.9.4

Virginia, II.46.3
Visconti, Valentina, II.68.3
Vitellius, II.49.3
Volscians, I.24.1, II.15.1, II.34.1
Vulcan, I.34.4

Xanthippe, II.21.1
Xerxes, I.21.2

Ytheron, II.16.1

Zenobia, I.20.1